Library of Congress Cataloging-in-Publication Data

Shields, John M.
An eschatological imagination: a revisionist Christian eschatology in the
light of David Tracy's theological project / John M. Shields.
p. cm. — (American university studies. Series VII, Theology and religion; v. 274)
Includes bibliographical references and index.
1. Eschatology—History of doctrines—20th century.
2. Tracy, David. I. Title.
BT821.3.S55   236—dc22   2008006321
ISBN 978-1-4331-0227-1
ISSN 0740-0446

Bibliographic information published by **Die Deutsche Bibliothek**.
Die Deutsche Bibliothek lists this publication in the "Deutsche
Nationalbibliografie"; detailed bibliographic data is available
on the Internet at http://dnb.ddb.de/.

The paper in this book meets the guidelines for permanence and durability
of the Committee on Production Guidelines for Book Longevity
of the Council of Library Resources.

© 2008 Peter Lang Publishing, Inc., New York
29 Broadway, 18th floor, New York, NY 10006
www.peterlang.com

Printed in the United States of America

John M. Shields

An Eschatological Imagination

A Revisionist Christian Eschatology in the Light of David Tracy's Theological Project

PETER LANG
New York • Washington, D.C./Baltimore • Bern
Frankfurt am Main • Berlin • Brussels • Vienna • Oxford

american
university
studies

Series VII
Theology and Religion

Vol. 274

PETER LANG
New York • Washington, D.C./Baltimore • Bern
Frankfurt am Main • Berlin • Brussels • Vienna • Oxford

An Eschatological Imagination

With gratitude to my wife Marianna for her love and steadfast support and to John P. McCarthy, mentor and colleague.

TABLE OF CONTENTS

ABBREVIATIONS

AI   *The Analogical Imagination: Christian Theology and the Culture of Pluralism.* New York: Crossroad, 1981.

BRO   *Blessed Rage for Order: The New Pluralism in Theology.* Chicago: University of Chicago Press, 1996.

DWO   *Dialogue with the Other: The Inter-Religious Dialogue.* Grand Rapids, Michigan: Eerdmans, 1990.

ONP   *On Naming the Present: God, Hermeneutics, and Church.* New York: Orbis, 1994.

PA   *Plurality and Ambiguity: Hermeneutics, Religion, Hope.* Chicago: University of Chicago Press, 1987.

INTRODUCTION

In 1957, the noted Swiss Roman Catholic theologian, Hans Urs von Balthasar, introduced what has become a classic discussion of Christian eschatology with the following statement:

> Eschatology is the storm center of the theology of our times. It is the source of several squalls that threaten all the theological fields, and makes them fruitful, beating down or reinvigorating their various growths. Troeltsch's dictum: "The bureau of eschatology is usually closed" was true enough of the liberalism of the nineteenth century, but since the turn of the century the office has been working overtime.[1]

For twentieth century Christian systematic theologians, eschatology did become a "storm center" as it moved to the forefront of Christian theology. It triggered reinvestigations and reinterpretations of various other topoi of Christian systematic theology in the light of that very movement and in spite of the dismissals of cool and rational liberal thought.

Ironically, however, it is not the twentieth century systematic theologians who first stirred up the eschatological storm clouds but rather the nineteenth century liberals themselves as they called for the application of modern, rational, and "scientific" standards to the historical examination of the classic texts of the Christian tradition. The movement on the part of late nineteenth and twentieth century biblical scholars toward a scientific historical consciousness in approaching New Testament studies led to the re-discovery of the fundamental eschatological – indeed, to some, apocalyptic – nature of the central character of Christianity: Jesus the Christ. That very discovery demanded that eschatology be reckoned with and be allowed to make its influence felt within Christian systematics. With eschatology at the forefront of systematics, theological inter-pretations of such Christian doctrines as the doctrines of creation, of reconcili-ation, and of grace all had to be rethought in the effort to make for a coherent and ordered Christian systematics. This would be no easy task for Christian theologians who for centuries had tended to place eschatological assertions – sometimes quite bold and incredible assertions – at the very end of systematic texts, often as a sort of afterthought.

There is another irony lying within the move toward a greater apprecia-tion of the eschatological character of Christianity. For then present scientific investigations into the past, i.e., scientific historical methodology applied to the basic texts and faith claims of Christian theology, ironically ended up pointing Christian theologians towards a Christ who is thoroughly eschatological as the "Coming One" and, in doing so, towards the future. For the future must figure largely in any discussion of the "doctrine about the final reality"[2] and about the One who is to usher in that final reality. After all, the final reality is ahead of us precisely as final, and the eschatological Christ is ahead of us precisely as the One who is to come and to bring into fruition that final reality. The past has thrown us finally and ironically into the future!

We therefore have passed through and embraced modernity's critical ratio-nality and, in that passing and embrace, we have discovered once again the eschatological character of Jesus the Christ and the future orientation inherent in the aspirations of the earliest of Christian communities. These discoveries now confront the critical spirit within contemporary theology with the respon-sibility of making sense of these discoveries for a modern and postmodern world. This is the task of a revisionist approach to Christian theology; for a revisionist perspective takes seriously both the faith claims of the tradition and contemporary understandings of the human situation and allows claims and understandings to speak to each other critically. Thus, however much the way in which eschatology came to the forefront of Christian theology may be a matter of ironies, bringing eschatology to center stage has had the effect of forcing Christian theologians to accept the fact that the future orientation of the Christian tradition must be reckoned with in a critical revisionist manner.

Yet the question of the future points up a problem for Christian theo-logians and especially systematic theologians as they attempt to create an ordered whole or a coherent set of inter-related theological assertions. The problem is this: the future is an object of concern for us both as human beings and Christians living within time. However, we also know that the future is also objectively unavailable to us, no matter what our religious faith claims may be about past, present, and future. The future is ambiguous to us. In fact, concern for the future often unsettles and interrupts our present comforts. As unavailable, the future can never be thought of or spoken of in the language of certainty, the language of propositional assertion. How then can a critical and reasonable Christian eschatology framed within a revisionist spirit speak to the uncertainty of the future in a responsible way? Can we now honestly speak about the future in terms of certain systematic assertions or propositions as some theologians have tended to do through the ages and even to this very day? Would not our modern (and, for that matter, postmodern) critical spirit become rightly suspicious of such certainty claims? Might not the language of cautious but hopeful possibility be better suited to eschatological reflection? And might not the very notion of future as possibility rather than certainty point to a different and revised way of thinking eschatologically and a more effective genre for discussing Christian eschatology than that of systematic assertion? Alternatively, might not the language of rhetoric or persuasion better serve the contemporary eschatological task when viewed from a perspective that attempts to revise understandings of the Christian tradition in the light of what we now know of human history and the uncertainty of the future?

Along this line of thought, Charles Hardwick made the claim, albeit somewhat strongly and critically, that "At no point is contemporary theology more lacking in candour than in its pronouncements about the 'last things.'"[3] It has tended to make certainty claims and, in doing so, has suffered from the tendency to reduce eschatology to systematic assertions about the last things in terms of what Zachary Hayes has labeled a strange "supernatural geography"[4] for a future beyond time.[5] Stephen Williams, echoing the thoughts of the process theologian Schubert Ogden, contends that standard treatments of eschatology are often "incredible" because "eschatological statements have no sound basis in human experience or knowledge... the mythological elements they contain lack clear conceptual meaning."[6] In a word, Williams, by way of Ogden, claims that many treatments of eschatology fail to measure up to two essential conditions for the truth value of theological assertions made from the perspective of revisionist theology: meaning as internal logical coherence and meaningfulness as existential significance to human beings.

Christian eschatology may have indeed become a "storm center" in the middle of the twentieth century in that it forced systematic theologians to return attention to the eschatological nature of the person of Jesus Christ and in doing so to reinterpret traditional related Christian doctrines. However, as we move further into the twenty-first century with a greater appreciation of the critical and oftentimes suspicious role that contemporary human experience and thought can and must play in conversation with the Christian tradition, the storm that Christian eschatology unleashed is a storm that may require revising or changing the very way in which we think and live eschatologically precisely because of a ready and candid admission of the uncertainty of the future.

This present study recognizes this problem for Christian eschatology: the issue of the tension between the need to speak eschatologically and the difficulty in doing so because of future's unavailability. Building on the theological project of the Roman Catholic theologian David Tracy, this study also offers a new and revised way of thinking and living eschatologically. It does so from the perspective of "revisionist" Christian theology, a perspective that answers the criticism that traditional systematic eschatological reflection lacks candor and credibility by permitting the contemporary human situation to engage in a mutually informative and critical dialogue with the faith assertions of the Christian tradition. This perspective recognizes and deals with the problem of the future in an honest and critical way and in doing so envisions a new and non-systematic role for the Christian tradition on eschatological reflection wherein that tradition can offer a preferred, encouraging direction for possible action into the future rather than make eschatological certainty assertions.

This way of thinking and living eschatologically can be distilled into the following thesis: a contemporary and revisionist Christian eschatology, what I ultimately will name an *eschatological imagination*, is best constructed as a rhetoric of virtue, an exhortation to live in active Christian hope in a world that has passed from modernity into critical postmodernity and that continues to pass into a future that is objectively unavailable yet still of crucial human concern. In its classic sense, rhetoric is a genre of expression employed to exhort to action in a preferred direction and into the future. It is a genre that moves beyond the logic of speculation leading to further related speculations; for rhetoric's logic discovers a preferred way of acting and delivers an exhortation or persuades one to act on the preference.[7] A Christian eschatological imagination as a rhetoric of virtue – a rhetoric of hope – activates hope in the direction of working towards a Christian eschatological future.

At this point, the creative theological work of David Tracy can be called into service for the construction of an eschatological imagination. Tracy is the retired Andrew Thomas Greeley and Grace McNichols Greeley Distinguished Service Professor of Roman Catholic Studies at the University of Chicago Divinity School. He held that particular position within the Divinity School of the University of Chicago since 1987, although he had been on its faculty since 1969 after having previously served for two years on the theology faculty of the Catholic University of America.[8] For more than thirty years, David Tracy has made significant contributions to contemporary Christian theology, most particularly by way of his commitment to the hermeneutical nature of theological reflection in the face of the challenges of pluralism to Christian theology in the modern/postmodern world. The pluralism of thought in contemporary theological reflection as well as in modern and postmodern culture has stimulated his theological project almost from the very beginning. Tracy has sought to carry on a public and mutually critical and enriching conversation between the revelations and faith affirmations of Christianity and the liberating and penetrating insights of modern and postmodern thought. He has done so with a view to developing methods that would both "eliminate the merely mystifying components of [the Christian] vision and yet restore with contemporary integrity Christianity's central vision of God and humanity."[9] In a word, in claiming for theological reflection a public contributory role to society, history, and culture, Tracy has always maintained that an authentic Christian vision must be explicated within the context of the modern/postmodern fidelity to the "morality of scientific knowledge,"[10] a genuine openness to critical thought and conversation with plurality. This is the perspective of a revisionist Christian theologian. Thus John P. McCarthy notes in a summary statement about Tracy's scholarly theological project:

> All of [Tracy's] scholarship has been stamped by the transcendental imperatives rooted in his early study with Bernard Lonergan: "Be attentive, be intelligent, be rational, be responsible, develop and, if necessary, change." From his earliest work on an analysis of Lonergan's work, through his texts on fundamental theology, systematics, hermeneutics, church history, the dialogue with non-Christian religions, and currently, on the naming of God, Tracy has displayed a careful scholarship, judicious evaluation, and bold planning that few scholars have been able to accomplish.[11]

Tracy's careful scholarship, judicious evaluation, and bold planning in all aspects of his theological project are fueled by an adherence to that "morality of scientific knowledge" in fidelity to Lonergan's transcendental imperatives and a genuine willingness to carry on intellectually honest conversations with the plural voices of Christianity and modern/postmodern culture. Tracy's hope ultimately lies in mutually critical conversations, in genuine and open dialogue with the other.[12]

Tracy's critical and public openness accompanied by critique of any and all "mystifications" of religion is an especially important attitudinal position to take when engaging in critical reflection on Christian eschatology. Such a doctrine, resting as it does on rich but often alien and disturbing mythological language in the scriptures (that has unfortunately at times fueled apocalyptic fanaticism throughout history), can easily lend itself to the mystifications which Tracy as revisionist decries. Tracy himself would thus resonate with the critiques of traditional treatments of Christian eschatology noted above, i.e., the criticisms of Hardwick, Hayes, Williams, and Ogden. Therefore, Tracy's revisionist position, worked out in his modern/postmodern theological namings and animated by the morality of scientific knowledge, provides a direction that is committed, in principle at least, to making a non-mystifying contribution to a revisionist construction of Christian eschatology as an eschatological imagination shaped in the form of a rhetoric of virtue. For Tracy brings his theological reflections to a close with a call to action, a call toward "risking" human existence as Christian eschatological existence. Tracy's contribution then to the present study is foundational and supportive. The contribution of the study itself is the construction of an eschatological imagination as a rhetoric of virtue.

This present study will be structured along the following lines of inquiry. First, in Chapter One we will selectively review the contours or shapes that contemporary Christian eschatological thought has taken in the twentieth century in order to set the controlling themes which have surfaced within that discussion. In that review, we will come to see the essentially but not wholly systematic orientation of much contemporary eschatological reflection. Secondly, in Chapters Two, Three, and Four, we will examine David Tracy's three major texts, *Blessed Rage for Order: The New Pluralism in Theology*, *The Analogical Imagination: Christian Theology and the Culture of Pluralism*, and *Plurality and Ambiguity: Hermeneutics, Religion, Hope*, in order to discover the eschatological dimensions of his thought in these, his major and most well-known writings. In that process, we will investigate the eschatological dimensions of Tracy's namings of God and the human situation. My claim is that those very namings in their eschatological dimensions all point in a certain direction, the direction of response, action, ultimately "risking a life" of virtued existence.

Finally then in the concluding chapter, I will offer a revisionist construction of a contemporary Christian eschatology that is creditable, non-mystifying, and praxis oriented, an "eschatological imagination" in the form not of a systematics of Christian eschatology but in the form of a rhetoric on behalf of hope as action. This is an eschatological imagination that respects the ambiguity and uncertainty of the future, yet still exhorts the Christian to exercise hope on behalf of the Christian narrative in order to work towards the liberation which that Christian narrative offers as a real and therefore plausible possibility. If this revisionist construction is a successful one, then it offers one clear direction for allowing eschatology to play a significant role in Christian thought, life, and practice.

Notes

1. Quoted from Hans Urs von Balthasar, "Some Points in Eschatology," *Explorations in Theology*, Volume I (San Francisco: Ignatius Press, 1989), p. 255. The article is a reprint from von Balthasar's *Fragen der Theologie heute* (Einsiedeln, Switzerland: Benziger, 1957), pp. 403–421.
2. Zachary Hayes, *Visions of a Future: A Study of Christian Eschatology* (Collegeville, MN: The Liturgical Press, 1989), p. 11.
3. Cited in Stephen Williams' article, "Thirty Years of Hope: A Generation of Writing on Eschatology," in *Eschatology in Bible and Theology*, Kent E. Brower and Mark W. Elliot, eds. (Downers Grove, IL: Inter-Varsity Press, 1997), p. 243. See Hardwick's *Events of Grace: Naturalism, Existentialism and Theology* (Cambridge: Cambridge University Press, 1996) pp. 267ff.
4. Zachary Hayes, "Visions of a Future: Symbols of Heaven and Hell," *Chicago Studies* (1985), p. 147.
5. Within the Christian tradition, there are a multitude of examples of eschatological "certainty" claims in spite of the objective unavailability of the future. One classic example would be Bonaventure's treatment of the topoi of Christian eschatology in his *Breviloquium* (Patterson, New Jersey: St. Anthony Guild Press, 1963), translated by José de Vinck. In Book VII of that text, the Seraphic Doctor describes the "last things" in great detail and with an easy confidence in his particular hermeneutic of the Christian scriptures. Thus, for instance, Bonaventure describes – and makes his case for – the "consummating by fire of all worldly things" on pp. 289ff of the *Breviloquium*. While Bonaventure may not predict the actual time of the Final Future and End of all creation, he describes its nature in the language of assertion. One can even find the language of certain assertion in contemporary discussions of Christian eschatology. The relatively recent but brief *Letter on Certain Questions Concerning Eschatology* of the Congregation for the Doctrine of the Faith issued in 1979 and published by the Daughters of St. Paul is replete with faith assertions about the last things. Furthermore, even though Jürgen Moltmann began his classic text *Theology of Hope* (Minneapolis, MN: Fortress Press, 1967) with the cautionary claim that there can be no "logos" or certain understanding about the eschaton and eschata, he too concluded his own later systematic study of Christian eschatology, *The Coming of God: Christian Eschatology* (Minneapolis, MN: Fortress Press, 1996), with "certainty" descriptions of the Final Reality as a "joyful

perichoresis" of God, humanity and cosmos where all time and space will be "de-restricted."
See pp. 323ff.

6. Stephen Williams, "Thirty Years of Hope," p. 243. Williams' reference point for this statement is Schubert Ogden's essay "The Promise of Faith" in *The Reality of God* (New York: Harper and Row, 1963). See especially pp. 209ff of that text.

7. This is the movement of classic rhetoric from *inventio* or discovery to *pronuncio* or delivery. See a discussion of the stages of classic rhetoric as outlined by Edward P.J. Corbett and Robert J. Connors in *Classic Rhetoric for the Modern Student* (New York: Oxford University Press, 1999), beginning on p. 16.

8. See John P. McCarthy's brief biographical sketch of David Tracy in A *New Handbook of Christian Theologians* (Nashville: Abingdon Press, 1996), edited by Donald W. Musser and Joseph L. Price. McCarthy's article begins on p. 468.

9. *Blessed Rage for Order: The New Pluralism in Theology* (Chicago: University of Chicago Press, 1996), p. 5. Excerpts throughout totaling ca. 5.5. pages from *Blessed Rage for Order: The New Pluralism in Theology* by David Tracy. Copyright © 1975 by the Seabury Press, Inc. Reprinted by permission of HarperCollins Publisher. Hereafter identified as *BRO*.

10. *BRO*, p. 6.

11. John P. McCarthy, "David Tracy," p. 468.

12. These conversations and open dialogue are engaged then by means of such methodological strategies as "mutually critical correlations" between "the meanings present in common human experience and the meanings present in the Christian fact" in *Blessed Rage for Order* (see pp. 43ff), the engagement of an "analogical imagination" that discovers "similarities in difference" in *The Analogical Imagination* (see pp. 405ff), and a hermeneutic of "retrieval, suspicion, and critique" of classic texts, symbols, and events in *Plurality and Ambiguity* (see p. 100). *The Analogical Imagination: Christian Theology and the Culture of Pluralism* (New York: Crossroad, 1981). Used with permission of Crossroad Publishing Company from *The Analogical Imagination: Christian Theology and the Culture of Pluralism* by David Tracy. Permission conveyed through Copyright Clearance Center, Inc. Hereafter identified as *AI*. *Plurality and Ambiguity: Hermeneutics, Religion, Hope* (Chicago: University of Chicago Press, 1987). Excerpts throughout totaling ca. 7.3 pages from *Plurality and Ambiguity: Hermeneutics, Religion, Hope* by David Tracy. Copyright © 1987 by David Tracy. Reprinted by permission of HarperCollins Publisher. Hereafter identified as *PA*.

· 1 ·

THE CONTOURS OF CONTEMPORARY ESCHATOLOGICAL REFLECTION

As noted in the "Introduction," during the middle of the twentieth century, Hans Urs von Balthasar characterized Christian eschatology as a veritable "storm center of the theology of our times,"[1] and this in contrast to Ernst Troeltsch's claim that nineteenth century Protestant theology had generally closed the door on eschatological reflection when it reduced Christianity to ethics in fidelity to the "modern concept of development."[2] While Charles Hardwick[3] may claim that contemporary studies of Christian eschatology are lacking in candor, a claim that other thinkers may perhaps contest, there is no doubt that eschatological reflection, reflection on the nature and content of Christian hope, has come to the forefront of the theological scene. In *On Naming the Present* published in 1994, David Tracy himself made the assertion that "neither optimism nor pessimism but hope is at the heart of the Christian vision of both nature and history," and that "all theologians would do well to focus again on that central category of hope."[4] Such an assertion reflects the thinking of much of the latter half of the twentieth century, thinking that perhaps took its cue from the classic statement of Karl Barth in his 1922 commentary on Romans that "if Christianity be not altogether thoroughgoing eschatology, there remains in it no relation whatever with Christ."[5] For instance, in his introduction to *Hope and the Future of Man* published in 1972, Ewert Cousins made a related assertion when he noted that "eschatology has been singled out as the distinctive element in the Christian vision, and hope the central Christian virtue."[6] So too quite recently, Carl Braaten and Robert Jensen made a similar claim when they noted in the preface to *The Last Things: Biblical and Theological Perspectives on Eschatology*, that "the twentieth century will be remembered in the history of theology for its rediscovery of the centrality of eschatology in the message of Jesus and early Christianity."[7] Braaten himself intensifies that claim by noting that contemporary Christian churches and traditions have "largely lost the apocalyptic imagination" of Jesus,[8] a "revolutionary imagination"[9] fired by cross and resurrection that must be retrieved in fidelity to the life and teaching of Jesus and that must be lived out as a resistance movement in the world, transvaluing all ordinary values.[10]

Structuring the Discussion of Contemporary Christian Eschatology

The effort to structure any discussion of contemporary theological reflection on Christian eschatology is no small task. The sheer volume of texts and articles touching upon Christian eschatology demands judicious selection of studies for review.[11] Limits must be set. Therefore, in the following pages: first, there will be an investigation of the thought and contributions of leading contemporary Protestant and Roman Catholic theologians to the discussion of Christian eschatology today in order to register controlling issues and themes; secondly, and with a view towards synthesis of contemporary eschatological themes, four major points of convergence in contemporary eschatological thinking as identified by Stephen Williams[12] will be reported out and reflected upon. The immediately following pages then will focus primarily on key insights from selected authors who have "recently" published texts devoted exclusively to Christian eschatology, i.e., Gerhard Sauter and Jürgen Moltmann on the Protestant side, and Zachary Hayes and Dermot Lane from the Roman Catholic perspective. Such a selection, however, will also give proper attention to the critical eschatological thinking of many of the leading theologians of the twentieth century who were at the center of the eschatological "storms."[13] The chapter will continue with a reflective registering of key twentieth century theologians against William's points of convergence for the sake of pointing out the changing direction of contemporary eschatological thinking. In concluding this analysis and before moving on to a detailed analysis of David Tracy, I will show finally that Christian eschatological reflection, largely and traditionally a systematic and therefore a speculative task, has more and more begun to shift greater emphasis towards practice, towards actions in this world.

Gerhard Sauter

In his most recent study of Christian eschatology, *What Dare We Hope: Reconsidering Eschatology*,[14] and taking his cue from von Balthasar, Gerhard Sauter chose to structure his discussion of Christian eschatology – what he in a response to 1 Peter 3:15[15] defines as "a theological discipline consist[ing] of intellectual experiences with the confession of hope"[16] – by conducting a historical analysis of the contributions of leading twentieth century Christian thinkers to eschatological reflection. In developing such a structure, Sauter places these theologians into general schools of eschatological thought. He initiates his discussion with due attention to the "consistent eschatology" that rose out of the historical critical studies of both Weiss[17] and Schweitzer[18] at the turn of the twentieth century. In Sauter's estimation, Weiss's and Schweitzer's historical critical studies of the New Testament leading to the determination of the apocalyptic character of Jesus and his preaching initiated the eschatological storms and gave rise to consistent eschatology. This is an eschatological stance that calls for Christians to remain faithful to the spirit of the teachings of Jesus in the face of the failure of Jesus' own expectations of an immanent eschaton. Sauter himself views consistent eschatology with its cry of "on in the spirit of Jesus" as having some positive benefit if that battle cry recognizes the role of the creative power of the Spirit of God in an eschatological existence lived in the light of the delay of the Parousia.[19]

Sauter then passes on to the "radical" eschatological thinking of such diverse theologians as Barth, Bultmann, and Rahner and generally identifies their eschatologies as radical because of their common claim for the interruptive eschatological in-breaking action of the Transcendent God into history in the person and event of Jesus Christ.[20] For theologians such as Barth and Bultmann, the radical in-breaking of the Christ event not only underscores the interruptive nature of eschatology but also lends to eschatological thinking a "presentist" orientation where the "eternity" of God cuts into temporal history in a radical way through God's salvific action in Christ. In this process, eschatology, christology, and soteriology are linked in a systematic way. For Bultmann, for instance, "Christ is the 'end of the law,' he is also the 'end of history' – not in the temporal sense but existentially,"[21] in the radical demand for a personal and existential faith decision for Christ. Sauter then concludes this particular structured approach to twentieth century Christian eschatology with an analysis of the eschatological reflections of the equally diverse "theologians of history:" Pannenberg, Moltmann, Metz, and Gutierrez.[22] The theologians of history, in contrast to the proponents of radical eschatology, highlight the future orientation of Christian eschatological reflection, albeit in different ways. Theirs is a more teleological and therefore future-oriented approach to Christian eschatology, hoping for the realization of a "future" Kingdom of God.

Such a structuring, the historical analysis of the development of "schools of thought" in the twentieth century, while helpful to a great degree, may however run the risk of losing sight of different nuances among and within theological as eschatological perspectives in the very effort to identify general characteristics. For instance, Karl Rahner and Rudolph Bultmann stand very much apart from each other in the matter of eschatological time;[23] yet they both clearly identify God as the Transcendent Other and Jesus Christ as the key to any Christian eschatological discussions. They both also place great emphasis on the free decision of the human being. Moreover, Jürgen Moltmann and Gustavo Gutierrez have a much more "this worldly" and action oriented eschatological sense than has Wolfhart Pannenberg. Yet, there is some conceptual value in being able to identify certain convergent and divergent streams of eschatological reflection.

On another level, the interpretation of the very meaning (or meanings) of the "final reality" (and/or "realities") in contemporary theological reflection heightens the complexity of the task and yet permits another structured approach to eschatological reflection. While attending to great historical figures giving rise to general trends in eschatological reflection, Sauter also notes that the final reality about which eschatological reflection concerns itself is a pluriform concept. The final reality may be interpreted in terms of a doctrine of "last things," the *eschata*, of the "end-time" or the *eschaton*, and/or of the Final as Coming One, i.e., Jesus Christ as the *Eschatos*, the One who has come but who will come again.[24] Moreover, some Christian thinkers have blurred the distinction between *eschaton* and *Eschatos* by radically collapsing the end-time into the very person of Jesus Christ as the Final One, a move made very early in the tradition by Origen when he identified Jesus as *hē autobasileia*, "the Kingdom in person."[25]

Throughout the centuries, each dimension or aspect of the final reality – the *eschata*, the *eschaton*, or the *Eschatos* – has taken on lesser or greater emphasis in the life of the Church and in its critical eschatological reflection, oftentimes as a result of historical circumstances. As Ernst Käsemann noted in *New Testament Questions of Today,* "an authentic theology never comes into existence as an intellectual construction in a vacuum."[26] Thus Käsemann's own historical critical reading of New Testament texts led him to conclude that the primitive Christian communities to whom Paul and the gospel authors wrote were animated by an apocalyptic eschatological orientation, apocalyptic in the sense that the Easter experience ushered in an entirely new aeon. After the Easter experience, in faith and hope the primitive Christian community expected an "immanent Parousia," an *eschaton* ushered in by the immanent return of the *Eschatos* to rule over a new kingdom of not wrath but grace.[27] In other words, an Easter faith operative in that particular historied community, the primitive Christian community, gave rise to an emphasis on *eschaton* ushered in by *Eschatos.*

However, Wolfhart Pannenberg in his discussion of the Kingdom of God, the core animating feature of Jesus' teaching in the New Testament and that which has been identified as the *eschaton,* claims with some amazement that the Kingdom "has not played as dominant a role in Christian eschatology as one might expect."[28] Indeed, he notes that very early on the term *basileia* or Kingdom became rare in the Apologists and very quickly was replaced with a focus on such *eschata* as "the resurrection of the dead and the last judgment."[29] The mellowing of apocalyptic expectations of the immanent return of Jesus as Lord and as *Eschatos* in primitive Christianity strongly influenced the directing of eschatological hope to such final realities or *eschata* as individual death, judgment, heaven and hell, as well as towards speculation about the more communally oriented last things, i.e., "the resurrection of the dead…and the second coming of Jesus Christ."[30] Thus, as Joseph Ratzinger has pointed out, the plaintive cries of *Maranatha,* the "Come Lord Jesus" of the primitive Christian communities, evolved into the medieval chant, *Dies Irae.*[31]

Such an orientation, the focusing of attention on the private and communal *eschata,* remained strong even into the twentieth century in both the life of the church and in the eschatological thinking of some Christian theologians. This is the case in spite of radical eschatology's re-focusing of attention on Jesus Christ as the *Eschatos* with the accompanying shift in eschatological thought from concern for the future to faith decisions in the present. Rudolph Bultmann's eschatological thinking demonstrates this shift in particular.[32] Thus, even Karl Rahner, and in spite of his own re-interpretation of all eschatological thinking by way of asserting that Jesus Christ is the *Eschatos* and the lens through which Christians must see the future,[33] begins his discussion of Christian eschatology in his classic *Foundations of Christian Faith* with a retrieval of the notion of the last things or *eschata*, both communal and individual.[34] Thus too, Joseph Ratzinger in *Eschatology: Death and Eternal Life* continues to make the case for Christian eschatology as a critical reflection on the *eschata* or last things (both individual and communal) as he criticizes theologians of history for their futurist emphasis on the *eschaton*[35] and radical eschatologists for their emphasis on the *Eschatos* leading to (in his mind) a purely presentist, actualist or existential interpretation of Christian eschatology.[36] What Ratzinger strives for is a balance in Christian eschatological thought, a balance that makes room for continued reflection not only on Jesus Christ as the *Eschatos* but also on the last things or *eschata* in a realistic tension between past, present, and future. He notes that "Jesus proclaimed the good news of the Kingdom of God as a reality which is both present and still to come."[37]

Structures chosen for clarifying eschatological reflection such as those identified by Sauter are not mutually exclusive; rather, they often interpenetrate each other. Thus, one could readily make the case that the twentieth century historical schools or strands of eschatological thinking as identified by Sauter can, in some part, find a correlative resonance with the pluriform meanings of the final reality(ies). One could make the claim, for instance, that radical eschatology has as its primary focus Jesus Christ as the *Eschatos* and that eschatologies as theologies of history have as their primary focus the end-time, the *eschaton*. Yet the qualifier "primary" is very important here. There is much sharing and nuancing at work in any structuring of the discussion of eschatological thinking on the part of systematic theologians. Perhaps Gerhard Sauter himself says it best in the following: "The various types of eschatology balance each other, and this is for the good. [However] they all have a tendency to overemphasize statements while ignoring disturbing questions which, in the long run, cannot be left aside."[38] It is perhaps for this reason that Sauter himself closes his study with what he believes to be enduring commonalities gleaned from structured analyses of eschatological reflection. Such commonalities are all expressed as the objects of eschatological hope: hope for "the consummation of all creation . . . the fulfillment of God's promises . . . [and] the constitution of new human beings and their transformation into eternal life."[39] He also concludes with three key eschatological affirmations which he believes to be essential to any and all eschatologies no matter how they are structured: 1) the belief that hope is the central eschatological virtue and as such is sheer gift from God; 2) the belief that hope grounds itself on God's promise; and, 3) the belief that Jesus is the Coming One, the one who comes from God as victor.[40] Yet Sauter fully recognizes that his commonalities and key eschatological affirmations themselves invite interpretations. It is no wonder then that he concludes *What Dare We Hope?* with questions, questions inviting further dialogue on accounting for eschatological hope.

Jürgen Moltmann

Like Gerhard Sauter, Jürgen Moltmann wrote a major text devoted exclusively to Christian eschatology in the closing days of the twentieth century. In *The Coming of God: Christian Eschatology*,[41] he too attempted to structure his discussion of Christian eschatology along clearly defined lines but with eschatological hope focused primarily on future in terms of an *adventum novum* as the controlling feature of the discussion. Gerhard Sauter's structured analysis of Christian eschatological reflection concludes with the claim for eschatological hope as the freely given grace promised and given in Jesus Christ as the Coming One, the victorious one coming from God. Such an eschatological theme animates Sauter's claim that God in Jesus Christ as the *Eschatos* "justifies" the Christian by faith and in hope.[42] In this way, Sauter casts the shape of eschatology into a re-interpretation of the classic Protestant doctrine of justification. In this, essential Christian eschatological claims are linked to soteriology. Sauter takes Paul's claim in Romans 8: 23 that in hope we are saved quite seriously. Moltmann, however, begins and concludes his own structured analysis with the key eschatological concept of *adventum*, the advent or coming of God ushering into all creation a true *novum*.[43] Moltmann's central eschatological theme is very clear: "In the end is the beginning,"[44] a truly new beginning inaugurated by the dialectic of the death and resurrection of Jesus Christ warranting an advent oriented hope. Thus Moltmann very clearly gives a decidedly forward and dynamically future-oriented direction to his eschatological thought. Although Sauter does speak of Jesus Christ as the "Coming One," his final claim that Christians are justified in hope and that Jesus is the Coming One precisely as the One who comes from God delivering the "verdict of justification"[45] echoes the more presentist orientation of radical eschatologists such as Barth and Bultmann. One senses that Sauter is more sympathetic to Bultmann's claim that the eschatological event of Jesus Christ brings about an essential and ultimate "change in self-understanding" in the individual believing and hoping Christian[46] rather than to a future *novum* for all humankind and all creation, the kind of *novum* that occupies much of Moltmann's future as advent orientation. Yet Moltmann does not leave the past behind entirely; he states at the outset that "Christian eschatology is the *remembered* hope of the raising of the crucified Christ, so it talks about beginning afresh in the deadly end."[47] This beginning afresh is a true *novum* rising from the dialectic of death and the new life of resurrection into the Kingdom of God where, ultimately, "the whole earth is full of [God's] glory."[48]

Moltmann's claim that eschatological hope ultimately focuses on the very "glorification" of God as the Coming One is actually an expansion of his eschatological thought from the time of *Theology of Hope*, his first text on Christian eschatology published in English in 1967. That theme, the glorification of God, clearly surfaces in his summary of the content of Christian eschatological hope in the following statement, a statement which also structures the ordering of the eschatological sub-themes of his text:

> This glorifying of God in the world embraces the *salvation* and eternal life of human beings, the *deliverance* of all created things, and the *peace* of the new creation. Christian eschatology has four horizons:
>
> 1. It is hope in God for God's glory.
> 2. It is hope in God for the new creation of the world.
> 3. It is hope in God for the history of human beings with the earth.
> 4. It is hope in God for the resurrection and eternal life of human people.[49]

It is important to note that Moltmann's structuring of Christian eschatological reflection begins with hope in God's glory yet also takes into account both historical eschatology by way of discussion of the Kingdom of God and its distortions over time into political millenarianisms,[50] and cosmic eschatology as hope in "the end of time in the eternity of God" and in the "end of space in the presence of God."[51] Moltmann also makes room for a discussion of a theology/philosophy of death when he addresses hope for the "resurrection and eternal life of human people."[52] While Moltmann's overall eschatological orientation is advent oriented and thus oriented primarily towards a discussion of the *eschaton*, he does not fail to address the question of the *eschata*; nor does he ignore Jesus. Jesus' death and resurrection underscore the dialectic and anticipatory nature of Christian eschatology.

Yet while Moltmann, like Sauter, references (and criticizes) leading Christian thinkers from the twentieth century, and thus gives attention to the historical development of eschatological thought, his major goal is to forge a Christian eschatology that remains faithful to Revelations 1: 4, "Peace to you from him who is, and who was and who is to come," and Revelations 21: 5, "See, I am making all things new," by distilling itself into the eschatological concept of *adventum novum* informed by the christological, i.e., the death and resurrection of Jesus Christ. Thus, hope in future as the *adventum novum* animates all of his thought. Such an orientation demands that he deals not only with history but also with cosmos[53] as the structuring of his reflection clearly demonstrates. Such an orientation also reflects an advent expectation not of annihilation of world and cosmos but of their transformation into the fullness of God's eternity and presence.

Yet again, as was noted above, what Moltmann has particularly added to his discussion of Christian eschatology is the claim that eschatological hope is hope in God for God's own glory.[54] In this sense, God precisely as the Coming God is Moltmann's *Eschatos*. This advent theme appears at the very beginning of *The Coming of God* and serves as the capstone of his Christian eschatology. In Moltmann's final reflections, the eschatological self-glorification of God in the future should be viewed as divine glorification that neither excludes nor swallows up human and cosmic involvement. Rather God's glorification as the truly *adventum novum* will take the shape of "the prodigal communication of God's own fullness of life"[55] to history and cosmos. This communication, prefigured in the resurrection of Jesus, will bring about the "interplay of all blessing and praise, singing, dancing, and rejoicing creatures in the community of God,"[56] like "a great song or a splendid poem or a wonderful dance of [God's] fantasy, . . . [in] the communication of his divine plenitude."[57] Thus in contrast to his "exodus" theme in *Theology of Hope*, Moltmann concludes *The Coming of God* with a more aesthetic and speculative eschatological hope, a faith and hope in the advent of a joyful perichoresis of God and all of God's creation. Within that very conclusion, Moltmann offers a speculative vision of and about the final future; it will be a perichoresis.

The Roman Catholic Discussion: Zachary Hayes, Dermot Lane, and the Debt to Karl Rahner

Other contemporary theologians, particularly from the side of the Roman Catholic tradition such as Zachary Hayes and Dermot Lane, have structured their texts on Christian eschatology along lines similar to that of Jürgen Moltmann in many ways. For instance, in *Visions of a Future: A Study of Christian Eschatology*,[58] Hayes, like Moltmann, places great emphasis on tracing the development and expansion of eschatological hope through the concept of "promise" in the Hebrew and Christian scriptures.[59] Moreover, as the title of Hayes's text indicates, he too casts the discussion of Christian eschatology primarily in terms of the future. Yet Hayes's understanding of Christian eschatology is not exclusively future oriented; nor does it focus eschatological hope entirely on an eschatological existence above and beyond this present creation.[60] Rather, Hayes's claim for the need for a "dialectical" understanding of Christian eschatological assertions is reflected in his discussion of the debate between what he calls the Roman Catholic "incarnationalists"[61] with their emphasis on the presence of God's transforming grace in the present world as a result of the divine gift of the incarnation of Jesus Christ and the "eschatologists"[62] with their emphasis on a discontinuity between history and the eschatological Kingdom. He notes that for the "eschatologists" the "final goal of human history is not the city of humanity but the city of God," and that "the only Christian decision... [has] to be the decision to have faith in God alone. The collapse of culture may be a summons to purify one's faith. A purified faith would be a faith in God and not in culture."[63] Such a Roman Catholic perspective resonates with a Barthian crisis eschatology as well as a Bultmannian reduction of eschatology into a present faith decision for God calling for a reversal of values. Hayes's own position on this matter, perhaps reflecting the influence of his teacher Joseph Ratzinger, is that "both sides of this debate can claim a strong basis in Scripture" and that there is a need for "dialectical sensitivity in Christian eschatology."[64] This dialectical sensitivity arises from the recognition of what David Tracy himself has characterized as the "already-not-yet" dimension of the Christ event and of Christian as eschatological existence.[65] Christian eschatology, for Hayes, entails a dynamic tension between both present and future.

In his structuring of the discussion of Christian eschatology, Hayes also shares with the Moltmann of *The Coming of God* the speculative assertion that the final reality, the *eschaton*, is and will be the reality of a peace-filled relationship with the divine life. Both speak of a certain hoped for perichoresis between and among the divine, the human, and the cosmic. While Moltmann speaks of such a hope particularly in terms of the final glorification of God, and of a "de-restricted" humanity and cosmos as participation in that very glorification, Hayes makes a related assertion about the nature of the final reality when he claims in his discussion of heaven (and of the doctrine of the beatific vision) that "the rich and diverse imagery of the Scriptures suggests that heaven is more a quality of life than a place that could be located somewhere. Heaven is the symbol for the full maturity and perfection of human life in the presence of God."[66]

The final reality is asserted as a communion, a relationship characterized by the "total penetration of the human person by the loving presence of God."[67]

While we note that Hayes shares with Moltmann similarities in his structuring of a contemporary discussion of Christian eschatology, we must also note that Hayes's thought is greatly indebted to the thinking of Karl Rahner and this on two fronts. First, Hayes bases his discussion of Christian eschatological hope not only on the revelations of both the Hebrew and Christian scriptures but also on what he calls the "philosophical basis for systematic eschatology."[68] In doing so, Hayes references the thought of Gabriel Marcel and Ernst Bloch in a dialogue with the Christian anthropology of Karl Rahner, a Christian anthropology of human self-transcendence animated by "transcendental hope."[69] The value of such a methodological turn permits Hayes to make the claim that there is a resonance between human aspirations, human hopes, and the distinctly Judeo-Christian hopes of revelation. For Hayes, there is a certain continuity between the human as secular and human as religious drive for fulfillment as self-transcendence. Such a stance clearly reflects Rahner's thinking.

On a second and related front, Hayes, clearly influenced by Rahner's theology of grace, demonstrates a tendency to structure eschatological reflection by way of retrieving that very theology (wherein "grace" is "the self-communication of God"[70]) to inform eschatological reflection. The eschatological reality is the reality of the presence of God's grace both here and now and into the future. Such an interpretation has the benefit of moving the understanding of eschatological finality beyond the merely temporal to include the understanding of finality in terms of "ultimacy," an ultimacy born of the Ultimate Presence of God as grace both in the present and into a future of fulfillment. Eschatological finality as ultimacy then may hold within itself both a temporal and depth dimension where present and future are held in dynamic tension. This is also von Balthasar's perspective of eschatological time. Perhaps the following not only serves to summarize Hayes's eschatological perspective but also points up his recognition of the dialectical tension of eschatological assertions within the perspective of a Rahnerian graced anthropology:

> Christian eschatology, from the beginning, has been characterized by a tension between the present and the future. The experience of faith and grace in the present is already an experience of eschatological reality. But the mystery of grace is not completely realized in any historical experience. There remains a future fulfillment which is the object of hope. This tension between the present experience of grace and the future fulfillment of grace in the Kingdom must remain as a dimension of Christian eschatological awareness throughout history.[71]

Hayes is not alone in this mode of eschatological thinking. In his own discussion of the eschatological nature of salvation in Christ Jesus, the liberation theologian Gustavo Gutierrez echoes Hayes's theme – admittedly for the purpose of making the case for an "in the world" Christian eschatology of liberation – when he (Gutierrez) speaks of the eschatological promises of God in terms of partial fulfillment in the present with hope for total fulfillment into the future.[72]

Dermot Lane in his text on Christian eschatology, *Keeping Hope Alive: Stirrings in Christian Eschatology*,[73] echoes a similar theme when he notes that John Henry Newman "reminds us [that] grace is glory in exile whereas glory is grace fulfilled."[74] Lane structures much of his own eschatological reflection on the basis of a theology of grace giving rise to a Christian eschatology as the expression of a Christian anthropology in the mode of fulfillment. Like Hayes, Lane is a clearly influenced by the Roman Catholic theological as eschatological perspective of Karl Rahner. Perhaps the following both summarizes Lane's perspective and demonstrates the influence of Rahner on that very perspective.

> Eschatology is not something additional or extrinsic to anthropology. Instead, escha-
> tology is, as Rahner frequently points out, anthropology in the mode of fulfillment;
> that is, anthropology conjugated in the future. Eschatology completes what is already
> going on in history and taking place in human experience....Eschatology is the ful-
> fillment of promises implicit in human hope and the flourishing of the innate human
> capacity to become. In other words, eschatology is the full realization of something
> already set in motion from the very beginning, namely the gift of a graced existence in
> creation....Eschatology is about the full flowering of the gift and grace of historical
> existence in eternity.[75]

All of the above clearly reflects a Rahnerian view of Christian eschatology. Note the clear resonance with Rahner's own claim that "eschatology is man's view from the perspective of his experience of salvation, the experience which he now has in grace and in Christ. It is a view of how the future has to be if the present as the beginning of the future is what man knows it to be in his Christian anthropology."[76] Thus for Rahner and for Lane as his disciple, eschatological knowledge of the future "...insofar as it is still to come, is an inner moment of the self-understanding of man in his present hour of existence – and *grows out of it*."[77] What is perhaps most significant about Lane's comment above – in line with Rahner's thinking and whole theological project – is his claim that Christian eschatology is all about fulfillment as continuity, a fulfillment continuous with what has already been set in motion by the creative and salvific grace of God. The systematic doctrines of graced creation, salvation, and eschatological fulfillment are all of a piece in this particular perspective, and the interruptive dimension of eschatological reflection of radical Protestant theologians such as Barth and Bultmann is muted in this particular Roman Catholic perspective.[78]

What Lane perhaps adds to the discussion of Christian eschatology is his recognition of the postmodern critique of the modern "turn to the subject." This, ironically, is the turn which informs much of the transcendental Christian anthropology of Rahner. Lane holds firm to a doctrine of grace leading to a fulfillment eschatology. However, aware of the postmodern critique of what David Tracy calls the "purely autonomous ego" of modernity[79] and in spite of his overall fidelity to Rahnerian themes, Lane does assert along with postmodern thinkers that the postmodern human being existing in this world can best be described by way of an anthropology of "relationality" caught in the tension between identity and difference/otherness. Lane takes his cue from Paul Ricoeur at this point.

> It is perhaps Paul Ricoeur who provides the most coherent philosophical framework for describing the different tensions within this important first step in the construction of an alternative anthropology. According to Ricoeur in *Oneself as Another* the unity of relationality and individuality can be summed up as a "dialectical tie between selfhood and otherness." Within this dialectic, otherness is not something simply added on to selfhood to overcome the danger of solipsism; instead otherness belongs to the "ontological constitution of selfhood." The advantage of this dialectic "is that it keeps the self from occupying the place of foundation." Further, this particular dialectic reminds us that the "selfhood of oneself implies otherness to such an intimate degree that one cannot be thought of without the other."[80]

Lane's appreciation for the postmodern critique of the modern turn to the subject with its accompanying ontological determination of the relationality of human beings allows him to speak of Christian eschatology not only in terms of a Rahnerian sense of continuity but also by way of the categories of difference and otherness.[81] Such categories permit Lane ultimately to allow feminist, ecological, and cosmological critiques of Christian theology in general and Christian eschatology in particular to inform the eschatological discussion.[82] Such categories of postmodern thought are also reflected in Lane's final claim that a creditable contemporary Christian eschatology ought to be "life-enhancing," must affirm "the value of human actions and social praxis both for this life and for the next life," and thus "should have an emancipatory thrust"[83] for human beings in relation to each other and to cosmos. In Lane's thinking, then, the systematic task of eschatological reflection, the task of linking Christian eschatology to the Christian doctrine of grace, begins to point towards Christian eschatology as more than a systematic venture. Christian eschatology now also begins to take on a practical or action dimension. It is true that Lane treats of the same standard topoi of Christian eschatology much like Moltmann and Hayes. But what Lanes also contributes to the discussion is a greater appreciation of postmodern thought concerning the nature of the human person and its implications for a Christian eschatology. This would be a Christian eschatology that must concern itself with ethical praxis in the present world characterized as it is by difference and otherness and by the dynamism of the individual always in tensive relationship with the otherness of humanity, cosmos, and God. Lane's eschatology calls for a "turn to the other" – be that humanity or cosmos – in "solidarity."[84] Praxis must figure into all Christian theological reflection, including the eschatological. Hence Lane is sympathetic to the unsettling eschatological cries of liberation and feminist theologians and their demands for liberations in this world both now and into the future. And with that sympathy, Lane's Christian eschatology as a further interpretation of a theology of graced anthropology perhaps begins to signal, however inchoately, the need to move the eschatological discussion beyond systematics to action, to practice.

In summary then, I have attempted, in an admittedly brief fashion, to sketch out the general contours or shapes that eschatological reflection has taken in the writings of selected Christian theologians in the last days of the twentieth century. While Moltmann is perhaps the theologian most widely recognized for his contributions to the discussion of Christian eschatology, particularly by way of his claim for the primacy of hope in an *adventum novum* as the key to eschatological reflection, Sauter, Hayes, and Lane have also made important contributions to the present discussion. Gerhard Sauter's penetrating text, *What Dare We Hope?* is an excellent example of critical scholarship structured in such a way as to attend to the key perspectives of twentieth century schools of eschatological reflection as well as to the inner relationships between and among the *eschata*, *eschaton*, and *Eschatos*. As Sauter notes, an eschatology exclusively focused on the *eschata* robs them of their relationship to Christ the *Eschatos*, and an eschatology exclusively focused on the *eschaton* may fall prey to an overly optimistic sense of development in history.[85] Sauter himself contributes to the discussion by way of the retrieval and eschatological interpretation of the classic Protestant doctrine of justification, a retrieval that tempers any predilection for a completely futurist eschatology by reminding us that the Barthian and Bultmannian contributions to the discussion of Christian eschatology should not be dismissed lightly because of their presentist and soteriological orientations.

With their shared reliance on a methodology taking as its starting point philosophical and anthropological reflections on human hope and with their tendency to structure eschatological reflection along the lines of the fulfill-ment mode of a theology of grace, Hayes and Lane offer the discussion the opportunity to shape the contours of eschatological reflection by way of the Catholic doctrine of analogy. Even Hayes's affirmation of the dialectical tension between the present and the future in eschatological assertions is a "both-and" tension, an implicit affirmation of the continuity between human as secular and religious hope. Such an affirmation somewhat mutes the more interruptive eschatological tenor of some Protestant theologians by defin-ing the eschatological relationship between present and future in terms of hope for fulfillment. Yet Lane, certainly more than Hayes, has begun to take seriously the postmodern critique of the modern self and the reality of inter-ruption present to postmodern consciousness. As we shall see, this critical stance will be echoed in the thought of David Tracy also and will ultimately point Christian eschatological hope less in the direction of speculations about the nature of a final future and more in the direction of acting on behalf of a preferred future.

Each of these contemporary theologians, in their own way, also reminds us that critical reflection on Christian eschatological claims is a complex task invit-ing varied interpretations. Because eschatology ultimately focuses its attention and hope on God, who is Mystery, and the future, which is also a matter of mys-tery in many ways, it demands conversations characterized by openness. Thus, Karl Rahner characterizes hope as a fundamental openness to the Mystery of God and to our future in God. "Hope ... is a process of constantly eliminating the provisional in order to make room for the radical and pure uncontrollability of God.... In this sense hope is that which endures"[86] because hope in God must be an ongoing openness to the Mystery of God who endures eternally and who can never be controlled by humanity. Naming God as the Absolute Mystery carries with it the naming of God as Absolute Future.

If, as Rahner notes, God as Mystery is the "absolute future of man,"[87] hope as openness to the Ultimate Mystery who is God then demands a certain measure of modesty when the person of hope makes eschatological assertions. Rahner's student, the political theologian Johannes Baptist Metz, echoes that same understanding of eschatological hope when he speaks of the "eschatological reservation" which must qualify any and all human political and social hopes to structure the future.[88] As Origen warned Christian theologians back in the third century of the common era, any and all talk of the "the end or consummation" of the future of humanity and cosmos with God is a matter of "dealing with subjects that call for discussion rather than definition."[89] So too in the waning days of the twentieth century, Dermot Lane began his contemporary discussion of Christian eschatology with the claim – reminiscent of Origen's caveat – that "we need to arrive at a stage of 'learned ignorance' (*docta ignorantia*) in most matters theological and this is particularly the case in eschatology"[90] because of both the Mystery of God and the objective unavailability of the future. Yet in spite of and at the same time because of our "learned ignorance" in the matter of Christian eschatology, Lane continues to claim that we must "keep hope alive." The revelations of scripture demand this.

Four Thematic Convergences Along the Contours of Eschatological Reflection: The Work of Stephen Williams and the Contemporary Discussion

When Karl Rahner made the eschatological claim that God as Absolute Mystery is the "absolute future of man," he was articulating a significant – perhaps primary – point of convergence along the contours of contemporary eschatological reflection. Karl Barth made the very same claim in his brief essay in *Death to Life*.[91] when he observed that "God alone is [man's] future and his hope."[92] Barth also made that same claim in *Church Dogmatics* IV.1 in the context of discussing the Christian doctrine of reconciliation,[93] and he further concretized that claim into the assertion that Jesus Christ as the final, definitive act of God and verdict on mankind is "the absolute and final future."[94] And Schubert Ogden, the process theologian, made a related claim when he noted that "it is God himself who is the only final end even as he is also the only primal beginning, both of man and of the world."[95] In a word, the claim that it is the God of Jesus Christ who is the final and thus eschatological reality for humanity and cosmos serves as the primary convergent contemporary eschatological assertion, an assertion that links Christian eschatology with the doctrine of God and christology.

Yet other convergences have also emerged. In the article, "Thirty Years of Hope: A Generation of Writing on Eschatology," Stephen Williams contends that, despite divergences and nuances in eschatological thinking, certain converging themes or eschatological assertions have indeed surfaced. Relying on his own interpretation of Moltmann's *Theology of Hope* as the starting point for making that claim, Williams identifies four enduring, highly inter-related eschatological assertions: first, the affirmation of the *centrality* of eschatology for contemporary theological reflection; secondly, the claim that the *point* of Christian eschatology is to stimulate "this-worldly action;" thirdly, the notion that the *content* of eschatological reflection is hope in God's promise(es); and fourthly, the appropriation of *christology* as the methodological tool with which to make Christian eschatological assertions. These are Williams's four converging points.[96] In the following pages, I will explore these points of convergence in the light of previous analysis of the eschatological reflections of leading contemporary Christian theologians. The ordering of that exploration, however, will be adjusted to demonstrate more clearly how contemporary reflection on Christian eschatology has begun to move beyond systematics alone to include eschatology as practice, as a task in this world. In this sense, Williams's points one and four reflect convergence along the lines of systematics while points two and three reflect a greater interest in eschatology as practice.

There is a certain relationship between Rahner's eschatological assertion that God is Absolute Mystery and Future, and thus the Final Reality and Williams' converging eschatological assertions. While it is true that Rahner's retrieval of the notion of God as Absolute Mystery and as the Absolute Future of mankind and cosmos lends to eschatological assertions a certain modesty demanding an openness to the future,[97] it is also true that there is neither modesty nor tentativeness in that very theological/eschatological claim. In his own language and informed by his over-arching theology of grace, Rahner summarizes this theological as eschatological claim in his "future oriented creed" which concludes *Foundations of Christian Faith*:

> Christianity is the religion which keeps open the question about the absolute future which wills to give itself in its own reality by self-communication, and which has established this will as eschatologically irreversible in Jesus Christ, and this future is called God.[98]

Such a faith statement is important to the present discussion because it can serve as the *theological* foundation for the attendant claim on Williams' part that eschatology stands at the forefront of Christian theological reflection. The profession of the Christian community that Jesus as the Christ/Messiah manifests this very claim in a definitive, (i.e., for Rahner "irreversible"), historical, and incarnate way reinforces that claim by way of christology. Thus Moltmann notes quite strongly in his *Theology of Hope*:

> The eschatological is not one element of Christianity, but it is the medium of Christian faith as such, the key in which everything in it is set, the glow that suffuses everything here in the dawn of an expected new day. For Christian faith lives by the raising of the crucified Christ, and strains after the promises of the universal future of Christ. Eschatology is the passionate suffering and passionate longing kindled by the Messiah. Hence eschatology can not really be only a part of Christian doctrine. The eschatological outlook is characteristic of all Christian proclamation, of every Christian existence and of the whole church.[99]

Moltmann's observation taken in tandem with Rahner, Barth, and Ogden's theological as eschatological assertions serves to illustrate then what Stephen Williams sees as two key and intimately related points of convergence in eschatological thinking over the past thirty years: the "centrality of eschatology" in contemporary Christian theological reflection and the claim that christology concretely informs that claim.[100] The *theological* claim for God as the Absolute Future of humanity and cosmos accompanied by the concomitant Christian claim for God's eschatological as final action in Jesus as the Christ demands, as Barth noted in 1922, that eschatology must stand at the center of Christian faith and Christian theology. This is the case because the object of eschatological hope is neither an "object" nor "objects" that can be described by way of some "supernatural geography" but is rather "Subject." God, the Subject and Ultimate Concern of all of theology, is the Absolute Future of humanity, the final and thus eschatological goal of humanity. And, to the Christian, it is the final action of God in Jesus Christ which reveals this most fully.

Yet *historical* analysis of this *theological* claim points up the fact that Christian thinkers have come to affirm that claim for the centrality of eschatology by following divergent paths along the contours of eschatological reflection. For instance, the pioneering work of Weiss and Schweitzer in turn of the century historical critical studies of the Christian scriptures led to the realization that, in the words of Rudolph Bultmann, "it has become more and more clear that eschatological expectation and hope is the core of the New Testament preaching throughout."[101] According to Joseph Ratzinger, the work of Weiss and Schweitzer led to the "awareness that Jesus' preaching was soaked through with eschatology."[102] In this sense, the historical achievements of biblical scholarship served to point out that eschatology lies at the very heart of the New Testament and that any and all efforts to remain faithful to the core of New Testament teaching demand a reckoning with that eschatological centrality. Biblical scholarship at the turn of the twentieth century catapulted God and God's eschatological Kingdom and Jesus Christ as its eschatological prophet to the forefront of all Christian theology.

Yet the radical eschatologies born of such Protestant theologians as Barth and Bultmann in the early decades of the twentieth century, while cognizant and appreciative of the contributions of historical critical biblical studies, really developed out of a re-affirmation of the "transcendence of God,"[103] that totally Other God standing dialectically in judgment of the sinfulness of humanity. Barth had a wealth of historical evidence from which to support this insight and, in doing so, to affirm humanity's crucial need for liberation by the eschatological God. Barth looked out into modern history and saw not only what he perceived to be the failures of nineteenth century liberal Protestantism but also the historical reality of, as George Steiner has put it, "a period since August 1914 [that] has been…the most bestial in recorded history."[104] This is the historical reality of a sinful humanity bent on the self-assertion of human interest to the detriment of God's will and of the flourishing of humanity and creation. It is no wonder that radical eschatologists see the eschatological action of God in Jesus Christ as an interruption, not only as an in-breaking of the eternal God into time but also as an in-breaking of an always and everywhere judging justification of humanity in the face of the reality of historical sin. It is also no wonder that the theme of faith in and hope for liberation follows closely upon eschatological assertions, faith and hope in God as the Final Reality who liberates sinful humanity through God's action in Christ Jesus.

What is really important to note by way of implication deriving from the theological foundation of the claim for the centrality of eschatology to theology today, i.e., the belief that the object of eschatological hope is ultimately the Subject we call God, is that a new understanding of time, an eschatological sense of time, emerges out of this foundational belief. Eschatological time disrupts the ordinary human sense of time by holding past, present, and future in a new, related tension. If indeed the eternal God is eternally and eminently temporal in the sense of being always and everywhere present to humanity and creation, then that God is Absolute Presence to both present and future. This is the God who, in the thought of the radical eschatologists, justifies in the present – in *my* existential eschatological present according to Bultmann – and reverses the order of sin to the order of grace. And this is the God who, in the thought of eschatological theologians of grace, offers both a presence in the present and a future as consummation/fulfillment of the present.[105] Moreover, when that consummation/fulfillment is seen in contrast to the destructiveness of sin and suffering, it takes on the shape of consummation/fulfillment as liberation. The eschatological God who is the object of eschatological hope disrupts history with liberating judgment/salvation in Christ and with the divine competence to be both Presence and Future, an Ultimate Reality then in both depth (or height in von Balthasar's language) and temporality.

Moreover, the notion that the method of carrying out Christian eschato-logical reflection is "adumbrated" (to use Williams' term)[106] or structured after christology is clearly evident in the eschatological reflections of most if not all of twentieth century Christian eschatologists and itself reinforces the claim for the centrality of eschatology in Christian theology. One need not be a radical eschatologist such as Barth, Bultmann, or Rahner to affirm that the way to Christian eschatology necessarily passes by the way of christology (and, for that matter, soteriology). Yet, it is clear that Barth's radical eschatology hinges on the christological (and soteriological) doctrine of reconciliation. For Barth, Jesus Christ is "the divine pledge as such.... He himself as the eternally living God is also the eternally living man" and "the absolute and final future."[107] It is also clear that Bultmann claims that "Jesus Christ is the eschatological event."[108] If that is indeed the case, if in the words of David Tracy, the person and event of Jesus Christ, precisely as eschatological, is the "focal meaning"[109] for Christianity, then eschatology most certainly lies at the center of all Christian theology. Moreover, Rahner's classic assertion that eschatological "fulfillment is the perfection of the salvation already assigned and granted by God in faith to man and humanity in Jesus Christ"[110] also further serves as evidence of Stephen Williams' claim for that second theme of convergence in contemporary eschatological reflection.

Furthermore, and within his theology of hope and *adventum novum* eschatology, Moltmann sees in the dialectic of Jesus' crucifixion and resurrec-tion the "eschatological *anticipation* of the coming of God and the liberator of a bound humanity."[111] Despite other differences of interpretation, Moltmann and Pannenberg share this same claim that the christological shows the way to eschatological finality. Pannenberg thus notes that "in the coming of Jesus the future of God and his reign that Jesus proclaimed were present by anticipation."[112] Quite recently, Carl Braaten has made a related statement by way of an interesting turn of phrase, one that highlights the eschatological intensity and finality of the christological as eschatological. "He [Jesus] made present the reality of God's future in a concentrated way."[113] Regardless of differing eschatological interpretations of the Christ event – interpretations for instance, such as Bultmann's presentist existential interpretation as set over against Pannenberg's anticipatory "proleptic" interpretation – von Balthasar's observation that "God is the 'last thing' of the creature" and "Jesus Christ [is] the whole essence of the last things"[114] reflects a true convergence in con-temporary Christian eschatological thinking. Moreover, the very fact that the eschatological event of God in the person and work of Jesus is viewed as a past/present reality pointing to a future – either as liberating fulfillment or consum-mation of the hopes of humanity – further reinforces in a concrete and historical way the notion that eschatological time is tensive. And as such it encompasses and demands of Christians both a present faith and an anticipatory hope, in the words of Moltmann, a "believing hope" where "hope is the inseparable companion of faith."[115]

William's third point of convergence is the claim that the "content" of Christian eschatological hope can be distilled into the concept of "promise,"[116] a pledge of the coming of a positive state of affairs at God's hands. While it is true that contemporary theologians speak readily of both hope and prom-ise when engaging in eschatological reflection, it is also true that their over-arching eschatological as theological perspectives inform and influence their understandings of both hope and promise. It is also true that their differing understandings of hope in promise have implications for and nuance their understandings of Williams' final observation concerning the point of Christian eschatology. This "point" can be put in the form of the practical question: what is the task of the authentic Christian in the world in the light of the centrality of eschatology to Christian theology and to lived Christian existence?

Jürgen Moltmann's understanding of promise would be a case in point. Much as is the case with others, Moltmann grounds his understanding of escha-tological promise on a reading of the Hebrew and Christian scriptures[117] and then defines promise accordingly. In *The Experiment Hope*, he defines promise in the following manner:

> What then do we mean by a promise? A promise is a pledge that proclaims a reality that is not yet at hand. A promise pledges a new future, and in the promise this new future is already *word-present*. If a divine promise is involved, it means that this future does not result from those possibilities which are already inherent in the present, but that it originates from God's creative possibilities. God's promise always points to a new creation as the word for divine "creation" in the Old Testament, *barah*, indicates.[118]

It is important to note that Moltmann's Christian eschatology of the *adventum novum* rings through in his definition of eschatological promise, and this in spite of the fact that *The Experiment Hope* was written midway between his *Theology of Hope* and *The Coming of God*. There is a clear future orientation to Moltmann's understanding of promise as well as an insistence on his part that the divine promise involves something totally new born of God's creative possibilities. There is an element of discontinuity in Moltmann's understanding of eschatological promise in the sense that the "the future does not result from those possibilities which are already inherent in the present." The dialectical nature of Moltmann's eschatological thought, a dialectic made eminently clear in the sharp contrast of cross and a resurrection born entirely of God's creativity, surfaces here in his understanding of eschatological promise, an understanding that reinforces his distinction between *futurum* and *adventum*. Yet because of his claim that expectation of the "fulfillment [of divine promise] remains open for moments of *surprise*,"[119] he, like Rahner, comes to define eschatological hope in terms of openness to the future, particularly the future of the Coming God. While Rahner characterizes hope as an essential openness to future primarily from the perspective of a transcendental theology, that is, from his claim that God is the transcendental as absolute future of humanity and cosmos, Moltmann does so from the perspective of a reading of the story of God's promise in the scriptures.

Despite the fact that Moltmann views hope in God's promises in terms of stark dialectic, and thus in terms of a certain measure of discontinuity or contrast in the sense that his ultimate hope is for God's coming and final liberating and transformative action bringing about something entirely new,[120] such hope does not diminish Christian as eschatological responsibility in this present world. Moltmann's eschatology is a mission driven one calling for a "rectifying" hope,[121] a co-responsibility for liberations in this world. Thus he notes in the effort to indicate that eschatological promises of God permit neither escapism nor deferral:

> One does not move to another country to find freedom and God. One remains where one is in order to correspond to the conditions of the coming kingdom of God through the renewal of the heart and by practical transformation of social circumstances. The front line of the exodus is not emigration but liberation through transformation of the present. For in the present, where we always are, the powers of the past wrestle with the powers of the future, and fear and hope struggle for domination. By changing ourselves and the circumstances around us, by anticipating the future of God, we emigrate out of the past and into the future.[122]

In the light of the eschatological promises of God, we do not escape or emigrate from this world; we do our part to help transform ourselves and this

world. This same theme, the marrying of the eschatological promises of God
with liberating practice in this world, echoes in the eschatological reflections
of the liberation theologian Gustavo Gutierrez. In *A Theology of Liberation*, and
in his effort to connect creation, salvation, and eschatological consummation
into one movement which ultimately defines the final reality as "communion"
with God and humanity,[123] Gutierrez also points out that "the Bible is the book
of the Promise." It is the book of *epangelía*, a word pledged, an announcement
and notification of the *evangelion*, the Good News. And as book of promise, it
"orients all history toward the future and thus puts revelation in an eschatological perspective,"[124] a perspective which must lead to a "renewal of the theology
of hope"[125] as the gift of openness to the future.[126] As Gutierrez observes, "...
Promise lies behind the whole Bible, and it makes it the book of hope."[127]

However, Gutierrez's perspective, focused as it is on biblical promise, hope,
and thus future, is not totally future oriented. He does not permit eschatology to be reduced to an escapist deferral of hope towards a distant future and
another better world. He is very clear on this point. An accurate understanding
of Christian eschatology demands the recognition that it is "an intrahistorical
reality."[128] Gutierrez's perspective reflects an appreciation for the already-not-
yet tension in Christian eschatology precisely because the core of the New
Testament promise is the promise, word-present, which we call Jesus Christ, the
definitive and final Word of God. He is also liberator of humanity and history
and calls Christians to share in the liberations which he has begun by inaugurating the eschatological Kingdom. Thus Gutierrez claims quite strongly that "the
struggle for a just world in which there is no oppression, servitude, or alienated
work will signify the coming of the Kingdom." Christian eschatological hope
orients the Christian "towards the future because it transforms the present"[129]
in a "single convocation to salvation."[130] Thus, both Gutierrez and Moltmann
see in eschatological promise not only hope for the future but also eschatological co-responsibility for liberation of the present from all personal and societal
impediments to – in the words of Moltmann – the "interplay of all blessing and
praise...in the community of God"[131] and – in the words of Gutierrez – "the
communion of human beings with God and among themselves."[132]

This theme of the promise of communion with God as the hope and final
goal of humanity also echoes in the eschatological reflection of Karl Barth as it
does in the thought of Rudolph Bultmann, both radical eschatologists. This is
the case in spite of the fact that critics of Barth and Bultmann claim that their
emphasis on faith as the authentic response to the eschatological act of God in
Jesus Christ may minimize the significance of hope and future for them. It is true

that Bultmann speaks primarily in terms of the concrete and personal existential decision of faith in response to the eschatological action of God in Jesus Christ. "To live in faith is to live an eschatological existence" where "the acting grace [of God] is present now as the eschatological event."[133] Hence, Bultmann's famous statement at the conclusion of *History and Eschatology*: "In every moment slumbers the possibility of being the eschatological moment. You must awaken it."[134] This is all presentist language. Yet Bultmann is realistic enough to realize that the human being is "on a journey, on the way" in her/his present existence, and both defines the eschatological goal in terms of a communion which can be characterized by "an untroubled relationship with God" and hope as being "open to God's future."[135] Bultmann, however, tends to "merge" faith and hope in the future of God when he notes that "this hope or this faith may be called a readiness for the unknown future that God will give."[136]

Unlike Moltmann and Gutierrez however, Bultmann does not see eschatological existence as specifically entailing a program of social liberation in this world. Indeed for Bultmann, "history and the world do not change" as a result of the eschatological act of God in Christ and in the authentic faith response of the individual; rather "man's attitude to the world changes."[137] In spite of the fact that Bultmann, like both Moltmann and Gutierrez, speaks of the eschatological act of God in Jesus Christ as an event of liberation, he does so in terms of the free choice of faith in the individual, and one senses a rejection of the world rather than a mission to the world in Bultmann's personal and existential Christian eschatology. Moltmann and Gutierrez, perhaps more intensely influenced by the observation of global suffering and injustice at the turn of the twenty-first century, invest Christian eschatology with more of a social and this worldly liberation as task orientation. In the late twentieth century writings of both Moltmann and Gutierrez, and in contrast to Bultmann, we see eschatological thinking beginning to take on a more social action or task orientation while yet remaining within a systematic discussion.

Within his systematic discussion of Christian theology, Karl Barth shares with Bultmann a decidedly christologically and soteriologically oriented eschatology. And he too sees the ultimate eschatological goal of humanity as communion with God. He calls this hoped for communion "fellowship with God,"[138] a fellowship of service, a "participation of man in the being and life of God."[139] Yet Barth, clearly more than Bultmann, invests the eschatological act of God in Jesus Christ with a greater teleological, future orientation, at least in *Church Dogmatics*. Here Barth freely speaks of the "promise" of the New Testament revelation and eschatological hope. To Barth, "man is the bearer of the divine promise" and thus "the being of man consists in Christian hope."[140] Barth makes this assertion within the context of his discussion of what he considers to be a full and integral understanding the eschatological nature of the doctrine of reconciliation. This doctrine has, to Barth, three inter-related movements: judgment/justification as God's "verdict" on humanity evoking Christian faith, direction/sanctification calling for the praxis of Christian love, and promise or pledge of "a depth of fellowship with God which has yet to be disclosed" giving rise to eschatological hope. He thus ultimately characterizes the faithful, loving, and hopeful Christian as "an eschatological being."[141] Within this eschatological understanding of the doctrine of reconciliation, a doctrine that necessarily includes hope in promise as pledge, Barth shares with Hayes and others the realization that Christian eschatology contains within it that sense of eschatological time as an inclusive tension between past, present, and a hoped for future of fulfillment.

While Barth, like Bultmann and unlike Moltmann and Gutierrez, does not specifically invest Christian eschatology with the task of co-responsibility for the liberation of humanity in this world, he does not fix eschatological hope entirely on an eternal life after death and beyond this world, although he claims that this is the promise made to the Christian as eschatological being and the goal of that being.[142] What Barth does do, however, is make the claim that the "great" hope of the Christian for the fellowship of service to God in eternal life must qualify and give direction to the day to day "small" hopes of the Christian. In the following lengthy citation, he makes his point:

> But ... we must take note of an important distinction. Christian hope is a present being in and with and by the promise of the future. But in the one hope there will always be the great hope and also a small hope. All through temporal life there will be the expectation of eternal life. But there will also be its expectation in this temporal life. There will be confidence in the One who comes as the end and new beginning of all things. There will also be confidence in His appearing within the ordinary course of things as they still move towards that end and new beginning. There is joy in anticipation of the perfect service of God which awaits man when God is all in all. But in this joy there is also joy and zest for the service which to-day or to-morrow can be our transitory future. The promise and therefore our calling are in two dimensions. They refer to the last and ultimate things, but also to the penultimate and the provisional. They refer to the whole, but also concretely to the details, to the one in all but also to the all in one. The promised future is not only that of the day of the Lord at the end of all days, but because it is the end and goal of all days it is also to-day and to-morrow. In Christian hope there is no division in this respect, but again the one hope is the measure of the other .... The small hopes are only for the sake of the great hope from

which they derive.... Where there is the great hope, necessarily there are small hopes
for the immediate future.[143]

Ultimately then for Barth, while Jesus Christ – or rather the eschatological
justifying action of God on humanity in Christ Jesus – is the "content of the
promise and the object of hope [which] cannot be replaced by any other,"[144] his
eschatology does not end in the dismissal of small hopes in present temporal
existence but rather demands that the great hope qualifies and gives direction
to any and all small hopes of Christians. Thus he will say that "hope takes place
in the act of taking the next step; hope is action."[145] In this, and writing some
years before both Moltmann and Gutierrez, he too begins to invest Christian
eschatological existence with a task or service orientation although that orientation is not Barth's dominant focus.

Yet it is important to reiterate that for Barth as well as for Gutierrez (and
Moltmann) the great hope truly does qualify all small hopes; it acts as the
criterion upon which to judge and act upon all small hopes. As Gutierrez
puts it by way of reference to co-responsibility to the Kingdom of God as the
criterion qualifying all temporal hopes of liberation, "temporal progress...and
the growth of the Kingdom both are directed towards complete communion of human beings with God and among themselves. They have the same
goal.... But the process of liberation [i.e., in temporal progress] will not
have conquered the very roots of human oppression and exploitation without
the coming of the Kingdom"[146] Karl Rahner echoes this same line of thinking when he posits that there are two dimensions or orientations to human
concern for the future wherein a "mutually conditioning relationship consists
in...man's orientation towards his 'this-worldly' future and his orientation
towards the absolute future." He notes – and in doing so echoes Barth's
observation that the great hope qualifies and directs small hopes – that "these
two orientations, towards the 'this-worldly' future and the absolute future,
mutually condition one another in such a way that the Christian attitude
towards the absolute future which is God neither diminishes nor eliminates
the responsibility it entails for a 'this-worldly' future, but rather imparts a
radical dimension to it."[147] It is for this reason that Rahner also claims that
Christians, precisely as people gifted with eschatological hope, are "people of
a holy utopia," "the utopia of God," wherein "each of us has to answer to God
questions of whether we have fulfilled our political task, whether we have
loved our neighbor, whether we have respected people's freedom and treated
them with justice."[148]

Finally, then, Stephen Williams is quite right in noting that there is a real convergence – admittedly by way of nuanced thinking – in contemporary eschatological reflection on both the sense that hope in God's promise animates Christian eschatology and that this very hope fuels a co-responsibility for Christian acts of justice and love, of liberating and fulfilling justice and love, in this world. Theologians such as Moltmann, Gutierrez, Barth, and Rahner have all have come to affirm that ultimate hope in fellowship with God into an eternal life does not permit escape from the present reality but rather spurs on hope-filled actions of liberation in this world. In this sense, the movement of Christian eschatology to the center of Christian systematics has also had the effect of pointing eschatology beyond the speculative assertions of systematics and towards eschatology as praxis. Thus, as Nicholas Lash has put the matter, "eschatology is a stimulant and not a narcotic."[149] It is a stimulant and not a narcotic because eschatology as praxis grounds its trust and its hope ultimately in God as the Final Reality, the Absolute Presence and Absolute Future which, in the words of David Tracy, is the eternal power of "Pure, Unbounded Love" as both gift and command[150] in this world. In this sense then, all of Williams' converging themes share a resonance with and indeed are grounded in the primary assertion of contemporary eschatology that God is the final and thus ultimate Reality with which humanity must reckon both now and into the future.

Concluding Remarks

In the introductory chapter of this study, I made several over-arching observations. First, I noted that eschatology came to the forefront of Christian theological reflection in the twentieth century. In that movement it has become a "storm center," signaling the drive on the part of Christian systematic theologians to re-think Christian doctrines in the light of that movement's future orientation. Secondly, I noted that eschatology's concern for the future must be dealt with adequately from a revisionist perspective that takes seriously the future's ambiguity and uncertainty. Thirdly, I noted that David Tracy's modern/postmodern revisionist stance and thought – precisely as revisionist – can serve as a possible foundational base for revising Christian eschatological reflection not in the direction of systematic reflection alone but ultimately in the direction of a rhetoric of hope as action.

In the present chapter, I have presented the eschatological claims of leading representative twentieth century theologians in order to support the first observation noted above. Yet, in that analysis I have come to claim that, while eschatological hope has moved to the forefront of Christian theology, the interpretation of its meaning(s) has and continues to be a complex and stormy task. The contours of contemporary eschatological reflection have been influenced by a critical re-affirmation of and accompanying appreciation for the Christian tradition's eschatological spirit and future orientation. Yet the eschatological task has largely been a systematic one wherein theologians have made the effort to link the various topoi of Christian theology to eschatology as it moved to the center and, in doing so, to establish a certain conceptual coherence of the Christian position with eschatology at the center. This is a *partial* revision wherein the Christian position itself is re-thought in the light of its eschatological center.

However, contemporary and revised eschatological reflection must be influenced as well by the contemporary and burning yearning of the human spirit for liberation and fulfillment in a world and a history where hopes in the modern myth of human rational progress and development have been dashed time and time again[151] and where present interruptions to human progress and development underscore the ambiguity and uncertainty of the future. Thus, in the more recent years, some systematic theologians have also begun to imply, if not assert directly, that there must be an action and this-worldly oriented dimension to Christian eschatological reflection. In this sense, the systematic task becomes a practical task as well, reflecting William's convergent "point" that Christian eschatology must serve to stimulate actions in this world on behalf of the future.

These influencing factors have served to motivate Christian theologians to take on the task of revising and exploring the meanings and meaningfulness of *eschata, eschaton,* and *Eschatos* for the contemporary Christian. These explorations have led, in the mind of Gerhard Sauter, to the surfacing of schools of eschatological thought, each with their own judgments about the roles that *eschata, eschaton,* and/or *Eschatos* must play in the discussion of a contemporary Christian eschatology. Moreover, and in varying degrees, Christian thinkers of the recently past century have sought to re-integrate the Christian doctrine about the final reality into the doctrine of creation as well as into the doctrine of reconciliation, both of which doctrines being ultimately integrated into a theology of grace. These are all systematic moves, efforts to integrate eschatological assertions into the whole Christian vision with varying consequences depending on points of emphasis. Thus, eschatology as theology of grace in reconciliation can lend to eschatological thinking not only a presentist time orientation but also a clear sense of the eschatological as disruptive, discontinuous, and interruptive of the ordinary state of affairs with the in-breaking of God's eternity as judgment into time. An eschatology as theology of graced creation, while never willing to side-step the soteriological or the presence of God in the present, has the tendency to imagine hope by way of an understanding of the present continuous with a future of de-restricting fulfillment of all that is good and gracious in the present. In either orientation, however, the presence of God as grace brings a liberating newness to Christian eschatological existence and drives systematic theologians in the direction of making certain claims about the nature of a final future, i.e., the final future as perichoresis, as communion, or as de-restriction of time and space.

What is quite important to remember in all of the discussions is that twentieth century theologians readily affirm that God and a positive and life-giving relationship of love with God are the ultimate objects of both eschatological faith and hope. This is the case despite differing points of emphasis in eschatological reflection making for von Balthasar's "storm centers." Eschatology converges into assertions about God as the Final Reality and into linked speculative assertions about the nature of the future. For systematic theologians, the object of our hope is the Subject who is God, the God of Jesus Christ, the eschatological God by whom we are justified and with whom we then will certainly share "de-restricted fellowship," "untroubled relationship," or "communion" in the future. In this, systematic claims from the Christian tradition give rise to further logical speculative claims about the nature of a final future.

However, these claims might still be viewed suspiciously by the modern/ postmodern subject who may not be comforted by the confidence of Christian systematic theologians in defining the nature of the final future because of the more immediate future's ambiguity. This lack of confidence about the future may yet serve to alert us to the fact that eschatology in the mode of systematics may indeed serve a purpose, but a limited purpose because of its tendency to make speculative and certainty assertions about a none too certain dimension of existence: the future. And postmodern uncertainty about the future may ultimately force eschatological reflection into a new construction for eschatological discourse more appropriate for dealing with an ambiguous and unavailable future, as I will ultimately contend through further analysis. This would be a construction that must encompass both the language of speculation and of action that has begun to emerge and that would reflect a revisionist appreciation for both tradition and contemporary human experience and concerns.

Eschatological themes do converge in the contemporary discussions of Christian eschatology, each open to interpretation along the contours of eschatological reflection. These themes reflect the twentieth century effort to re-interpret and revise the Christian position to make a central space for eschatology. This itself is a revision of sorts. Yet, as I have demonstrated through analysis, this partial revision has begun to point Christian eschatology in the direction of systematics expanding into eschatology as practice on behalf of the future. A fully revisionist theological position must give due attention to both the tradition and the contemporary situation. The contemporary situation remains concerned about an ambiguous and threatening future, and eschatology must find a way to deal with that concern.

In the succeeding chapters, we will have the opportunity to be exposed to and explore David Tracy's revisionist theological project as it opens up for us the eschatological dimensions of his thought, eschatological dimensions that, as revisionist, have a sound basis in human experience and knowledge, exhibit conceptual clarity, and thus can make a constructive contribution to the ongoing discussion of Christian eschatology. For David Tracy's growing eschatological sense is informed by central conceptual themes in the form of revisionist namings emerging from his theological project. And these namings can make their own unique contributions to the discussion begun in this present chapter. Most importantly, I contend and will thus demonstrate that these namings, ultimately eschatological namings, call for active human as Christian responses, and thus serve as a clue as to the direction that contemporary Christian eschatology should take in a postmodern world suspicious of the certainty claims of an exclusively systematic Christian eschatology. These revisionist namings, in their eschatological dimensions *and* action orientation, will serve as a foundation ultimately for constructing an eschatological imagination as a rhetoric. For a rhetoric has action as its goal and encompasses both speculation and action wherein speculation gives direction to action on behalf of an eschatological future. This construction first demands analysis of Tracy's thought; this will be the task of the succeeding chapters.

Notes

1. See again Hans Urs von Balthasar, "Some Points of Eschatology," *Explorations in Theology*, Volume I (San Francisco: Ignatius Press, 1989), p. 255. Von Balthasar must have struck a powerful cord with this statement, for many major contemporary texts begin the discussion of Christian eschatology from von Balthasar's claim as a starting point.

2. See Troeltsch's famous quote that "the bureau of eschatology is generally closed these days" in his series of lectures delivered at the University of Heidelberg in 1912 and 1913 entitled *The Christian Faith* (Minneapolis: Fortress Press, 1991), p. 38.

3. See again Hardwick's *Events of Grace*, pp. 267ff.

4. *ONP*, p. 81.

5. Karl Barth, *Der Römerbrief, The Epistle to the Romans* (Oxford: Oxford University Press, 1968), p. 134.

6. Ewert H. Cousins, "Introduction," *Hope and the Future of Man* (Philadelphia: Fortress Press, 1972), p. vii.

7. Carl E. Braaten and Robert W. Jensen, eds. *The Last Things: Biblical and Theological Perspectives on Eschatology* (Grand Rapids, MI: Eerdmans, 2002), p. vii.

8. Carl E. Braaten, "The Recovery of Apocalyptic Imagination" in *The Last Things*, p.15.

9. Braaten's point of reference for this determination of apocalyptic as revolutionary revelation is John J. Collins's *The Apocalyptic Imagination: An Introduction to Jewish Apocalyptic Literature* (Grand Rapids, MI: Eerdmans, 1998). See p. 283 of that text where, however, Collins "qualifies" apocalyptic as revolutionary in imagination rather than in program.

10. See Braaten's claim to this effect also on p. 51 of his article, "The Significance of the Future: An Eschatological Perspective," in *Hope and the Future of Man*.

11. While Dermot Lane in his recent text about Christian eschatology, *Keeping Hope Alive: Stirrings in Christian Theology*, laments the fact that few major texts have been devoted to the study of Christian eschatology, the fact remains that the various topoi of Christian eschatology have been embedded in the writings of many twentieth century Christian theologians such as Barth, Bultmann, Rahner, and Moltmann. See *Keeping Hope Alive: Stirrings in Christian Theology* (New York: Paulist Press, 1996), p. ix.

12. Stephen Williams, "Thirty Years of Hope: A Generation of Writing on Eschatology," *Eschatology in Bible and Theology*, Kent E. Brower and Mark W. Elliot, eds. (Downers Grove, IL: Inter-Varsity Press, 1997), pp. 243–262.

13. In "Some Points of Eschatology," von Balthasar particularly identifies de Wette, Weiss, Schweitzer, Barth, and Bultmann as theologians at the center of the "storms." See p. 255.

14. Gerhard Sauter, *What Dare We Hope: Reconsidering Eschatology* (Harrisburg, PA: Trinity Press International, 1999).

15. "Always be ready to give an explanation to anyone who asks you for a reason for your hope." *NAB* Version.

16. Gerhard Sauter, *What Dare We Hope*, p. 217.

17. Johannes Weiss, *Jesus' Proclamation of the Kingdom of God* (Chico, CA:, Scholars Press, 1985). The original text was published in 1892.

18. Albert Schweitzer, *The Quest of the Historical Jesus: A Critical Study of Its Progress from Reimarus to Wrede* (New York: Macmillan, 1964). The original text was published in 1910.

19. Gerhard Sauter, *What Dare We Hope?* pp. 56ff.

20. See Sauter's discussion of "radical" eschatology beginning on p. 68 of *What Dare We Hope?*

21. As noted in Jürgen Moltmann's in *The Coming of God: Christian Eschatology* (Minneapolis, MN: Fortress Press, 1996) beginning on p. 13.

22. In his 1957 article cited above, von Balthasar himself identified the "storm centers" with de Wette, Weiss, Schweitzer, Werner, Barth, and Bultmann. See again "Some Points of

Eschatology," p. 255. Writing long after 1957, Sauter has added the "theologians of history" to the discussion, theologians who cast the eschatological in terms of a teleology of history. Sauter's discussion of the theologians of history begins on p. 119 of *What Dare We Hope?*

23. Rahner sees the eschatological future as present in Christ but hidden and pointing toward a future fulfillment; Bultmann seems to collapse eschatology into an existential present in the act of faith in the eschatological God of Jesus Christ.

24. See particularly Chapter 1 of *What Dare We Hope* beginning on p. 1.

25. Referenced on p. 34 of Joseph Ratzinger's *Eschatology: Death and Eternal Life* (Washington, DC: CUA Press, 1988).

26. Ernst Käsemann, *New Testament Questions of Today* (London: SCM Press, 1969), p. 127.

27. Ernst Käsemann, *New Testament Questions of Today*. See pp. 108ff. In Käsemann's view, what makes the primitive Christian Easter community apocalyptically eschatological is the nature of Jesus' teaching about conversion to a new aeon of grace. See his discussion of the contrast between John the Baptist and Jesus, the contrast between conversion/wrath and conversion/grace beginning on p. 111. Käsemann also points out in his study of Paul beginning on p. 124 that the Hellenistic Pauline communities very early on began to experience a certain tension in apocalyptic as eschatological expectation because of the delay of the Parousia leading to a "compromise between present and future eschatology." See p. 131. Käsemann's identification of the primitive Christian community as apocalyptic is based primarily on the claim that an apocalyptic orientation rests on the perception of a realization of an entirely new world, a new aeon cut off from an older one. This is the world of grace and joy. However, in his summary article on "Apocalypticism" in *The Interpreter's Dictionary of the Bible*, Supplementary Volume, (Nashville: Abingdon Press, 1982), pp. 28–34, Paul Hanson notes that the whole apocalyptic movement in Jewish and Christian thought is a much more complex phenomenon, more complex in that it is characterized not only by the recognition of and hope for a new aeon but also by the construction of a new symbolic universe, often laced with images of ultimate struggles as a defensive response to persecution by a dominant religious culture. See also John Collins' discussion of the book of Revelation in his *The Apocalyptic Imagination* beginning on p. 256 in which Collins notes that Jesus as the Christ appears as a victorious "warrior" figure. Joy is present, but so too is mortal combat between opposing forces.

28. Wolfhart Pannenberg, *Systematic Theology*, Volume III, G. W. Bromiley, trans. (Grand Rapids: Eerdmans, 1998), p. 527.

29. Wolfhart Pannenberg, *Systematic Theology*, Volume III, pp. 528ff.

30. See Pannenberg's essay "The Task of Christian Eschatology," in *The Last Things*, p. 4.

31. Joseph Ratzinger, *Eschatology: Death and Eternal Life*, p. 8.

32. See particularly Rudolph Bultmann's Gifford Lectures publication, *History and Eschatology: The Presence of Eternity* (New York: Harper and Row, 1957) where he claims that "Jesus Christ is the eschatological event, the action of God by which God has set an end to the old world..." and that "the advent of Christ is an event in the realm of eternity which is incommensurable with historical time" and, finally that the Christian "who is in Christ" is "already above time and history." See pp. 151–153. Bultmann is not alone in this shifting orientation. Von Balthasar's claim in "Some Points of Eschatology" that "God is the 'last thing' of the creature" and that "Jesus Christ... [is] the whole essence of the last things"

(see pp. 260–261) is based on his qualified support for the "realized eschatology" of the Johannine text of the New Testament (a Bultmannian interpretation also). As von Balthasar also notes in *Theo-Drama: The Last Act*, Volume V (San Francisco: Ignatius Press, 1998), p. 25, "The Christ event, which is always seen in its totality, is the vertical irruption of the fulfillment into horizontal time; such irruption does not leave this time – with its present, past, and future – unchanged, but draws it into itself and thereby gives it a new character." In this sense, both Bultmann and von Balthasar really change metaphors for eschatological reflection from the temporal to a sort of spatial one, that of "depth" or "height." Along these lines of thought, eschatological finality can take on the shape of finality as an "ultimacy" transcending ordinary time.

33. This is the core "thesis" of Rahner's classic article, "The Hermeneutics of Eschatological Assertions" in *Theological Investigations*, Volume IV (Baltimore: Helicon, 1966). See particularly Rahner's fourth thesis on pp. 332–333 where he states: "All that can really be said about this future [the real future of man] is that it can and must be the fulfillment of the whole man by the incomprehensible God, in the salvation hidden in Christ which is already given us."

34. See Karl Rahner, *Foundations of Christian Faith: An Introduction to the Idea of Christianity* (New York: Crossroad, 1993) beginning on p. 431.

35. A "this worldly" eschaton informed by political theology which Ratzinger believes belongs under the control of moral rather than eschatological theology. See pp. 57ff of *Eschatology: Death and Eternal Life*.

36. Joseph Ratzinger, *Eschatology: Death and Eternal Life*. See particularly Chapter 3 wherein he criticizes Barth, Bultmann, and liberation and political theologians such as Moltmann beginning on p. 46. Ratzinger's whole goal is to point out that "the classical themes of the doctrine of the last things – heaven and hell, purgatory and judgment, death and the immortality of the soul" are inappropriately diminished in significance by such "storm center" theologians as Barth, Bultmann, Moltmann, and Metz.

37. Joseph Ratzinger, *Eschatology: Death and Eternal Life*, p. 44. He expands on his claim in the following: "By gazing on the risen Christ, Christianity knew that a most significant coming had already taken place. It no longer proclaimed a pure theology of hope, living from mere expectation of the future, but pointed to a 'now' in which the promise had already become presence. Such a present was, of course, itself hope, for it bears the future within itself." See pp. 44–45.

38. Gerhard Sauter, *What Dare We Hope?* p. 213.

39. Gerhard Sauter, *What Dare We Hope?* p. 215.

40. Gerhard Sauter, *What Dare We Hope?* pp. 216ff.

41. Published in 1996 by Fortress Press, this work is, in many ways, a continuation of and expansion upon Moltmann's classic eschatological text, *Theology of Hope: On the Ground and Implications of a Christian Eschatology*, first published in English in 1967 by SCM Press Ltd. and re-published in 1991 by Harper Collins Publishers. In his introduction to *The Coming of God*, Moltmann makes that very assertion. "This eschatology, written thirty years after the *Theology of Hope* (1964; ET 1967), is entirely in line with that doctrine of hope." See p. xii.

42. Gerhard Sauter, *What Dare We Hope?* See p. xiv especially.

43. See pp. 22ff of *The Coming God*. See Moltmann's particular effort to make the case for coming or advent as the preferred eschatological concept when speaking about God in contrast to the concept of future or *futurum*. He does so to highlight his claim that one may not necessarily hope in a future but one can hope in a coming God who can save, deliver, and bring a new realm of peace.

44. Jürgen Moltmann, *The Coming of God*, p. x.

45. Gerhard Sauter, *What Dare We Hope?* p. 176. Note the resonance with Karl Bath's language of "verdict." See Barth's *Church Dogmatics*, Volume IV.1 (Edinburgh: T. & T. Clark, 1956) beginning on p. 128.

46. See Sauter's referencing of Bultmann in this regard in the closing pages of *What Dare We Hope?* on p. 221. This is perhaps in reference to Bultmann's statement in *History and Eschatology* that "history and the world do not change, but man's attitude to the world changes." See p. 153.

47. Jürgen Moltmann, *The Coming of God*, p. xi.

48. Moltmann quotes Is. 6:3 on p. xvi of *The Coming of God* in support for this claim.

49. Jürgen Moltmann, *The Coming of God*, p. xvi.

50. See, for instance, Moltmann's critiques of reductions of the concept of God's Kingdom into the "Holy" Roman Empire, into the "Redeemer Nation," i.e., the United States, the great experiment of modern progress, the Church as "the Mother and Preceptress of the Nations," and into "Epochal Millenarianism," i.e., the birth of modernity into the Enlightenment. See Section III of *The Coming of God* beginning on p. 159.

51. See particularly Section IV beginning on p. 279.

52. See Section II of *The Coming of God* beginning on p. 47. In this section, Moltmann treats the *eschata* in a rather thorough and judicious manner. The core of his own perspective on death and eternal life can be summarized in the following: "We cannot say either that death is the separation of the soul from the body, or that death is the separation of the human being from God.... Death has to be seen as the transformation of the person's spirit, that is to say his or her Gestalt and life history; and this means the whole person." See p. 76. Moltmann then rejects the Greek concept of the immortality of the soul and opts for an understanding of death as the de-restricting of the "human being's spirit in both time and space." See p. 77 of *The Coming of God*. Further, Moltmann rejects the notion of a penal purgatory experience as well as reincarnation. See his essay "Is there Life after Death?" in *The End of the World and the Ends of God*, John Polkinghorne and Michael Welker, eds. (Harrisburg, PA: Trinity Press International, 2000), pp. 238–255. Moltmann's consistent use of the language of the "human being's spirit" can give one the sense that he rejects any doctrine of a "bodily resurrection." Yet that is not the case; Moltmann's over-arching eschatological theme is that of *novum*, *novum* for the "whole" individual, including the "transformation and transfiguration" of the bodily form. He takes his cue in this regard from the resurrection of Jesus as referenced in Philippians 3: 21.

53. Hence, the reference to Rev. 21: 5. "Behold, I make all things new." *NAB* version.

54. In a sense, this concluding claim for the nature of Christian as eschatological hope is definitely an addition to his thought. It is interesting to note that Moltmann concludes *Theology of Hope* with a retrieval of the biblical notion of "exodus," liberation. Moltmann takes leave of the eschatological community as identified with Church in *Theology of Hope*

by way of a strong critique of modern humanist and transcendental thinking as well as with a critique of the history and effects of the industrial revolution. This movement leads him to calling to mission the eschatological community "to criticize and transform the present because it is open towards the universal future of the kingdom." See *Theology of Hope*, p. 335. He thus ends *Theology of Hope* with an "in the world" eschatological project of critique and transformation.

55. Jürgen Moltmann, *The Coming of God: Christian Eschatology*, p. 336.

56. Jürgen Moltmann, *The Coming of God: Christian Eschatology*, p. 336.

57. Jürgen Moltmann, *The Coming of God: Christian Eschatology*, pp. 338–339. This concentration on God's free sharing of God's plenitude or fullness is based on Moltmann's reading of such New Testament citations as John 1: 16 and Eph. 3: 19.

58. Zachary Hayes, *Visions of a Future: A Study of Christian Eschatology* (Collegeville, MN: The Liturgical Press, 1989).

59. See particularly Hayes's first and second chapters of *Visions of a Future* beginning on p. 15. There is a parallel discussion of "promise" in Chapters 2 and 3 of Moltmann's *Theology of Hope*.

60. In this matter, Hayes also resonates with Moltmann, especially the Moltmann of *Theology of Hope*, for Moltmann's concept of "rectifying hope" in *Theology of Hope* along with his concept of "exodus Church" and eschatological mission in this world echoes a refusal to relegate the eschatological exclusively to an other world hoped for in a distant future. See Moltmann's *Theology of Hope*, p. 34 and pp. 329ff. See also Hayes's final resonating observation in *Visions of a Future*, p. 204: "It is precisely because we believe that the world has a future of ultimate significance that Christian hope ought to turn us actively to the world with deep love and concern for the gift of God which it is."

61. Hayes would place such Roman Catholic thinkers as de Lubac, Chardin, Thils, and Dondeyne in this "incarnationalist school." See pp. 127 ff. of *Visions of a Future*.

62. Hayes places such theologians as Bouyer, Daniélou, Guardini, and Pieper in this particular "eschatological school." In this way and like Sauter, Hayes also structures eschatological reflection along the lines of "schools" of thought, albeit from a Roman Catholic perspective.

63. Zachary Hayes, *Visions of a Future*, p. 129.

64. Zachary Hayes, *Visions of a Future*, pp. 129ff.

65. See David Tracy's characterization in what is perhaps his first foray into the examination of Christian eschatology in his 1968 article "Horizon Analysis and Eschatology" *Continuum* 6 (Summer, 1968), pp. 166–179.

66. Zachary Hayes, *Visions of a Future*, p. 192.

67. Zachary Hayes, *Visions of a Future*, p. 197.

68. See particularly Chapter 3 of *Visions of a Future* beginning on p. 69.

69. See Hayes's discussion of Rahner's transcendental hope in relation to both the atheist Bloch and Marcel beginning on p. 77 of *Visions of a Future*. Hayes sees a clear parallel between Rahner's theological/philosophical transcendental hope and Marcel's philosophical "absolute" hope.

70. Zachary Hayes, *Visions of a Future*, p. 195. See Rahner's *Foundations of Christian Faith*, particularly Chapter 4 beginning on p. 116.

71. Zachary Hayes, *Visions of a Future*, p. 66.

72. See Gutierrez's *A Theology of Liberation* (New York: Orbis Books, 1988), p. 96. Interestingly, Gutierrez rests his case for the "one call to salvation" on Rahner's theology of grace. See his discussion to that effect beginning on p. 43. Hayes and Gutierrez are both influenced by Rahner.

73. Dermot Lane, *Keeping Hope Alive: Stirrings in Christian Theology* (New York: Paulist Press, 1996).

74. See Lane's reference to Newman in *Keeping Hope Alive* on pp. 23 and 38.

75. Dermot Lane, *Keeping Hope Alive*, p. 38.

76. Karl Rahner, *Foundations of Christian Faith*, p. 433.

77. Karl Rahner, "The Hermeneutics of Eschatological Assertions," p. 331.

78. This is the case in spite of the fact that Rahner, Barth, and Bultmann all see eschatology, christology, and soteriology as mutually interpenetrating doctrines informing each other.

79. David Tracy, PA, p. 82.

80. Dermot Lane, *Keeping Hope Alive*, pp. 33–34. Lane quotes from Ricoeur's *Oneself as Another* (Chicago: University of Chicago Press, 1992), pp. 317–318.

81. These are, as we shall see, the very categories that inform much of David Tracy's own postmodern reflections. Such categories serve as the springboard for Tracy's discussion of plurality and ambiguity in PA.

82. See his comments to that effect in *Keeping Hope Alive* beginning on p. 33.

83. Dermot Lane, *Keeping Hope Alive*, p. 17.

84. Dermot Lane, *Keeping Hope Alive*, p. 37. As an aside and in anticipation, I note that such a postmodern "turn to the other" echoes in the thought of David Tracy as well. It is reflected in Tracy's admiration both for his former colleague, Paul Ricoeur, and the Jewish philosopher Emmanuel Levinas. There is a resonance between what Lane has to say in an inchoate way in his structuring the discussion of Christian eschatology and what Tracy has to say in his own struggle to "name" the present of postmodernity. Tracy himself notes in *On Naming the Present*, "Levinas knows that the issue is the issue of otherness, not more of the same. But unlike many postmoderns, Levinas also knows that the issue must be ethical-political." See ONP, p. 17.

85. See Sauter's argument to this effect on pp. 8 and 11 of *What Dare We Hope?*

86. Karl Rahner, "On the Theology of Hope," *Theological Investigations*, Volume X (London: Darton, Longman & Todd, Ltd., 1973), pp. 245–259.

87. Karl Rahner, "The Question of the Future," *Theological Investigations*, Volume XII (New York: Seabury Press, 1974), p. 182.

88. Johannes Baptist Metz, *Faith in History and Society* (New York: Seabury Press, 1980), p. 91.

89. Origen, *De Principiis, On First Principals* translated by G. W. Butterworth (Gloucester, Mass: Peter Smith, 1973), p. 52.

90. Dermot Lane, *Keeping Hope Alive*, p. ix.

91. *Death to Life* (Chicago: Argus Communications, 1968). Barth's essay begins on p. 38.

92. See pp. 42, 44–45.

93. See Karl Barth's *Church Dogmatics*, IV.1 (Edinburgh: T. & T. Clark, 1956), p. 109 where he identifies "God as his [humanity's] future."

94. Karl Barth, *Church Dogmatics*, IV.1, p. 324.

95. Schubert Ogden, *The Reality of God*, p. 221.

96. See Stephen Williams' discussion to this effect in "Thirty Years of Hope," beginning on p. 245.

97. Again, this is precisely the case because of the uncontrollability of God as Mystery and Absolute Future. This Rahnerian theme is echoed analogically in Rahner's discussion of "future" in general. See Rahner's "A Fragmentary Aspect of a Theological Evaluation of the Concept of the Future" in *Theological Investigations*, Volume X (New York: Herder and Herder, 1973) beginning on p. 235. Rahner notes: "One of the characteristics of futurity is that it is mysterious.... The future, with its incomprehensibility and uncontrollability, may be there and may manifest itself and conceal itself at the same time.... The true future, the ultimate which itself cannot be constructed, takes place quite simply. It comes to meet us. It is intended to be imparted to us as the incomprehensible mystery." For Rahner, God as Absolute Mystery and Absolute Future obtains these same characteristics eminently.

98. Karl Rahner, *Foundations of Christian Faith*, p. 457.

99. Jürgen Moltmann, *Theology of Hope*, p. 16.

100. Stephen Williams, "Thirty Years of Hope," pp. 246–247 and pp. 258ff.

101. Rudolph Bultmann, *Jesus Christ and Mythology* (New York: Charles Scribner's Sons, 1958), p. 13.

102. Joseph Ratzinger, *Eschatology: Death and Eternal Life*, p.1.

103. Rudolph Bultmann, *Jesus Christ and Mythology*, p. 22.

104. Quoted from George Steiner's *Errata: An Examined Life* in *Hoping Against Hope: Christian Eschatology in Contemporary Context* by Richard Bauckham and Trevor Hart (London: Darton Longman & Todd, 1999), p. 15.

105. While "fulfillment" may be the term of choice with which to describe the future hope of humanity from the perspective of an eschatology as a graced anthropology, one might note that an eschatology along the lines of a theology of history – as in the thought of Wolfhart Pannenberg – opts for describing future hope in terms of "consummation." See Pannenberg's *Systematic Theology*, Volume III, p. 453 where he notes that "the eschatological future of consummation... [is] the goal of the eternal counsel of the divine plan for history." See also Pannenberg's accompanying claim for the centrality of the role of Jesus Christ in that consummation. "All things are to be summed up in him as the Son."

106. Stephen Williams, "Thirty Years of Hope," p. 246.

107. Karl Barth, *Church Dogmatics*, IV.1, pp. 115, 324.

108. Rudolph Bultmann, *Jesus Christ and Mythology*, (New York: Charles Scribner's Sons, 1958), p. 81.

109. *AI*, p. 423.

110. Karl Rahner, "The Hermeneutics of Eschatological Assertions," p. 333.

111. Jürgen Moltmann, *The Experiment Hope* (London: SCM Press, 1975), p. 54.

112. Wolfhart Pannenberg, *Systematic Theology*, Volume III, p. 435.

113. Carl Braaten, "The Recovery of Apocalyptic Imagination," p. 20.

114. Hans Urs von Balthasar, "Some Points of Eschatology," pp. 260–261.

115. Jürgen Moltmann, *Theology of Hope*, pp. 20–21.

116. Stephen William, "Thirty Years of Hope," p. 246.
117. He notes in *The Experiment Hope* ((London: SCM, 1975), p. 45, that "The writings of the Old and New Testaments comprise the history book of God's promises."
118. Jürgen Moltmann, *The Experiment Hope*, p. 49.
119. Jürgen Moltmann, *The Experiment Hope*, p. 49.
120. This is perhaps evidenced by his claim in *The Coming of God* that ultimate hope lies in "de-restricting" human finitude in terms of the ending of time into the eternity of God and the ending of space into the full presence of God. See pp. 279ff and 296ff. "Transformative" is seen here as real change into something new and not the fulfillment of what is already partly present. In this, there is a difference between his eschatological perspective and that of those who would see a greater correlation between human secular and religious hopes such as Rahner, Hayes, and Lane although Lane too speaks of eschatological hope in terms of transformation. See Lane's *Keeping Hope Alive*, p. 70, where he notes that "the ultimate aim of God's plan for the world is not simply a glorified kingdom of disembodied spirits contemplating God's Self but rather a new heaven and a new earth embracing the transfiguration of the cosmos as well as the transformation of humanity."
121. See Moltmann's *Theology of Hope*, p. 34.
122. Jürgen Moltmann, *The Experiment Hope*, p. 59.
123. Gustavo Gutierrez, *A Theology of Liberation*, p. 32.
124. Gustavo Gutierrez, *A Theology of Liberation*, p. 91.
125. Gustavo Gutierrez, *A Theology of Liberation*, p. 123.
126. Gustavo Gutierrez, *A Theology of Liberation*, p. 125.
127. Gustavo Gutierrez, *A Theology of Liberation*, p. 91.
128. Gustavo Gutierrez, *A Theology of Liberation*, p. 96.
129. Gustavo Gutierrez, *A Theology of Liberation*, p. 123.
130. Gustavo Gutierrez, *A Theology of Liberation*, p. 45.
131. See again Moltmann's *The Coming of God*, p. 336.
132. See again Gutierrez's *A Theology of Liberation*, p. 85.
133. Rudolph Bultmann, *Jesus Christ and Mythology*, pp. 81–82.
134. Rudolph Bultmann, *History and Eschatology*, p. 155.
135. Rudolph Bultmann, *Jesus Christ and Mythology*, pp. 29 and 31.
136. Rudolph Bultmann, *Jesus Christ and Mythology*, p. 31.
137. Rudolph Bultmann, *History and Eschatology*, p. 153.
138. Karl Barth, *Church Dogmatics*, IV.1, p. 111.
139. Karl Barth, *Church Dogmatics*, IV.1, p. 113.
140. Karl Barth, *Church Dogmatics*, IV.1, p. 108.
141. Karl Barth, *Church Dogmatics*, IV.1, pp. 108ff.
142. See Barth's claim to that effect with his reference to John 3: 16 on p. 111 of *Church Dogmatics*, IV.1.
143. Karl Barth, *Church Dogmatics*, IV.1, pp. 120–121.
144. Karl Barth, *Church Dogmatics*, IV.1, p. 121.
145. Karl Barth, *Church Dogmatics*, IV.3, p. 938.
146. Gustavo Gutierrez, *A Theology of Liberation*, p. 104.

147. Karl Rahner, "The Question of the Future," pp. 190–191.

148. Karl Rahner, "Utopia and Reality: The Shape of Christian Existence Caught Between the Ideal and the Real," *Theological Investigations*, Volume XXII (New York: Crossroad, 1991), pp. 27, 29, and 36.

149. Quoted in Stephen Williams' article, "Thirty Years of Hope," p. 247. This quotation is taken from Lash's book, *A Matter of Hope: A Theologian's Reflections on the Thought of Karl Marx* (London: Darton, Longman & Todd, 1981), p. 161.

150. *AI*, p. 331.

151. Thus N. T. Wright can claim that "the cosmos as a whole is simply not evolving towards a golden future." See his critique of the "myth of progress" in his *Surprised by Hope: Rethinking Heaven, the Resurrection, and the Mission of the Church*, (New York: Harper Collins, 2008), pp. 79–91.

ESCHATOLOGICAL DIMENSIONS IN DAVID TRACY'S *BLESSED RAGE FOR ORDER*

As the previous chapter has shown, contemporary discussions of Christian eschatology have shifted away from the traditional placement of the topic at the conclusion of texts on systematic theology, i.e., as summary systematic discussions of the "eschata" or the "last things," and brought them to the forefront of critical theological reflection. Although David Tracy has not joined many of his theological colleagues in producing a specific text on Christian eschatology reflecting that shift, eschatological thinking has come, more and more, to the forefront in his theological project also. In his brief discussion of "conversion," for instance, in an article published in 1968 entitled, "Horizon Analysis and Eschatology," Tracy contended that a Christian "interpretation of human existence" is "eschatological" at heart. This is a strong claim which resonates with Barth's famous dictum in *Der Römerbrief*. In that same article, Tracy made two summary eschatological assertions based on the findings of then contemporary biblical scholarship. He noted:

> First, there is general agreement – by means, it remains true, of various Christian formulations – of the transcendent, final, unique indeed once and for all character of God's eschatological act in Christ Jesus. Second, there is general agreement contra Schweitzer-Weiss on the one hand and the early Dodd on the other, on the presence of both present and future elements in the eschatological existence of Jesus, of his church and of all truly Christian existence.[1]

For Tracy, any adequate Christian eschatology, any discussion of the "content of our Christian hope,"[2] must recognize and take into account these two fundamental claims: the claim that God, the Ultimate Reality, has acted with eschatological finality in Jesus as the Christ and that both the present and the future figure into any adequate eschatological reflection. Here then, we have a possible interpretive starting point for understanding Tracy's later eschatological reflections.

More recently, Tracy clearly "names" the present, that postmodernity which has passed through Enlightenment modernity via the suspicion of modern optimism and scientism, as "interruptive eschatological time before the living God."[3] Thus, time when viewed eschatologically is interruptive of the ordinary. Moreover, Tracy contends that the theodicy question, the question of God in the face of massive human suffering echoed in the voice of the suffering "others," calls for a rediscovery and return to the "eschatological God who disrupts all continuity and confidence."[4] This is the "God who comes first as empowering hope . . . a God promising to help liberate and transform all reality and promising as well to challenge and overcome the self-satisfied *logos* of modernity."[5] The eschatological God of David Tracy is then the God of hope who disrupts the ordinary and optimistic complacency, the God of promise, liberation, and transformation. In turn, Jesus Christ is the "eschatological prophet bespeaking the Other [who is God] for the sake of all others"[6] both in the present and on behalf of the future. For Tracy then as a revisionist Christian theologian, both the God of Jesus Christ and the human temporal situation have eschatological dimensions, and those dimensions are "interruptive."

Tracy's major works have been devoted largely to the development of reasonable and adequate theological methods with which to engage contemporary theological questions and make possible applications of those methods to those key questions raised by contemporary plurality. Yet these same works have also made implicit and explicit references to the eschatological dimensions of theological reflection, and *Blessed Rage for Order* is no exception. Therefore, the purpose of the present chapter is to engage in an analysis of Tracy's thought in *Blessed Rage for Order* in order to discover those eschatological dimensions. This analysis will thus proceed by way of the preliminary discussion of "plurality" and "limit," both central themes and keywords in *Blessed Rage for Order* and thus necessary entry points for the discovery of the implicit and explicit eschatological dimensions of Tracy's work. In *Blessed Rage for Order*, one could claim that the eschatological dimensions are – to employ a musical metaphor – played in two keys: the keys of metaphysics and of hermeneutics.[7] The metaphysical key of transcendence and process plays the eschatological dimensions more implicitly, more subtly; the hermeneutical key plays those eschatological dimensions more explicitly, intensely, and transformatively.

Plurality

Blessed Rage for Order: The New Pluralism in Theology was David Tracy's first major text on theological method in the face of modern/postmodern pluralism. It was published in 1975 and was acclaimed, in the words of Avery Dulles, as a "piece of creative scholarship"[8] that willingly reckoned with the reality of pluralism in theological reflection. Hence, as Ted Peters advises anyone reading Tracy's works, one must do so with a full recognition of David Tracy's commitment to accepting and working through the contemporary challenges with which an intellectually honest pluralism confronts the theological project. When reading Tracy, "we must recognize and embrace pluralism."[9] This is indeed the case. If one were to name, in a general way, the contemporary postmodern situation from Tracy's perspective, such a naming would necessarily have to include Tracy's full recognition, acceptance of and appreciation for theological pluralism. This is one of Tracy's primary assumptions in *Blessed Rage for Order*.[10]

Tracy's second principle assumption in *Blessed Rage for Order* is a function of his critical appreciation of that pluralism: "That assumption holds that each theologian must attempt to articulate and defend an explicit method of inquiry, and to use that method to interpret the symbols and texts of our common life and of Christianity."[11] Such a method of inquiry demands the appropriation of critically sound intellectual frameworks with which to carry on that inquiry. Both transcendental and process philosophies are important – albeit, in the minds of some thinkers, disparate – metaphysical frameworks which Tracy employs in his analysis of the plurality inherent in human experience. For Tracy, the recognition and acceptance of pluralism may indeed require multiple, critical appropriations, and this present study shows how both interpretive turns contribute to understanding the eschatological dimensions of Tracy's theological project in *Blessed Rage for Order*.

Furthermore, as Tracy notes, "...critical...mean[s] a fidelity to open-ended inquiry, a loyalty to defending methodological canons, a willingness to follow the evidence wherever it may lead."[12] Herein lies his "modern" fidelity to the "morality of scientific knowledge,"[13] what Bernard Lonergan calls "the self-correcting power of reason"[14] In this sense, Tracy stands at a crossroad as it were between modernity and postmodernity. In his preface to the most recent edition of *Blessed Rage for Order*, published in 1996, he applauds what he considers to be the "unfinished, emancipatory side of the project of modernity," its willingness to critically review the basic traditional assumptions of theological, philosophical, and scientific thought.[15] However, in recognition of the ambiguities and discontinuities of the postmodern world, Tracy also refers to the nineteenth and twentieth century "masters of suspicion," i.e., Marx, Freud, Nietzsche, and Kierkegaard, those "paradigmatic postmodern analysts,"[16] in order to temper and interrupt the optimistic "illusions" of the modern project. Indeed, Tracy's final chapter in *Blessed Rage* as well as his later reflections in *Plurality and Ambiguity* point up the fact that modern history is riddled with interruptions – failures and violence – which contradict any overly sanguine and optimistic view of "progress." Thus, modernity and postmodernity can work their emancipations, their liberations. And emancipation or liberation in the midst of pluralism is a key theme that will also surface as an eschatological dimension in Tracy's thought.

Within the context of modernity (and postmodernity), Tracy points to certain disturbing ambiguities which are born of that double-edged sword of enlightened modern reason: cognitive, ethical, and existential crises that give rise to "that strange *pathos* which seems to characterize both the crisis of meaning and the struggle for authentic humanity operative in our contemporary period."[17] These three crisis situations for theology ultimately serve as the structural starting points for the correlation of his metaphysical and hermeneutical reflections in *Blessed Rage*. Tracy makes the claim that there is a universal religious dimension to secular human existence, that this dimension is best described as "limit" reflecting a commitment to a "basic trust" or faith in "the full affirmation of the ultimate significance of our lives in the world,"[18] and that this descriptor resonates quite adequately with both common religious language and specific New Testament eschatological disclosures. Through a careful method of correlation by way of the exploration of modern/postmodern crises on these three levels, Tracy ultimately comes to re-affirm the Christian claim that Christianity provides "the authentic way to understand our common human existence."[19]

Most importantly, Tracy claims that the responsible and authentic revisionist Christian theologian must be freed from a supernaturalism or a mystification of religion as well as a purely naturalist or secular understanding of God, humanity, and reality. He writes:

> ...such theologians wish to deny the purely secularist negation of any real ground of meaning outside ourselves which assures that faith is not simply illusion. They also intend to negate any essentially positivist "revelational" affirmation of our supposed ability to transcend this faith in this world in favor of some presumably greater, indeed supernatural world. They believe that neither secularism nor supernaturalism can adequately reflect or appropriately ensure our commitment to the final worthwhileness of the struggle for truth and honesty in our inquiry, and for justice and even agapic love in our individual and social practice.... This...is the situation of the modern Christian theologian. He finds himself disenchanted with the mystifications promulgated by too many church officials and the mystifications proclaimed with equal certitude by the secularist self-understanding of the age. He believes he shares the basic Christian faith of the former and the secular faith of the latter. Indeed, he believes that the Christian faith is at heart none other than the most adequate articulation of the basic faith of secularity itself.[20]

This lengthy citation is of extreme importance not only for understanding Tracy's revisionist theological position in the face of plurality but also for determining the eschatological dimensions of his thought in a number of ways. First, the final claim noted above, the claim that Christian faith is "at heart none other than the most adequate articulation of the basic faith of secularity itself," reflects Tracy's rejection of any mystifying dualism between supernatural and natural realms.[21] Thus Tracy notes:

> The theologian finds that his basic faith, his fundamental attitude toward reality, is the same faith shared implicitly or explicitly by his secular contemporaries. No more than they, can he allow belief in a "supernatural" realm of ultimate significance or in a supernatural God who seems, in the end, indifferent to the ultimate significance of our actions.[22]

This claim also puts the demand on him, especially later in his career as his concern for the suffering of the "other" intensifies, to emphasize the *praxis* dimension of any authentic theological project. What is most important to note here in terms of any eschatological claims regarding Tracy's theological project in *Blessed Rage* is that Tracy's interest lies in action in the world. One would be hard pressed to find any otherworldly eschatological dimensions in Tracy's thinking. Even in his hermeneutical analysis of New Testament texts and of the "christological fact" in *Blessed Rage*, the analysis in which he makes explicit eschatological claims, his focus is on Christian existence as the most authentic "mode-of-being-in-the-world." The language of transcendence and its imperative dimensionality is language about transcendence of limits to the human condition in the world. Finally, language which claims that Christian faith most adequately articulates basic secular faith warrants Tracy's later claim that the "limit language we call eschatological is an appropriate expression"[23] of the possibilities for human self-transcendence in authentic existence as Christian existence. In a word then, the liberating eschatological language of the Christian tradition resonates with the limit language of a secularity shot through with plurality.

The Notion of Limit

Early on in this chapter, the claim was made that the eschatological dimensions of Tracy's thought in *Blessed Rage for Order* are played implicitly in the key of the philosophical, i.e., via phenomenology and metaphysics, and explicitly in the key of New Testament hermeneutics,[24] both of which keys articulate Tracy's theme of "limit." This is Tracy's ultimate and controlling keyword for describing the religious dimension of human existence resulting from his analysis of the cognitive, ethical, and existential "crises" of modernity/postmodernity. Therefore, this dominant and recurring theme must be explored, not only in order to understand the meaning, meaningfulness, and truth value of disclosures about God and humanity, but also to gain entrée into the eschatological dimensions of Tracy's thought.

For Tracy, the method of a contemporary and revisionist fundamental theology should be that of a "mutually critical correlation"[25] where the theologian draws a given religious tradition into conversation with "common human religious experience and language."[26] In the very effort to articulate his method for doing fundamental theology, Tracy engages in a phenomenological or descriptive analysis of the religious dimension of common human experience and language and a metaphysical or transcendental effort to verify the results of the phenomenological analysis, that is, to affirm their conceptual coherence in meaning, their existential meaningfulness, and their true and universal adequacy to experience.[27] Thus, in fidelity to the modern "turn to the subject," Tracy begins with human experience.

The phenomenological analysis of human experience uncovers two fundamental and anthropologically descriptive keywords: "limit" and "basic trust" wherein basic trust is identified as the authentic human response to limit. Tracy's effort to identify these keywords with the religious dimension of common human experience via analysis of the three levels of contemporary crisis, i.e., the cognitive, the ethical, and the existential, lends to "limit" and "basic trust" a certain measure of universal applicability. Furthermore, Tracy's effort to explicate these key facets of human self-understanding and agency from a variety of philosophical worldviews[28] not only underscores his pointed effort to universalize his claims about the nature of the human being as religious but also reflects his recognition of plurality and his willingness to "reinterpret specific material positions from a broad spectrum of traditions."[29] This is phenomenology as thick description which focuses on phenomena from a wide range of angles.

In what sense then is the religious dimension of common human experience and language best characterized with the descriptors "limit" and "basic trust" and how are these descriptors disclosed at the three levels of cognitive meaning, ethics, and existence? Tracy begins his analysis of the religious dimension of common human experience by asking: "How and in what sense is the religious interpretation of our common human experience and language meaningful and true?"[30] There are two movements to his answer. First, Tracy makes the claim that religious experience (and language as reflective of that experience) is, by its very nature, limit experience, even though that experience may be expressed with some variability.

> My contention will be that all significant explicitly religious language and experience (the "religions") and all significant implicitly religious characteristics of our common experience (the "religious dimension") will bear at least the "family resemblance" of articulating or implying a limit-experience, a limit-language, or a limit-dimension.[31]

The question then becomes: why is that the case? Why is the religious element of human existence characterized by limit? Tracy answers in the following manner and, by doing so, sets his own limits for reflection in this matter:

> Now it seems sufficient merely to note a more ordinary usage of the category "religion." Employed in our common discourse, "religion" usually means a perspective which expresses a dominating interest in certain universal and elemental features of human existence as those features bear on the human desire for liberation and authentic existence. Such features can be analyzed as both expressive of certain "limits-to" our ordinary experience (e.g., finitude, contingency, or radical transience) and disclosive of certain fundamental structures of our existence beyond (or, alternatively, grounding to) that ordinary experience (e.g., our fundamental trust in the worthwhileness of existence, our basic belief in order and value).[32]

In other words, when human beings authentically engage themselves in reflection and discourse about religion, the dual characteristic of "limit-to" and "limit-of" (or "ground-to") surfaces. For Tracy, what also surfaces inherently within that twofold sense of limit is the human desire and drive for liberations. Tracy admits that other human experiences also disclose a sense of limit. Thus, "limit" does not equal or exclusively define religion but rather serves as an indispensable characterization of it.[33] The religious dimension of human experience and language reveals itself characteristically in the experiences and expressions of "limit-to" or boundaries upon human existence and "limit-of" or "ground-to" human existence as a "basic trust" or faith in the worthwhileness of human existence.

It is important to make a clarification at this point. For Tracy, limit is an essential and universal religious dimension of human experience that can be discovered by phenomenological analysis. Basic trust is the human response to the experiences of limit. In this sense, Tracy claims that the religious dimension of human experience is an existential trust in the face of limits. Moreover, in a transcendental, i.e., "truth claim" move, Tracy asserts that this faith as basic trust is not only an authentic human response to limit but also the very condition for the possibility of recognizing and living with limit. Herein lies Tracy's philosophical naming of the human situation. Furthermore, he claims, "... the object referent of all such language and experience is that reality which religious human beings mean when they say 'God.'"[34] God is thus philosophically named as the objective ground to all religious experience and guarantor of that basic faith/trust. For Tracy, any adequate critical reflection on the limit dimensions of human existence necessarily leads to the question of God.[35]

In a second move, Tracy makes his case for limit and basic trust by analyzing human existence on the three different levels of crisis for modern/postmodern consciousness which are also the three dimensions of human experience: the dimensions of scientific knowledge, of moral questioning, and of existential experience itself.[36] Thus, first and drawing upon the work of Bernard Lonergan, his mentor,[37] Tracy notes that an analysis of the human drive to know, the drive for scientific knowledge, phenomenologically discloses this sense of the human being as ever moving to the limits of scientific knowledge. What is most important for his argument, however, is his claim that the human being engaged in the pursuit of knowledge, in the pursuit for example of scientific discovery, asks fundamental questions, at least implicitly, in that very pursuit. These fundamental questions lurk in the background of all scientific inquiry. Thus, there is a transcendental, i.e., fundamental, dimension to human cognition. Limit points to transcendence at least as a real possibility.

This transcendental dimension is disclosed, for instance, in the formulation of three basic questions which for Tracy point out not only the "limit-to" character of scientific (and thus rational) questioning but also the "ground-to" that questioning. In the first place and appropriating Lonergan, Tracy asks: can scientific inquiry bear fruit? That is, "can these answers [the answers which result from scientific inquiry] work if the world is not intelligible? Can the world be intelligible if it does not have an intelligent ground?"[38] Secondly, can the scientist trust scientific judgment as "virtually unconditioned affirmation"[39] without recourse to a formally unconditioned ground? Thirdly, "... is it worthwhile to ask whether our goals, purposes, and ideals are themselves worthwhile (a limit-to question)? Can we understand and affirm such a demand for worthwhileness without affirming an intelligent, rational, responsible source and ground for them (a limit-of question)?"[40] Tracy's answer to all three of these basic questions is a resounding "no." Human experience with the world of science supports this response. We operate at the cognitive level with a prior sense that real knowledge is possible, with a basic trust in the very possibility of a real knowing. Scientists continue to conduct scientific inquiry with a certain measure of zest, success, and confidence. They both accumulate knowledge and continue to pursue it. Thus, when the human being engages in the very act of scientific reflection, when the human being makes cognitive scientific inquiry, she or he does so with an implicit sense or basic trust that there is some measure of security and value in that very engagement and that the knowledge secured by that activity is grounded and trustworthy.

In a sense, Tracy's phenomenological engagement with the scientific world via Lonergan is not all that novel. Augustine and Thomas also posited an *ordo* to all of creation because of its theistic ground. A "blessed rage for order" has often served to inform the theistic and Christian tradition. Yet, Tracy also makes an important additional point. "Since these limit-questions legitimately follow from scientific inquiry itself, they are not imposed extrinsically upon scientists by 'religious' types but rather are well within the scientific inquirer's own horizon."[41] In other words, and in fidelity to his over-arching methodology of correlation, Tracy sees the religious dimension of human experience as limit in a twofold sense[42] and he sees this twofold sense of limit operative in the very secular act of engaging in scientific inquiry itself. Thus, on both levels, the human being is disclosed as one who can live in basic trust in a fundamental way.[43]

This basic sense of trust in the face of the boundaries of limit-to questions is, to Tracy, also evident in a phenomenological analysis of the moral dimension of human existence. Referencing the thought of both Stephen Toulmin and Schubert Ogden,[44] Tracy makes the claim that the fundamental question "Why ought I keep my promise anyway?" i.e., why act in a morally righteous manner, uncovers this same character of limit-to and limit-of in the moral dimension of human existence. Tracy makes the point:

> In fact there is no moral argument for answering that question. Such questions, there-fore, may be described as limit-questions: questions emerging at the limit of the usual kinds of moral questions and arguments. More summarily, we cannot really produce a moral argument for being moral. The limit-character of the logic of such questions (and hence the type of arguments to which they will appeal) suggest to Toulmin that they be described as "religious" or "theological" questions. Our own natural "desire for reassurance, for a general confidence about the future" impels us to *use* religious language and to develop theological arguments.[45]

Thus, the fundamental question concerning the "why" of morally righteous language uncovers both the limit-to or boundary of human moral questioning and points to a limit-of or ground-to such questioning in the very act of asking "why?" However, Tracy does not see this sense of a fundamental moral ground as a merely human projection in the face of a desire for security. Citing the insights of Schubert Ogden, Tracy continues on:

> Ogden develops Toulmin's own insistence that we "reassure" ourselves that the "whole" and the "future" are trustworthy in order to argue that all religious *language* thereby bears the linguistic form of *re-presentation*. We misunderstand the function of religious language if we claim that it *causes* (presents) our general confidence or trust in the meaningfulness of existence. We understand such language correctly only when we recognize that the use of religious language is an *effect* (a *re-presentation*) of an already present basic confidence or trust.[46]

In other words, in the use of religious language to address questions of moral existence, the human being recognizes and expresses her/his limit/boundary and, ultimately, only makes sense out of morally righteous behavior in the light of a prior sensing and trusting a ground for that behavior. Religious language is not presentative but representative of a basic trust. Just as in scientific inquiry, in the matter of moral behavior there is this religious intuition of a ground (later to be identified by Tracy as the living God) which gives human existence a certain worthwhileness, wholeness, and potential for liberation. Moreover, Tracy's retrieval of Ogden's understanding of "re-presentation" serves as a guarantee in a sense of the possibility of countering the claim that religious language is merely a human effort towards self-security. Tracy's (and

Ogden's) claim is that the security lies not within the human fabrications of a secure ground for existence but rather on a basic faith in the wholeness, the worthwhileness of existence. In spite of and in the light of limit, the religious human being lives in a stance of basic faith or trust which makes possible self-transcendence.[47]

The two dimensions of human experience explored by Tracy thus far, and for which he makes the case of a religious as limit dimension to human existence, rise out of basic human questioning of existence. They are thus matters of human reflection, of human cognition and ethical action based on that cognition. The third dimension is existential; it discloses the religious in the situation, in lived experience. Drawing upon Karl Jaspers' existential analysis of human experience,[48] Tracy claims that the daily common experiences of human existence are also limit-to experiences (boundary experiences) and limit-of experiences (located in a basic trust in a trustworthy ground). Tracy makes the point in this way: "Fundamentally, the concept [limit-situation] refers to those human situations wherein a human being ineluctably finds manifest a certain ultimate limit or horizon to his or her existence."[49]

Tracy sees this twofold sense of limit evident in the realities of everyday experiences as limit-to, e.g., "guilt, anxiety, sickness, and the recognition of death as one's own destiny," and as limit-of, e.g., "ecstatic experiences – intense joy, love, reassurance, creation."[50] While momentary, the ecstatic experiences of human existence serve to verify the possibilities of human transcendence. "All such *ec-static*, i.e., transcendental, experiences may, by their 'limit-disclosing' character, serve as 'signals of transcendence,' as 'rumors of angels ....'"[51] Thus, the moments of shadow (limit-to situations) and the moments of light (limit-of situations), perhaps often in a dynamic tension or perhaps where one moment is embedded in the other, again uncover the possibility of this basic trust and self-transcendence of which Tracy speaks, and they do so in the very disclosure/recognition of human limitation. The limit experience of love is perhaps the most classic and poignant example of the transcendental nature of human limit experience. "Authentic love, both erotic and agapic, puts us in touch with a reality whose power we cannot deny. We do not work ourselves into a state of love, as we might into a habit of justice. We 'fall,' we 'are' in love. While its power lasts, we experience the rest of our lives as somehow shadowy."[52] This resonates positively with Tracy's later characterization of the religious dimension of human existence: the human being is "finite, estranged, and needing a liberation by a power not its own,"[53] as well as with the (negative) Heideggerian notion of existential anxiety as "a fear disclosive of our often forgotten but never totally absent consciousness of our own radical contingency" where "the final dimension or horizon of our own situation is neither one of our making nor under our control."[54]

Tracy summarizes his phenomenology of the religious dimension of human experience in *Blessed Rage for Order* in the following way: the religious dimension is "... a dimension which, in my own brief and hazy glimpses, discloses a reality, however named and in what ever manner experienced, which functions as a final, now gracious, now frightening, now trustworthy, now absurd, always uncontrollable limit-of the very meaning of existence itself."[55] And, again, the object referent of that gracious but frightening limit-of is, in *Blessed Rage*, Tracy's God. If the human being is religious at all, then she or he is religious precisely in asking the fundamental as transcendental questions inherent in the human pursuit of scientific knowledge and moral righteousness and in sharing in the limit experiences of existence (both of radical boundary and of ec-stasis), that is, in asking the fundamental questions and living in the fundamental situations which disclose or re-present limit-to as human boundary and limit-of as a trust in the reality of a gracious ground, i.e., God. Thus, "... the first and abiding issue for human beings is their faith or un-faith, commitment to value or failure to live a human life. A faith of this kind ... is most immediately experienced in boundary-situations and peak experiences and most clearly mediated or expressed in the limit language of an explicitly religious self-understanding."[56]

Here then from the perspective of philosophical analysis via the entry points of the cognitive, the ethical, and the existential, we see the human situation radically and fundamentally described as one of "limit." At the same time, we see God as the radical and fundamental or transcendental objective ground of all limits. And finally we see faith as a basic trust as both the warrant and authentic human response to this twofold nature of limit. Moreover, Tracy's appropriation of Ian Ramsey's descriptors for religious limit language serves, in his mind, to re-present limit as the fundamental religious dimension of common human experience at the linguistic and empirical level. Ramsey's categories of "odd personal discernment, a total commitment, and a universal significance"[57] with their "infinity" qualifiers serve as apt descriptors of religious language and experience. They attempt, by means of language, to capture the limit character of religious experience. Tracy thus notes: "Limit-language seems a correct way to indicate the logically odd character of religious language and the qualitatively different empirical placing for that language in our common experience."[58]

The Implicit Eschatological Dimension

It is clear from the above summary analysis that Tracy's effort to discover and appropriate an adequately universal descriptor for the religious element or dimension of common human experience (and, concomitantly, for God as the objective ground for that dimension) rests on philosophical reflection. The musical key at this point of the discussion is philosophical and thus, to Tracy, secular. Given that key then, what can be said about both God and humanity eschatologically? If limit in the twofold sense of limit-to or boundary and limit-of as fundamental ground is the key to unlocking the implicit and perhaps subtle eschatological dimensions of Tracy's thought in *Blessed Rage*, how is that the case especially in anticipation of Tracy's final claim that the "limit-language we call eschatological [as revealed in New Testament disclosures] is an appropriate expression" of the decision to "risk living a life-at-the-limits"[59] as an authentic and thus ultimately Christian as eschatological human being?

First and in a general sense, Tracy's naming of God as the object referent of limit-of or ground-to existence resonates quite well with the eschatological claim that God is the Final Reality for humanity as well as for all existence. In Tracy's own words, this is the One who has accomplished the "transcendent, final, indeed once and for all...eschatological act in Christ Jesus."[60] This itself is an eschatological claim. It is true that Christian theologians have adopted different formulations for describing God as the Final Reality for all existence. For instance, and appropriating the language of the Hebrew Scriptures, Jürgen Moltmann speaks of this Final Reality as the *"cosmic Shekinah,"*[61] as a final Presence that serves as the focus and ground of all eschatological images and metaphors. And as Gerhard Sauter has noted in *What Dare We Hope? Reconsidering Eschatology*, particularly in his discussion of the radical nature of Christian eschatology, eschatology is the "boundary marker of theology" because "eschatology is radicalized in order to bear witness to God as the 'wholly other' who cannot be deduced from the world or history."[62] Eschatology is the boundary marker for theology because it takes theological reflection to its final limit which is God. While such a decidedly Barthian stance can open itself to the critique that all theology is reduced to eschatology, Sauter's appropriation of the concept "boundary marker" when speaking eschatologically resonates well with Tracy's twofold sense of limit wherein the human being is confronted with boundaries (or limits-to) yet senses a Reality beyond those boundaries (a limit-of) guaranteeing the worthwhileness of existence despite those very boundaries or limits.

While Tracy, fully Catholic in his thinking, would perhaps have some difficulty with the radical claim that God as the wholly other cannot be deduced from the world and its history,[63] he would agree that God as the object referent of the ground to all existence is the Final Reality. When Tracy states that the religious dimension of human existence lived out in basic faith "discloses a reality…which functions as a final, now gracious, now frightening, now trustworthy, now absurd, always uncontrollable limit to the very meaning of existence,"[64] he implicitly makes the claim for the eschatological God via the philosophical perspective not only with the descriptor "final" but also with the reference to God's "uncontrollable" nature, a nature that "disrupts all continuity and confidence."[65] Here eschatological finality can be identified with limit in its function as an "ultimacy," as the very "condition of all possibility" beyond the control of human agency precisely because it grounds all human agency. Later in his writings, Tracy even names God as the "Ultimate Reality."[66]

This sense of finality does not necessarily exclude a temporal understanding of finality; yet the emphasis is on finality as ultimacy. We recall here von Balthasar's assertion in his discussion of eschatology that "God is the 'last thing' of the creature,"[67] as well as Barth's claim that "God alone is his [the human being's] future and his hope."[68] Regardless of whether one includes a sense of temporal finality in the designation "last thing" or not, the last thing is, eschatologically speaking, the ultimate thing. Tracy himself blends the notions of transcendence, the other side of limit, and finality as both temporal and yet ultimate in his claiming that God's action in Christ Jesus is the final eschatological act of God without limiting the idea of finality to the temporal.[69] To be the last thing is to be the ultimate uncontrollable Reality which grounds all reality and lends to it its trustworthiness. It is for this reason that Tracy asserts that the "final or ultimate horizon" of human existence is a "religious one,"[70] in which the limit-of existence or Final Reality graciously warrants faith in the worthwhileness of existence. If indeed there is a "final, now gracious…always uncontrollable limit to the very meaning of our existence," a limit-of which human beings sense in faith through their daily encounters with boundary, that limit-of or uncontrollable ground is the eschatological God, the Ultimate Reality.[71]

In *Blessed Rage for Order* however, Tracy does not rest with his naming of God as the ultimate final ground of all existence. Such a naming is ultimately somewhat antiseptic and in need of greater concretization in order to meet Tracy's goal of speaking of God in an existentially meaningful way that also ultimately correlates with a hermeneutic of the Jewish and Christian traditions. Therefore, adopting a process metaphysics in a deliberate second step beyond the transcendentalism of Bernard Lonergan (without, that is, abandoning its valuable constructs), Tracy appropriates the "dipolar" God, that "limit-concept" of God as Pure Unbounded Love, from process thought. Tracy does so because such a conceptualization of God resonates not only with his understanding of human relationality and temporality, but also because such a limit concept resonates with the Jewish and Christian scriptural naming of God, particularly the Johannine naming of God as Love.[72] In other words, Tracy claims that process categories of thought provide a logical and coherent understanding of God[73] and existence. They also account for God in a way meaningful to humanity. Finally, such process categories resonate with traditional Christian religious disclosures about God. Thus Tracy's understanding of the dipolar God is logically coherent in the light of the process understanding of human existence and all reality, an understanding that does not set "absolute" and "relative" in opposition. The process God is also meaningful for human existence as inherently relational because this God is social and relational. This God truly cares, affects and is affected by creation. Furthermore, this God as Pure Unbounded Love resonates faithfully with the scriptural disclosures of God as related to and caring of humanity and all creation.[74]

At its heart, Tracy's argument for the dipolar God is another argument from analogy but one which starts from a metaphysics of relation rather than one of substance. Critiquing "classical theism," Tracy makes his claim in the light of a series of fundamental religious questions and assertions:

> The troubling questions of the process thinkers cannot be silenced [by classical theism] even on an existential level: Is not the God of the Jewish and Christian scriptures profoundly involved in humanity's struggle to the point where God not merely affects but is affected by the struggle? Is Bonhoeffer's famous cry that only a suffering God can help merely a rhetorical flourish of a troubled man? Can the God of Jesus Christ really be *simply* changeless, omnipotent, omniscient, unaffected by our anguish and our achievements? Was the magnificent move of classical patristic and medieval Catholic Christianity from the *quoad nos* of the scriptural interest in God's relationship to humanity to the *quoad se* of the patristic and medieval interest in God-in-himself a fully positive move? Or did its impressive intellectual achievements conceal certain inherent religious and conceptual difficulties? My own suspicion is that all authentic Christians live and pray and speak as if God were really affected by their action. They live as if, to use the expression of one process theologian [Ogden], God really were Pure Unbounded Love struggling, suffering, achieving with humanity.[75]

While it is not necessary to review all the details of Tracy's argument in opposition to the God of classical theism and in favor of the process God, the dipolar

God as Pure Unbounded Love, an argument which admittedly has been critiqued by some colleagues,[76] it is important to note that Tracy makes this argument for the process understanding of God out of a certain dissatisfaction with the classic theist understanding of God as the "Wholly Absolute God, unrelated internally to creatures and thus literally unaffected by their actions."[77] This dissatisfaction rises from Tracy's fidelity to his revisionist goal of carrying on a critical theological reflection that is both adequate to human experience and appropriate to the tradition. The God of classical theism seems not to ring true in Tracy's mind because he cannot logically reconcile an unrelated and yet loving God.

At this point, a pertinent question may then be asked: how does this second naming of God, this naming beyond the claim for God as the transcendent object referent of limit-of, also disclose or help to fill out the eschatological dimension of Tracy's thought? If – and within the key of the philosophical as metaphysical/transcendental – God is the transcendent limit, the Final as Ultimate Reality grounding all basic trust or faith in the wholeness and worthwhileness of existence, what does the philosophical key of process contribute to an eschatology?

The understanding of God as Pure Unbounded Love interpreted by way of process metaphysics bespeaks an implicit eschatology in a significant way. The very move to eminence in the Tracy/Ogden language about the dipolar God resonates with the eschatological as final and ultimate and at the same time lends to that language a more concrete and meaningful understanding of the nature of that ultimacy or finality. We move from God as Ultimate Ground to God as Love in an ultimacy of purity and lack of boundary. God is God precisely as eminently pure and unbounded in God's very loving. This naming of God is a true move to eminence by way of analogy from human experience.[78] That is to say, Tracy contends that human existence is such that an essential element of that existence is relationality, the capability of self-transcendence through loving.[79] However, that relationality is bounded by finitude, contingency. The process theologians would contend that this is not the case for the dipolar God. God's relationality is unbounded, with all and for all. In other words, language about the dipolar God itself is eschatological language in that it attributes to God ultimacy in terms of relationality and concomitantly relationality as the ultimate reality.

Tracy's own language in describing the dipolar God takes on the shape of the language of limit, finality, and thus ultimacy when he poses the question: "… should we say that God is both absolute (as the one whose *existence* depends on no other beings) and relative (as the one whose *actuality* is relative to all other human beings)?"[80] Tracy answers that question affirmatively when he states that the dipolar God is absolutely and thus ultimately, finally and unparadoxically, relative because "God alone is relative to all. God alone affects all...and is affected by all."[81] Here relative takes on a texture of ultimacy as it refers to relationality and not to contingency.

This notion of God, the Ultimate Reality, also puts an eschatological claim on humanity. Human existence as ultimately relational, if truly faithful to its Ground as Pure, Unbounded Love, is called to the relationality of love. In other words, the eschatological limit of all existence disclosed implicitly in the analysis of human limit questions and existence, that limit-of or ground-to all existence which elicits the human response of faith as basic trust, is love itself. This limit-concept is made more concrete and meaningful to humanity by way of the process naming of God in that the eschatological limit-of or ground-to all existence is pure, unbounded love, agapic love.[82] That dipolar God who is Pure Unbounded Love then not only invites the human response of faith as a basic trust in the worthwhileness of existence and its call to self-transcendence but also invites the human response of love. For love is self-diffusive; it bespeaks an invitation to self-transcendence in love in response to its free offer.

David Tracy's naming of God as the dipolar God of Pure Unbounded Love from the perspective of process metaphysics characterizes God in eschato-logical terms wherein ultimacy takes on the shape of the relationality of pure, unbounded love. This is a significant contribution to the discussion of Chris-tian eschatology coming from a primarily philosophical perspective, a secular perspective, because it is an eschatological naming that resonates with and is meaningful for secular human existence. Such meaningful resonance under-scores Tracy's basic claim for coherence between the secular and the religious, a coherence that militates against theological mystifications. Moreover and quite importantly for a theologian who sees praxis as integral to the theologi-cal project, Tracy's namings of God from his philosophical and secular starting points also serve to point to the possibility of authentic human responses to that eschatological God, the response of faith as a basic trust and the response of love to the free offer of divine agape. There is then warrant for claiming that the very philosophical exercise which David Tracy engages in *Blessed Rage for Order*, an exercise that discloses namings of God, affords one the opportunity to see how Tracy's God functions eschatologically and how human beings may respond to that eschatological functioning. In sum, the meaning inherent in Tracy's naming of God as the object referent of Limit-of and Pure Unbounded

Love points to possible authentic human and Christian responses, e.g., in faith and love, to that eschatological God in the world. That very resonance then serves not only to reinforce Tracy's contention that the basic faith of authentic secularity correlates at heart with the basic faith of authentic Christianity but also that the eschatological can be discovered in the ordinariness of daily existence and not in a mystifying supernaturalism. And quite importantly for Tracy, eschatological disclosures or discoveries about God and human existence inherently point not towards thought or speculation alone but rather in the direction of active responses to the stimulus nature of those discoveries.

To this point, we have focused our attention on Tracy's disclosure of limit and basic trust in terms of "Limit-of" in order to discover some implicit eschatological dimensions to his thought. The focus has been on his naming of God, the Final as Ultimate Reality, in terms of transcendental and process analysis. Before moving from the philosophical key to that of the hermeneutical in Tracy's reflections on New Testament texts, we can also find other implicit eschatological themes on the second side of limit, i.e., "limit-to," for Tracy names the human situation as limit-to. Just as naming God in the philosophical and thus secular key affords the opportunity for eschatological interpretation of Tracy's thought, so too, naming the human situation in that same key affords a similar opportunity on a number of different but related levels, for limit-to ineluctably points to limit-of in Tracy's analysis.

The inevitable human confrontation with boundaries in the cognitive, moral, and existential dimensions of existence, the confrontation with "limit-to," affords one the opportunity to make a self-transcending act of faith in a transcendent and thus ultimate limit-of or ground-to the worthwhileness of all existence. Indeed, such confrontation demands this transcendental act of faith. The alternative would drive the human being down the path of solipsism and despair. And "opportunity" is a key word at this point because opportunity denotes "possibility" as opposed to certainty and opens the way for human hope.[83] Tracy's understanding of limits or boundaries to human existence at the level of cognitive and moral questioning as well as at the level of ordinary existence holds within it not only hope in the possibility of self-transcendence in spite of limit but also, and again referring both to Lonergan's "transcendental imperatives"[84] and to the postmodern "cry of illusion" against the complacencies of modernity,[85] the human challenge to accept the demand for self-transcendence inherent in the call to live an authentic human existence. This hope and demand for human self-transcendence in its cognitive, moral, and existential dimensions is implicitly eschatological in nature precisely because the human intuition of an affirming transcendent ground "reassures" – to use Toulmin's term – the human being of the very possibility of that self-transcendence, of moving through limit in a basic faith by the grace of the Ultimate Limit. Thus reassurance as a basic faith engenders hope, the predominant but not exclusive eschatological virtue.

Moreover, inherent of course in the eschatological notion of self transcendence are two other mutually related eschatological dimensions: eschatological transformation as a real newness and its uncontrollability by mere human agency.[86] The experience of limit-to disclosed in the phenomenological analysis of human cognition, ethical action, and ordinary existence again allows for the claim of an implicit eschatological dimension to Tracy's thought in *Blessed Rage* because that analysis also discloses hope in a newness not exclusively wrought by human control. For instance, we recall that Tracy's phenomenology of the aspirationally transcendental nature of the critical scientist, of her or his drive for scientific discovery, confronts the scientist with fundamental limit questions about the real possibility of achieving fruitful and valuable scientific knowledge. That very drive is inherent in the very nature of the human being.[87] We are seekers and interpreters of meanings, of understanding, and we carry out that search hoping to discover something really new and fruitful. Moreover, as Tracy has sought to point out, we do so because of a certain measure of confidence or trust in the possibility of achievement of new and potentially transformative scientific insights. We sense and have faith in an *ordo* guaranteed by a gracious ground warranting our efforts. That faith gives hope to move forward into a future of possible new discoveries. Moreover, we seek to discover that order, to recognize it and appropriate it. We do not create it. That underlying order is not of our making, nor entirely under our control.

One can note by example that Newton truly discovered some extraordinarily new insights into the physical *ordo*, insights which allowed for the transformation of the scientific world in the seventeenth century. One can also note that the drive for self-transcendence via scientific experimentation and discovery always impels the scientist to new insights, to greater discoveries. Einstein relativizes Newton. Thus, the secular human drive for knowledge itself as demonstrated by authentic scientific investigation echoes – at the level of secularity – the eschatological as self-transcendence in both its dimensionalities of real newness and uncontrollability. On this basically secular level, self-transcendence takes place for the authentic critical scientist when that scientist transcends herself/himself by risking scientific inquiry and achieving and appropriating new scientific insights. Moreover, for Tracy that self-transcendence becomes more authentic when the recognitions achieved and appropriated are put into the practical service of the human community, when they work their positive transformations and thus liberations on behalf of that human community.[88]

Tracy's analysis of limit-to and limit-of at the crisis point of the ethical is not all that extensive. Basically, he makes the claim that there is no adequate answer to the question of "why should I keep my promise to act in an ethical manner" without recourse to trust in a higher ground, a normative ground that reassures us "that the whole and the future are trustworthy."[89] As has been noted, he retrieves Toulmin's language of reassurance and Ogden's language of re-presentation to make his case and does not focus a great amount of attention on the ethical dimension of human existence per se.[90] Perhaps what is most important about his analysis for the present discussion is that, for Tracy, authentic ethical action cannot ultimately be governed by norms under one's own control. Indeed, one's own norms may be interrupted by a fundamental ground-to or limit-of human ethical action norming that action. This is the uncontrollable Ultimate Ground which theism and Christian eschatology name as God. Thus, to answer his basic ethical question, "Why ought I keep my promise anyway?" Tracy would respond with a faithful affirmation of the intuition of a prior Promise that authentic ethical action governed by a norm beyond human conception and interruptive finally of human control will result in a positive future. In other words, the limit-to of the ethical questions and situations point to the eschatological limit-of precisely as an ethical normative ground which is not of human making nor ultimately under human control. Here self-transcendence is worked out as ethical action that results from a going beyond one's own conceptions of the norms governing that action to a recognition and appropriation of a normative structure that is not of one's own making. It is transcendence in the very act of risking ethical action based on the intuition of an ultimate normative ground.

Tracy's phenomenological analysis of human existence in the "world of the everyday,"[91] that third point of crisis in modern/postmodern consciousness, perhaps most clearly reflects self-transcendence as at least implicitly eschatological by way of the dimensions of newness and uncontrollability. "Ecstatic experiences" such as the experiences of joy, creativity, and especially love are clearly existential examples of self-transcendence,[92] and human beings recognize them as such. Moreover, these experiences are such that a real newness enters into one's life, a newness via transcendental experiences which take hold of and transform one's situation, one's perspectives, and one's relationships dramatically. The newness and uncontrollability of these self-transcending moments is described by Tracy as limit of a decidedly "gracious character," as gift which really transforms the everyday:

> When in the grasp of such experiences, we all find, however momentarily, that we can and do transcend our usual lackluster selves and our usual everyday worlds to touch upon a dimension of experience which cannot be stated adequately in the language of ordinary, everyday experience . . . . We find ourselves affirming the reality of ecstatic experience, but not as something merely decided upon by us. In all such authentic moments of ecstasy, we experience a reality simply given, gifted, happened. Such a reality, as religious mystics remind us, maybe a taste of that self-transcending experience of a "being-in-love-without-qualification" familiar to the authentically religious person.[93]

It is also true, of course, that Tracy recognizes that everyday experiences can confront a person with intense anxiety as well as joy. Limit-to situations are, after all, boundary situations. Recall that Tracy notes in agreement with Martin Heidegger, "anxiety is a fear disclosive of our often forgotten but never totally absent consciousness of our own radical contingency."[94] Yet these moments when we find ourselves "poised over an abyss, a chasm"[95] are also opportunities, possibilities, for self-transcendence because they "disclose that the final dimension or horizon of our own situation is neither one of our own making nor one under our control."[96] If positive ecstatic experiences such as those of love signal self-transcendence in that they disclose a really new reality in the midst of the ordinary, then the negative existential experiences of boundary (such as radical illness, loss of a loved one, etc.) force us to recognize that, at root, all of our efforts to master our situations ultimately fail because they deny a final and thus eschatological dimension of existence out of our control. The eschatological God, the ground-to all existence, offers self-transcendence but not always on human terms. The eschatological God is interruptive and cannot be controlled, and the secular as the sometimes painful existential realization of limit-to does come to recognize this truth. This is a truth that calls for the basic trust in a gracious limit-of existence, that demands what Paul calls "hoping against hope" in Romans 4: 18 and rests on the realization that "all human attempts at self-aggrandizement, self-affirmation, and self-justification before God and humanity fail."[97] Limit-to situations confront us with boundary; they also offer the opportunity and hope for transformative self-transcendence.

In sum then, Tracy's analysis of the limit-to our knowledge, our moral doings, and our everyday experiences discloses both the confrontation of humanity with boundary and the offer of an opportunity for transformative newness through the exercise of a basic secular faith and hope. This opportunity is present only because of a prior basic faith and hope in the reality of a limit-of our knowledge, our moral agency, and our existential situations. Thus, there is an implicitly eschatological dimension to these fundamental secular human dimensions: the dimensions of cognition, morality, and everyday existence. However, this dimension does not rest on an eschatological accounting laced with supernatural dualism but on the analysis of human agency within the world. The other side of limit, transcendence played out in the unquenchable human desire for new meanings, in the keeping of an ethical promise, and in sharing in ecstatic experiences, ultimately rests on a faith which engenders hope, again that primarily but not exclusively eschatological virtue. As Sauter states from the perspective of systematic eschatology, "The confession of faith always implies hope."[98] From the perspective of a phenomenological analysis of limit, basic faith and hope are secular, that is, in the world, authentic human possibilities.

In this philosophical key, David Tracy names God in language which reflects eschatological affirmations about God's functioning as a Final Ultimate Reality, as the Ultimate Reality which is Pure Unbounded Love. These are the eschatological meanings implicit in limit-of, and these eschatological meanings ground and summon forth faith as basic trust and love as authentic human responses to the eschatological God. But Tracy also names the human situation as limit-to in the same philosophical key, the key that places the human being on the cusp between finitude and ultimate transcendence. It is the key where the human being sometimes faintly, sometimes strongly, senses "rumors of angels."[99] And because of such a sense, this is the key not only of faith and love but also of hope, hope in the real possibility of self and societal transcendence in spite of limits-to. This is the key which recognizes a certain measure of ambiguity to existence in the inter-play of limit-to and limit-of but, because of faith in love as the ultimate reality, also engenders hope as an imagination of the possibility of transformative transcendence. Thus it is no wonder that Bauckham and Hart call for the recognition of the "essentially imaginative nature of hope,"[100] for a faith engendering hope at the secular level of existence offers the possibility of imagining new and transformative meanings and experiences of transcendence. David Tracy's phenomenology of limit then in its two fold dimension bespeaks an implicit eschatology in his namings of God, of the human situation, and of what he perceives to be the authentic human response to those namings. The eschatological key of transcendence as real newness, ultimately uncontrollable by mere human agency, harmonizes with the eschatological key of Ultimate Reality as Pure Unbounded Love and points in the direction of an authentic revisionist eschatology – an active in-this-world and non-mystifying supernaturalist eschatology – of faith as basic trust, of love for love, and of hope enkindled by faith and love.

The Explicit Eschatological Dimension Disclosing an Eschatological Mode of Being-in-the-World

In *Blessed Rage for Order*, David Tracy also explicitly speaks of Christian eschatology in the course of carrying out his project of defining what he considers to be a critically reasonable and potentially fruitful method for fundamental theology in this modern/postmodern world. His explicit eschatological assertions are woven into his whole argument in favor of the method of critical correlation and of limit in its twofold dimension as the defining characteristic of human existence in relation to God. These assertions appear at four key points in the text: in his discussions of the "eschatological" theologians, of "history, theory and praxis," of the "religious language" of New Testament texts, and of the "re-presentative limit language of christology." First, and in a very preliminary way, Tracy identifies the eschatological theologians with the radical postmodern social and historical critique of the optimism of the modern liberal project of Enlightenment.[101] This is an important identification, for it discloses Tracy's belief that liberation is a concept inherent in the discussion of Christian eschatology. The imperative dimensionality of the modern/postmodern drive for transcendence requires liberating praxis. There is for Tracy then a clear connection between Lonergan's transcendental imperatives and authentic praxis in theology, and eschatological reflection is directed towards action.

That belief is reinforced in the very fact that Tracy concludes *Blessed Rage* with a discussion of "history, theory, and praxis." One of Tracy's goals in the final chapter of the text is to suggest that the theological method of critical correlation can be applied fruitfully to practical theology as well as to fundamental theology. Within that argument, Tracy identifies the eschatological theologians such as Jürgen Moltmann, Johannes Metz, Carl Braaten, Rubem Alves, Richard Shaull, Juan Segundo, Gustavo Gutierrez, and Dorothee Soelle[102] with the call for "a retrieval of the Jewish and Christian eschatological symbols...of societal, political, and religious liberation"[103] to criticize – via dialectic – the present oppressive social order evident in postmodern history. This is the eschatological call for real historical change not as development but as action on behalf of liberation on the social as well as individual levels. This is the kind of "persevering, rectifying hope that finds articulated expression in thought and action" which lies as the heart of Moltmann's theology of hope as eschatology.[104]

Yet Tracy also criticizes the eschatological theologians. At this point of his career, Tracy considers them to be "neo-orthodox" at heart in that they are primarily theologians of retrieval and fail to apply critical theory to their own traditional eschatological symbols. He notes: "Perhaps the principle reason for this failure can be traced to the eschatological theologians' seeming refusal to challenge the neo-orthodox model of their immediate theological predecessors."[105] Whether Tracy's critique of the eschatological as liberation theologians is justified or not, the point to keep in mind is that Tracy clearly identifies the eschatological with action in favor of liberation and not wholly with a passive certainty in some future consummation or fulfillment. Furthermore, he does so not in terms of liberation as retreat from the historical world of the everyday but in terms of liberation of self and world within history.

Tracy also makes explicit eschatological assertions at two other points in *Blessed Rage for Order,* and both points lie within his turn to the second pole of his methodological reflection in fundamental theology, the pole of the Christian tradition. He does so in his "historical and hermeneutical investigation" of "the Christian Tradition."[106] These are the points in *Blessed Rage for Order* at which he explores the "religious language" of the New Testament[107] and the "re-presentative limit-language of christology."[108] Tracy's discussion of New Testament language forms points to the explicit eschatological dimensions or senses inherent in selected New Testament genres. Further, Tracy's discussion of the "re-presentative" character of the "christological fact" also points to the final and thus ultimately significant re-presentation of what he considers to be the concrete authentic as Christian mode of being-in-the-world made possible for the believer through the words, deeds, and destiny of Jesus as the Christ.[109]

In his effort to make the case for religious language as limit language in the New Testament, Tracy selects three key New Testament genres for analysis at the historical and hermeneutical level: the New Testament proverbs, Jesus' proclamatory sayings, and the parables. Tracy's thesis is that these three forms, all of which are disclosive of a Christian eschatological world view,[110] serve to disclose, at the hermeneutical level, the radical religious experience of limit. With the support of historical-critical biblical scholarship,[111] he notes that "several recent interpretations of the New Testament uses of proverbs, eschatological sayings, and parables show how the *sense* of such language can properly be described as fitting the earlier description of religious language as a limit-language."[112] In his analysis, Tracy asserts that these selected New Testament forms or genres are expressive of limit, the key concept that serves as the major indicator of the religious dimension inherent in human existence. Furthermore, his claim that religious limit-language is "eschatological,"[113] coupled with the hermeneutic of these three genres, serves to disclose what Tracy sees as concrete, lived expressions of Christian existence as eschatological existence.

Tracy also characterizes the three New Testament forms or genres of proverb, proclamation, and parable as "breaking" forms.[114] As eschatological, these forms break through ordinary forms of expression. They interrupt our everyday understandings of existence, and they do so in three important ways: these forms intensify, transgress, and go to the limits of language.[115] As Tracy notes, Christian proverbs such as "Whoever seeks to gain his life will lose it, but whoever loses his life will preserve it" (Lk 17: 33; cf. Mk 8:35) are intense, jarring, paradoxical statements about an existence which takes up the challenge of Christian faith. They open up a radically new, ultimate, and thus eschatological understanding of reality and point to an entirely new possible mode of being in the light of Christian faith. They offer the possibility and challenge of transcending ordinary understandings.

Moreover, the eschatological proclamatory sayings of Jesus such as Lk 17:21, "the Kingdom of God is in the midst of you," both interrupt or transgress the ordinary and literal understanding of time and make the faith claim that an eschatological understanding of time is not apocalyptic in some fundamentalist (literalist) sense or totally future oriented but that such an understanding holds past, present, and future in a dynamic unity in tension. Implicit in this discussion of the tensive nature of eschatological time is the claim that Jesus as the Christ is the "eschatological prophet," the *Eschatos* who announces the in-breaking of the eschatological Kingdom of God. Transgression of ordinary understandings, and particularly the ordinary understanding of time, again ushers in the possibility of new understandings and a new mode of being in the world.

Furthermore as Tracy claims (by way of Paul Ricoeur), the parable not only "goes to the limits of language" but also does so within the world of the normal, the ordinary.[116] Here we see eschatological intensification and transgression in the extravagant behavior of parable characters, ordinary people operating in extraordinary ways with a new righteousness. They risk a life at the limits often in a generous, agapic love (as in the case of the Prodigal Father) which sets in motion real newness and superabundance. Tracy summarizes the eschatological meaning inherent in the parable stories in the following way:

> One need not appeal only to the general eschatological religious vision enunciated by Jeremias, Dodd, or Bultmann as the parabolic horizon of meaning in order to understand that eschatological, limit horizon. Rather one may note that, even linguistically these narratives, for all their ordinariness, force the underlying metaphor to a limit which can be described as a "religious" use of language. The parables, as stories, take the reader to the point where the course of ordinary life is broken; an intensification of the everyday emerges; the unexpected happens; a strange world of meaning is projected which challenges, jars, disorients our everyday vision precisely by both showing us the limits to the everyday and projecting the limit-character of the whole.[117]

Thus these three selected New Testament genres break and thus interrupt the form of the ordinary at the level of human understanding and at the level of expected moral agency. They also point to a new and demanding ethical responsibility within the world as they intensify through paradox, transgress the ordinary, and thus move us to the very limit. In this, they are disclosive of eschatological meaning. Furthermore, proverb, proclamation, and parable as disclosive of really and radically new ways of understanding existence and of living a life based upon those new understandings parallel the implicit eschatological dimension inherent in limit as the possibility of self and societal transcendence at the philosophical level. A correlative dynamic is operative in limit language and the explicit eschatological language of the New Testament. Limit offers the possibility of transcendence at the human levels of cognition, morality, and existence. The explicit eschatological genres of New Testament language add the further and very concrete claim that Christian existence as eschatological existence necessarily entails a sense of urgency, of intensification, and, most importantly, the challenge to appropriate a reversal of ordinary understanding and behavior in order that a real newness and, ultimately, superabundance unfold in the ordinary. Herein lies the liberating effect of an eschatological understanding of existence. Liberation comes about in the shocking and interruptive recognition and appropriation of a new and final understanding of reality that is often a reversal of the ordinary oftentimes anthropocentric view, a reversal that is disclosed by a ground or final power not of human creation or control.

What is perhaps most important to note in Tracy's position regarding the religious/eschatological nature of selected New Testament language forms is that these forms function as indicators of a real possible mode of Christian existence which breaks through and liberates the ordinary and gives to the ordinary an eschatological finality in this world. In a summary statement, Tracy notes:

> Religious language and religious experience promise, restore, and liberate a dimension to our lives....That language re-presents our always threatened basic confidence and trust in the very meaningfulness of even our most cherished and noble enterprises, science, morality, and culture. That language discloses the reassurance needed that the final reality of our lives is in fact trustworthy....Religious language, whenever it is authentically related to a religious insight of extraordinary force as in the New Testament, employs and explodes all our ordinary language forms in order to jar us into a recognition of what, on our own, can seem only a desirable but impossible possible mode-of-being-in-the-world. As proverbial, that religious language disorients us and forces us to see another, a seemingly impossible way of living with authenticity. As parabolic, that language redescribes our experience in such a manner that the sense of its meaning (its now limit-metaphor) discloses a limit-referent which projects and promises that one can in fact live a life of wholeness, of total commitment, or radical honesty and agapic love in the presence of the gracious God of Jesus the Christ.[118]

The shock of recognition which gives rise to the religious insight that existence can be authentically re-described in terms of a seemingly impossible possibility is a liberating reversal of ordinary understandings. It is offered to humanity as a revelatory and promissory gift in the "christological fact." From the perspective of hermeneutical analysis, the senses discovered in the New Testament forms point to a referent, a possible mode-of-being-in-the-world – a possible and plausible way of acting – which the "re-presentative" christological fact discloses, offers, challenges, and warrants. The christological fact stimulates action as it shapes a possible and preferred way of living in spite of limiting interruptions.

Tracy's discussion of the "christological fact" is thus the final point where he makes an explicit eschatological assertion in *Blessed Rage for Order*. He asserts:

> When the full disclosive force of that symbol [the christological fact of Jesus as the Christ] is existentially seen, one may realize that here any human being is asked to decide with an urgency for which that limit-language we call eschatological is an appropriate expression: to decide to risk living a life-at-the-limits, a faithful, hoping, and loving life, which the Christian gospel proclaims as both a true understanding of the actual human situation in its reality and its possibility and an ever-to-be-renewed decision.[119]

In other words, at this point Tracy joins eschatological assertions with christological assertions in making the claim that the "christological fact" presents again and again, time after time, the real possibility of choosing to live a life of seeming impossibility, the life of faith, hope, and agapic love in the eschatological God which the "words, deeds, and destiny"[120] of Jesus as the Christ disclose with interruptive, final, and gracious power. Like Barth and Rahner, Tracy finally claims that Jesus as the Christ is the key to all eschatological assertions precisely because Jesus as the Christ is radically "at the heart of Christian self-understanding."[121] However, he does so not via a traditional systematic analysis of christological doctrine nor by embarking on a new search for the historical Jesus. He does so by way of a hermeneutic of the New Testament texts that both ties the explosive, interruptive, eschatological senses or forms of New Testament genres of proverb, proclamation, and parable to the words, deeds, and destiny of Jesus and unites disclosure or discovery to action.

Moreover, Tracy asserts that there is a dramatic unity between the eschatologically oriented words and deeds of the Jesus who proclaimed the eschatological Kingdom of agapic love and his destiny in his "paradigmatic role as the crucified one."[122] Jesus' destiny as the crucified one is not what most warrants eschatological faith, love, and hope in risking a life at the limit; indeed, crucifixion standing on its own bespeaks the impossibility and futility of that form of life, a reversal of the ordinary view of existence that leads only to death. The complete christological fact is representative of true and final Christian existence only when warranted by the interruptive action of the eschatological God in Jesus' resurrection. As Tracy notes, "... the central representative symbol of the cross is always joined to the symbol of the resurrection."[123] The resurrection of the representative figure of a new mode of being-in-the-world who was/is Jesus the Christ gives rise to a plausible hope on which to live on into the future, to the real possibility of a final reversal. This is the reversal of death into a new life of ultimate superabundance which the Kingdom parables pre-figure in tensive metaphors of the extraordinary at the limit of the ordinary. Tracy summarizes thus:

> Whatever the historical occasion of the resurrection-belief so central to the New Testament may be, the basic existential meaning of that belief remains the same: the representative words, deeds, and teachings of this representative figure, this Jesus as the Christ, can in fact be trusted. He is the re-presentation, *the* Word, *the* Deed, *the* very Destiny of God himself. The God disclosed in the words, deeds, and destiny of Jesus the Christ is the only God there is – a loving, righteous Father who promises the power of this new righteousness, this new possibility of self-sacrificing love to those who will hear and abide by the Word spoken in the words, deeds, and destiny of Jesus the Christ.[124]

In a very real way then, Tracy's retrieval of the central Christian faith claim that Jesus as the Christ re-presents the core fact of human existence, i.e., the actuality in Jesus and the possibility for us of an eschatological as final mode of being in the world, brings to convergence the key eschatological themes, both implicit and explicit, which run through *Blessed Rage*. The re-presentative nature of the christological fact appropriated in faith as a basic trust points to a new understanding of eschatological time which transcends and breaks the ordinary linear and literal interpretation of time. Eschatological hope then is not relegated to an apocalyptic future beyond space and time but lives in the dynamic tension of past, present, and future in this world where the future becomes the realm of living on a Christian possibility. Resurrection, that ultimate transcendence, when joined to the intensifications and transgressions – indeed, the radical interruptive reversals – of the ordinary imbedded in the christological words, deeds, and cross both discloses and warrants the real possibility of eschatological self and societal transcendence wrought not by human agency but by the action of the interruptive eschatological God who is Pure Unbounded Love and the Ultimate Reality. Herein lies for Tracy true and authentic liberation, at least as a possibility and therefore as a stimulus for hope. It is a possibility because the eschatological action of God, the Final Ground-to or Limit-of all existence, was/is a reality in Jesus as the Christ, a reality which offers and warrants a life of risk, of faith, love, and hope at the limits.

Concluding Remarks

David Tracy's theological project in *Blessed Rage for Order* is primarily an exercise in determining a method for engaging in a Christian fundamental theology. His project is first and foremost an effort to describe and apply the revisionist method of mutually critical correlation to common human religious experience as seen through contemporary eyes and to the faith claims of the Christian tradition. I contend that this very effort has surfaced revisionist namings both of God and of the contemporary human situation that have eschatological dimensions. The controlling and interruptive keyword, "limit," as applied to both God and situation discloses the eschatological dimension of Tracy's revisionist perspective in *Blessed Rage for Order*. Thus, Tracy's theological project in *Blessed Rage for Order* takes us beyond fundamental theology per se and displays some of the dimensions of a non-mystifying Christian eschatology for a modern and postmodern world. A pattern of eschatological thinking has surfaced in *Blessed Rage for Order* wherein disclosed eschatological dimensions call for an action oriented form of discourse in response to the boundaries to everyday thinking and existence. Discovered "limit" namings, eschatological namings, are namings that recognize the ultimate dimensions of existence while, at the same time, confirm living – action – specifically within those dimensions.

Thus, Tracy's namings of God and the human situation in *Blessed Rage for Order* achieve a theology for the modern/postmodern world that affirms the radicality of Christian eschatological claims. This takes the shape of a philosophical description of the real possibility of a liberating, authentic life in the world, a life of virtued existence, a life of faith, hope, and love in the Ultimate and Final Reality re-presented in the words, deeds, and destiny of Jesus as the Christ. Herein then also lies a real and radical newness for existence and its liberation into the future. When Tracy sketches out his chapter on the christological fact, he points to the human need for fiction to attempt, however haltingly, to describe an uncontrollable Ultimate Reality and humanity's relationship to that Reality. He also points out the reality of sin in the world; sin interrupts but ultimately does not frustrate the eschatological *ordo* because it can be overcome by the reversal of the ordinary anthropocentric mode of being in the world with the theological/eschatological mode.[125] This is the mode-of-being-in-the-world which Jesus as the Christ re-presents, a real and concrete mode of being in the world which offers, finally, to a free humanity the possibility of liberating transcendence in hope if only appropriated and acted upon.

"Limit" in the midst of plurality then is the key to Tracy's thought in *Blessed Rage for Order.* It not only affords him the opportunity to make a critical correlation between secular and religious human existence in the face of plurality via philosophical and hermeneutical analysis; it also allows him, finally and thus eschatologically, to make the claim that authentic secular human existence is authentic precisely as religious and as Christian and thus eschatological. Transcendence as the other side of limit at the cognitive and ethical levels of human existence takes radical but concrete shape when directed towards living according to the christological disclosure. This form of existence is eschatological; it is grounded in a recognition and faith as basic trust in a Reality, a Power of the whole not under human control, which graciously offers self-transcendence in love and engenders hope, the eschatological response to the theological. It is transcendence as a real possibility in response to the gracious nature of Transcendence at the heart of all reality. And that response to the eschatological God of *Blessed Rage for Order* who is Transcendence or Limit-of at the very heart of all reality takes concrete shape first and foremost as the active response of faith. This would be faith as a basic trust in the worthwhileness of existence in and in spite of limit and faith as the shock of recognition that there is a real possibility of self-transcendence into a life of love and hope, the Christian eschatological life.

In *Blessed Rage for Order*, the eschatological life then is a "life-at-the-limits, a faithful, hoping, and loving life which the Christian gospel proclaims as both a true understanding of the actual human situation in its reality and its possibility and an ever-to-be-renewed decision."[126] In this sense, the Christian gospel or story both describes the present reality eschatologically and gives direction for acting on future possibilities. But that same form of life is a life of risk. Tracy's revisionist eschatological disclosures point to an offer, a possible mode of existence in this world both for the present and the future, that may be trusted, appropriated, and acted upon. However, competing non-eschatological forms of existence and the very nature of the future itself as a place of ambiguity and uncertainty both underscore the risk nature of eschatological existence. For eschatological existence as it faces the future is existence operating on possibilities rather than hard and fast certainties. As we delve further into the eschatological dimensions of Tracy's project in *The Analogical Imagination* and *Plurality and Ambiguity,* we will continue to see patterns of eschatological thinking upon which to build: eschatological dimensions as namings evoking action responses within the framework of a revisionist spirit and language. We will also see a modern become postmodern revisionist spirit of hopeful suspicion emerging in the face of risk. And ultimately, these discoveries will afford the final opportunity to construct a revisionist Christian eschatology that moves beyond the theological genres of fundamental and systematic theology, the genres of *Blessed Rage* and *The Analogical Imagination,* to a new genre, that of eschatology as a rhetoric.

Notes

1. David Tracy, "Horizon Analysis and Eschatology," *Continuum* 6 (Summer, 1968), p. 177.
2. This is how Monica Hellwig characterizes Christian eschatology in her summary article, "Eschatology," in *Systematic Theology: Roman Catholic Perspectives,* Volume II, Francis Schüssler Fiorenza and John P. Galvin, eds. (Minneapolis, MN: Fortress Press, 1991), p. 349.
3. *ONP,* p. 18.
4. David Tracy, "The Hidden God: The Divine Other of Liberation." *Cross Currents* 46/1 (Spring, 1996), p. 6.
5. David Tracy, "The Hidden God." p. 8.
6. David Tracy, "Theology and the Many Faces of Postmodernity," *Theology Today* 51/1 (April, 1994), p. 112. We recall that this title, "eschatological prophet," is Edward Schillebeeckx's preferred descriptor of Jesus the Christ. Refer to *Jesus: An Experiment in Christology* (New York: Crossroad, 1991), beginning on p. 401.

7. To be more precise here, the key is philosophical as both phenomenological and metaphysical. The reference to the musical metaphor of two keys, the key of the philosophical and the key of the hermeneutical, is an appropriate and informative one. That is, in *BRO* Tracy's controlling keyword is "limit," and he explores that controlling keyword both from a secular philosophical perspective and from a religious hermeneutical perspective much as a musician can play the same notes from two different starting points, i.e., in two different keys. Yet the same notes are played and determine a melody. Such a metaphor supports Tracy's "correlational" approach to the theological project and plays up a certain measure of coherence between the secular and the sacred/religious in Tracy's thought.

8. Avery Dulles, "Method in Fundamental Theology: Reflections on David Tracy's *Blessed Rage for Order." Theological Studies* 37/2 (June, 1976), p. 304.

9. Ted Peters, "David Tracy: Theologian to an Age of Pluralism." *Dialog* 26 (1987), p. 298.

10. Thus in the opening pages of *BRO*, Tracy states: "The present work operates on two principle assumptions. The first assumption insists that the present pluralism of theologies allows each theologian to learn incomparably more about reality by disclosing really different ways of viewing both our common humanity and Christianity." See p. 3.

11. See also *BRO*, p. 3.

12. *BRO*, p. 7.

13. *BRO*, p. 6.

14. *BRO*, p. xiv.

15. *BRO*, p. xv.

16. *BRO*, p. 11.

17. *BRO*, p. 4. In *The Analogical Imagination*, Tracy names this *pathos* our "not-at-homeness." See p. 356 of *AI*.

18. *BRO*, p. 8.

19. *BRO*, p. 44.

20. *BRO*, pp. 9–10.

21. *BRO*, p. 10. When applied to the concept of liberation theology, what Tracy calls "eschatological" theology (see Chapter 10 of *BRO*) in, for instance, the thought of Gustavo Gutierrez, this claim of Tracy's is played out in the discussion of the "crisis of the distinction of planes" and the affirmation of "the single convocation to salvation." See Gustavo Gutierrez, *A Theology of Liberation* (Maryknoll, New York: Orbis Books, 1988), especially pp. 39ff. Gutierrez cites de Lubac and Rahner as his (and Tracy's) theological predecessors in making that type of a claim. As an aside, Gaspar Martinez in his *Confronting the Mystery of God* sees both Tracy and Gutierrez as "children" of Rahner in both their modern move to historical consciousness and in their return to God as Absolute Mystery. That, indeed, is Martinez's whole thesis.

22. *BRO*, p. 8.

23. *BRO*, p. 223.

24. This, admittedly, is itself a philosophical perspective. This would be the Gadamerian and Ricoeurian stance on the status of hermeneutics and also Tracy's.

25. The "mutual" descriptor for Tracy's revisionist method of critical correlation was an addition made by Tracy post-1975 in order to "indicate the fuller range of possible correlations between some interpretation of the situation and some interpretation of the tradition.

This signals that theological correlation is not always harmonious...." See Tracy's "God, Dialogue, and Solidarity" in *Cross Currents* 107 (October, 1990), p. 900.

26. This strategy is fully outlined in Chapter 3 of BRO, pp. 43ff.
27. See Chapter 4 of BRO beginning on p. 64. On p. 71, he makes clear his three criteria for any acceptable phenomenological-transcendental analysis: "A particular experience or language is 'meaningful' when it discloses an authentic dimension of our experience as selves. It has 'meaning' when its cognitive claims can be expressed conceptually with internal coherence. It is 'true' when transcendental or metaphysical analysis shows its 'adequacy to experience' by explicating how a particular concept (e.g., time, space, self, or God) functions as a fundamental 'belief' or 'condition of possibility' of all our experience." Also see p. 55 in Chapter 3.
28. From Bernard Lonergan to Stephen Toulmin to Schubert Ogden and Karl Jaspers, that is, from transcendental method, linguistic analysis, process thinking, and existential phenomenology. See BRO, pp. 91ff and especially p. 94.
29. BRO, p. 91.
30. BRO, p. 91.
31. BRO, p. 93.
32. BRO, p. 93.
33. See Tracy's clarification in note 11 on p. 111 of BRO.
34. BRO, p. 109.
35. In this, Tracy is quite faithful to his mentor Bernard Lonergan. See p. 102 of Lonergan's *Method in Theology* (Toronto: University of Toronto Press, 1971).
36. These dimensions are crisis points precisely because the emancipations of modernity have called into question traditional understandings at these three levels. For example, Kant has turned the understanding of knowledge upside down; Enlightenment "freedom" has called into question traditional norms for ethical practice; and existentialist interpretations of the absurdity of existence (Sartre) have called into question the pre-Enlightenment positive teleological view of reality.
37. The pertinent reference to Lonergan here is pointed to by Tracy himself, Lonergan's own discussion of self-transcendence and religion in *Method in Theology*, pp. 104ff.
38. BRO, p. 98.
39. Note here Lonergan's language of the "virtually unconditioned" affirmation, that which later Tracy calls the "relatively adequate."
40. BRO, p. 98.
41. BRO, p. 99.
42. That is, as limit-to and limit-of.
43. This fundamental trust is universally human and at this point is not tied to a formalized set of dogmatic beliefs. Tracy is doing "fundamental theology," exploring the foundations of belief itself and not the particularized institutional concretizations of fundamental belief.
44. See pp. 102ff. In a sense, Tracy's primary conversation partner at this point is Schubert Ogden who discusses Toulmin at length in *The Reality of God* (New York: Harper and Row, 1966). See especially pp. 32ff of *The Reality of God*.
45. BRO, p. 102.
46. BRO, p. 103.

47. This stance is not so very different from that of that eminent English Roman Catholic theologian of the nineteenth century, John Henry Newman, who sought to make sense of the relationship between faith and reason in the face of Enlightenment scientism. A personal note following up a lively discussion with a friend and scientist, William Froude, crystallizes the point: "He [Froude] said that no truth had been arrived at without this habit of skeptical caution – it was the parent of discovery. I said no great thing would be done without the very reverse habit, viz that of conviction and faith...." See the quotation in Nicholas Lash's "Introduction" to *An Essay in Aid of a Grammar of Assent* (Notre Dame: University of Notre Dame Press, 1979), p. 6.

48. See notes 72ff on pp. 116–117 for Tracy's references to a number of Jaspers' texts. Tracy also refers to Abraham Maslow's discussion of "peak experiences" to fill out his discussion. See p. 105 of *BRO* also.

49. *BRO*, p. 105.

50. *BRO*, p. 105.

51. *BRO*, p. 106.

52. *BRO*, pp. 105–106.

53. *PA*, p. 89.

54. *BRO*, p.107.

55. *BRO*, p. 108.

56. *BRO*, p. 187.

57. *BRO*, p. 122.

58. *BRO*, p. 124.

59. *BRO*, p. 223.

60. See again, "Horizon Analysis and Eschatology," p. 176.

61. Jürgen Moltmann, *The Coming of God: Christian Eschatology* (Minneapolis, MN: Fortress Press, 1996) p. xiii.

62. Gerhard Sauter, *What Dare We Hope? Reconsidering Eschatology*, pp. 69, 19.

63. Analogy, after all, figures largely in Tracy's thought, and while Tracy ultimately joins Rahner in naming God as Mystery and thus ultimately beyond human comprehension and control, Tracy never espouses dialectic at the expense of analogy.

64. *BRO*, p. 108.

65. See again "The Hidden God: The Divine Other of Liberation," p. 8.

66. See, for instance, p. 110 of *Plurality and Ambiguity*.

67. Hans Urs von Balthasar, "Some Points of Eschatology" in *Explorations in Theology*, Volume I, p. 260.

68. Karl Barth in *Death to Life*, Adolf Portmann, ed. (Chicago: Argus Communications, 1968), p. 42.

69. "Horizon Analysis and Eschatology," p. 176. He notes: "First, there is general agreement – by means, it remains true, of various Christian formulations – of the transcendent, final, unique indeed once and for all character of God's eschatological act in Christ Jesus." This claim becomes the key theme in *The Analogical Imagination* and is thus greatly expanded in that later text.

70. *BRO*, p. 47.

71. Hence, Tracy claims: "but the final truth of religion, I believe, is in fact its objective ground in theism." See p. 163 of *BRO*.

72. Ogden's text, *The Reality of God* is a significant resource for Tracy here. Tracy's direct reference to Ogden appears in BRO, p. 179. See also Tracy's correlation of the bipolar God with the Johannine naming in BRO, p.189.

73. That is, as much as is possible given the finite nature of the human being.

74. Tracy makes that argument both in its critique of the classical theist position and in support of the process position in Chapter 8 of BRO beginning on p. 172.

75. BRO, p. 177. Schubert Ogden characterizes or names God in this manner in *The Reality of God*, p. 177.

76. See, for instance, Avery Dulles' brief critique in "Method in Fundamental Theology: Reflections on David Tracy's *Blessed Rage for Order*" on pp. 312–313.

77. BRO, p. 180.

78. Ogden's discussion of the temporality of God in *The Reality of God* (San Francisco: Harper & Row, 1977) is informative in a parallel way at this point. Based on his reading of Martin Heidegger in *Sein und Zeit*, Ogden claims that God's time is not an ever present eternity but rather a primal and infinite temporality. Ogden claims that the classical way of describing or naming God, the via affirmativa leading to the via negativa and the via eminentia, is consistent only if the claim is made that God is temporal, but eminently and thus infinitely temporal. See his argument beginning on p. 144.

79. See again Tracy's discussion of "authentic self-transcending human love" in BRO, pp. 106–107.

80. BRO, p. 179.

81. BRO, p. 179.

82. In this sense, then, Tracy's naming of God as Pure Unbounded Love clearly meets one of his two criteria for critical and revisionist theological assertions, that of adequacy to human experience. The bipolar God of process thought is an adequate meaningful limit-concept for God Who is the Ultimate Ground to all existence. As an aside, that very limit-concept also resonates quite appropriately with the Christian tradition. One again immediately thinks of the Johannine profession that God is Love in 1 John 4: 8 (which Tracy himself later references in BRO as well as in AI and later works) and of all of the succeeding affirmations of the Johannine profession within the tradition. For instance, in his *Itinerarium*, Bonaventure concludes this classic work that is an eschatology within theology as spirituality with the claim that the Triune God is "the highest good without qualification," the good of "supreme mutual intimacy" and "supreme mutual interpenetration." See St. Bonaventure, *The Soul's Journey into God*, translation by Ewert Cousins (Mahwah, NJ: Paulist Press, 1978), pp. 102ff.

83. This is a claim that runs through the secular understanding of hope in the thought of Ernst Bloch, that secular thinker who has so greatly influenced Christian eschatological reflection in the recently past century. Hope, possibility, and future are all inter-connected. See, for instance, Bloch's essay on "Man as Possibility" in *The Future of Hope* (Philadelphia: Fortress Press, 1970) beginning on p. 50.

84. See again Tracy's discussion of "self-transcendence as scientific authenticity" beginning on p. 96 of BRO where he appropriates the Lonerganian claim that "One lives authentically insofar as one continues to allow oneself an expanding horizon. That expansion has as its chief aim the going-beyond one's present state in accordance with the transcendental

imperatives: 'Be attentive, be intelligent, be reasonable, be responsible, develop and, if necessary, change.'"

85. We note that Tracy's argument for the revisionist theological method, the method of mutually critical correlation, itself rests on the imperative dimensionality of self-transcendence at the cultural level. He states on p. 11 of BRO: "By and large, the contemporary model can be described as a demand for 'self-transcendence:' a radical commitment to the struggle to transcend our present and individual and societal states in favor of a continuous examination of those illusions which cloud our real and more limited possibilities for knowledge and action."

86. Again at this point, one could also summon up evidence from the Christian tradition in support of the claim that the eschatological entails the notions of transcendence, real newness brought about by divine rather than mere human agency. One can, for instance, recall the Pauline profession that in Christ "the old has passed away, behold, the new has come." See II Cor. 5: 17. See also von Rad's discussion of the prophetic eschatology in the Hebrew scripture where the eschatological preaching of the various prophets point to a "new state," to the "message of the new thing" which is not under human control but rather is the work of God. See von Rad's Old Testament Theology, Volume II (New York: Harper and Row, 1965), beginning on p. 119. Classic prophetic texts such as Is. 44: 19, 66: 22 and Jer. 31:31 all support this claim for the eschatological as transcendence into a real newness not under human control. Refer again to Moltmann's claim that novum is at the core of Christian eschatology. See again Moltmann's The Coming of God, p. 28. These eschatological notions are then clearly appropriate to the tradition. However, again what is most important to note at this juncture is that these very eschatological notions are, to Tracy, implicitly present in the secular and thus are adequate to human experience and meaningful.

87. This is what Tracy's mentor Bernard Lonergan calls the human being's "drive to know" fueling the inherent drive towards self-transcendence. See Lonergan's Method in Theology, p. 101.

88. BRO, p.12. This emphasis on the need for transformative liberations especially reflects Tracy's postmodern side.

89. BRO, p. 103.

90. That is, at this point in the text. In a real sense, Tracy's final chapter in Blessed Rage for Order is all about human responsibility for ethical action in the world and in history.

91. BRO, pp. 105ff.

92. As an aside, a few years after Tracy first published Blessed Rage for Order, an article which he authored appeared in Concilium entitled "The Catholic Model of Caritas." His claim in that article is that the Catholic concept of caritas, that is, eros transformed into agape by grace, correlates well with the secular understanding of love as self-transcendence in transformation. The article is reprinted in ONP, beginning on p. 94.

93. BRO, pp. 105–106. A note, Tracy's use of the phrase "being-in-love-without-qualification" resonates with Lonergan's description of love of God. See his discussion of love as self-transcendence towards God in Method in Theology, pp. 105–106. This is agapic love.

94. BRO, p. 107.

95. BRO, p. 107.

96. *BRO*, p. 107.

97. Gerhard Sauter, *What Dare We Hope? Reconsidering Eschatology*, p. 222.

98. Gerhard Sauter, *What Dare We Hope? Reconsidering Eschatology*, p. 218.

99. *BRO*, p. 106.

100. Richard Bauckham and Trevor Hart, *Hoping Against Hope: Christian Eschatology in Contemporary Context* (London: Darton, Longman, and Todd, 1999), p. 84.

101. See p. 13 of *BRO* where he ties the goal of the eschatological theologians, the "praxis of human liberation," to the postmodern critique of the "oppressive horrors of the twentieth century" wrought by "modern scientific processes of demystification and rationalization."

102. *BRO*, p. 242.

103. *BRO*, p. 243.

104. See Moltmann's introductory "Meditation on Hope" in *The Theology of Hope* (Minneapolis, MN: Fortress Press, 1993), p. 34.

105. *BRO*, pp. 244–245. Later in his career, Tracy identifies his own project more closely with the eschatological as liberation theologians in that he considers the suffering of the oppressed as the proper starting point for any adequate critical theological reflection on the "theodicy" question. See, for instance, Tracy's address to the Catholic Theological Society of America in 1995 in *Proceedings of the Fiftieth Annual Convention* (Santa Clara, CA: Santa Clara University Press), pp. 15ff. See also Tracy's own "New Preface" to the second edition of *Blessed Rage for Order*, the 1996 edition, in which he points out the need to recognize and appropriate the liberationist insights of feminist theology into an adequate revisionist theology. See p. xiv.

106. *BRO*, p. 49.

107. That is, in Chapter Six.

108. That is, in Chapter Nine.

109. As an aside, we may note that much of Tracy's "historical and hermeneutical" discussion seeks to make the case for correlating limit in philosophical investigation with limit in hermeneutical investigation. This is after all the point of the whole exercise. Yet, that very discussion discloses – in Tracy's own use of language – eschatological assertions on Tracy's part.

110. His claim for their eschatological nature is based on the same claim made by contemporary biblical scholarship. See, for instance, his reference to the work of Norman Perrin on pp. 125–126.

111. Such as the scholarly work of Beardslee, Perrin, Dodd, Jülicher, Jeremias, and Ricoeur (from a philosophical perspective). See pp. 124ff of *BRO*.

112. *BRO*, p. 124.

113. *BRO*, p. 223.

114. *BRO*, p. 124.

115. *BRO*, p. 124.

116. *BRO*, pp. 129–130.

117. *BRO*, p. 130.

118. *BRO*, p. 136.

119. *BRO*, p. 223.

120. *BRO*, p. 219.

121. *BRO*, p. 221.
122. *BRO*, p. 219.
123. *BRO*, p. 220.
124. *BRO*, p. 220.
125. Here, Tracy shows his indebtedness to the insights and retrievals of neo-orthodoxy. See his discussion of the "fact of evil" on pp. 211ff of *BRO*.
126. *BRO*, p. 223.

· 3 ·

ESCHATOLOGICAL DIMENSIONS IN DAVID TRACY'S *THE ANALOGICAL IMAGINATION*

In 1981, David Tracy published his second major theological text, *The Analogical Imagination: Christian Theology and the Culture of Pluralism*. This text was the product of Tracy's revisionist effort to deal with contemporary pluralism within the context of systematic theology. Yet, commenting on the book, William M. Shea observed: "*The Analogical Imagination* is not a systematic theology; it is a fundamental theology of systematics. Tracy is still largely dealing with method questions."[1] Tracy's recognition of the emancipations of modern and postmodern critical thought and the pluralism which they set loose demands this focus on critical method in order to ensure that theological reflection does not lapse into the "repressive tolerance of a lazy pluralism."[2] In *The Analogical Imagination*, the mutually critical correlational method of *Blessed Rage for Order* partly gives way to another critical methodology, that of the hermeneutic of the "classic."

As one may recall from the analysis made in the previous chapter, many insights into the eschatological were derived from the implicit eschatological sense inherent in Tracy's philosophical analysis of the religious dimension of human existence. The more explicit eschatological statements as derived from an analysis of New Testament texts and the "christological fact" were seen as intensifications of an aspect of finality or limit of human existence. In the present chapter, I will explore Tracy's concrete and systematic eschatological claims by way of analysis of his understanding of the nature and disclosive power of the classic, the religious classic and the Christian classic, and finally the authentically Christian response to that Christian classic.[3] The chapter will conclude with a discussion of the shape that eschatological existence can take in the face of plurality within culture and even within the Christian tradition and in response to the Christian classic.

In this sense, the structural movement of the present chapter echoes Tracy's own movement into greater particularity with concomitantly more intense universal claims, such as his claim for the "wholeness" of Love as the Ultimate Reality finally and decisively manifest in the concrete person and event of Jesus as the Christ. For the movement from the secular to the religious and Christian classic is, for Tracy, not only a movement into greater particularity, and thus not a movement from one world to another, but also a movement to make more concrete and finally decisive universal claims about the relationship of God, self, and world through the classic event of Jesus Christ. Thus, a parallel claim can be made here that his analysis which discloses the nature of the classic, the religious classic, and the Christian classic carries with it its own sense of eschatological intensification in the movement from the part to the whole to the ultimately final. This is not to claim that the secular classic is wholly eschatological in nature in spite of the fact that it affords one the recognition of "the essential, the permanent, and…surplus of meaning."[4] The secular classic rather has the possibility of offering the opportunity to "grasp certain essential truths,"[5] but essential truths are not necessarily wholly final truths, the eschatological truths claimed by the religious Christian classic. As the following discussion will then demonstrate, there are faint "echoes of the eschatological" in the nature, production, and reception of the secular classic; yet the wholeness and finality of the religious and Christian classics disclose their more properly speaking eschatological character.

The Nature of the Classic and Its Appropriateness for a Public Systematics

In *The Analogical Imagination*, the over-arching method of choice is specifically hermeneutical and is explicitly indebted to Hans Georg Gadamer's discussion of the classic.[6] This is the case because *The Analogical Imagination* is a book about systematic theology wherein the theologian's "major task is the reinterpretation of the tradition for the present situation."[7] This necessarily involves the interpretation and reinterpretation of all of the classic texts, symbols, rituals, and events available in that tradition. Thus, Tracy claims: "The systematic theologian is the interpreter of religious classics."[8] However, the fact that systematic theology shares with both fundamental and practical theology a final focal interest in the question of God and of the relation of humanity and cosmos with that God makes it a particular but also public venture as it seeks to make universal claims. Tracy will not permit the "explicit religion" which Christianity is to retreat into a closed realm of privatization and "dogmatocracy."[9] Nor will he permit theological reflection about that explicit religion to fall into privatized isolation. This assertion of the public nature of theology informs Tracy's introductory discussion of the "social portrait of the theologian" in *The Analogical Imagination*.[10] It is based on the fundamental notion that the systematic theologian is a person living in a world, in a history and culture, with the responsibility of reinterpreting a particular religious tradition in a manner that makes public sense. To do theology is to think and engage in hermeneutics, and that is a matter of dialogue, conversation. It is public and thus open to critique and interpretation.

Therefore, given the pluralism of interpretations both within a particular religious tradition such as Christianity and in contemporary culture in general, Tracy continues to make the effort in *The Analogical Imagination* to explore substantive theological questions within a methodological framework which will, in his mind, make sense to the reasonable contemporary person open to plurality. Hence, Tracy appropriates the "interpretation of the classic" as his method. The idea of the classic and the illuminations and possible transformations which it affords are realities with which the public is familiar and accepts as a bearer of some essential truth about existence. Tracy's reading of human experience is such that human beings recognize the power of classic to bear truth. Furthermore, Tracy contends that the public also knows that classics continually invite reinterpretations not only because human beings are interpreters but also, and most importantly for Tracy, because of the depth of meaning(s) embedded within the classics. In sum, Tracy's claim for the hermeneutic of the classic, both in culture in general and in the particularity of systematic theology, is a claim for its critical publicness and thus its appropriateness as a methodological strategy with which to recognize and interpret both essential claims about the truths of existence and the fundamental systematic claims to truth in Christianity.

Tracy notes several key features of the nature and production of the classic which are hermeneutically important for consideration. For instance, Tracy along with Gadamer defines the classic as a "realized experience of an event of truth."[11] As such, the classic, whether as "text, event, gesture, image, symbol, person," is a "structured expression of the human experience"[12] which contains within itself an "excess of meaning [which] both demands constant interpretation and bears a certain kind of timeliness – namely the timeliness of a classic expression radically rooted in its own historical time and calling to my own historicity."[13] In this sense, the classic transcends time while remaining embedded in time.[14]

Moreover, for Tracy, the human interaction with the classic in which one "grasps certain essential truths"[15] is a participation,[16] a process of intense interaction and therefore a relationship which "envelops"[17] the human being because the classic as classic speaks to the finite human "hope for liberation to the essential."[18] It appeals to the human desire for some form of liberation and transformation. In speaking of the nature of the classic piece of art and its effects on the human being, Tracy notes:

> In allowing ourselves to experience art [as classic] we are transformed, however briefly, into the mode of being of the work of art where we experience the challenge, often the shock, of a reality greater than the everyday self, a reality of the paradigmatic power of the essential that transforms us. Here the back-and-forth movement of every game becomes the buoyant dialectic of true freedom: surprise, release, confrontation, shock, often reverential awe, always transformation. In our actual experience of the work of art, we move into the back-and-forth rhythms of the work: from its discovery and disclosure to a sensed recognition of the essential beyond the everyday; from its hiddenness to our sensed rootedness; from its disclosure and concealment of truth to our realized experience of a transformative truth, at once revealing and concealing.[19]

This long quotation contains all of the essential features of the classic in the mind of David Tracy, be it the classic of art or of a religious tradition. The classic exposes and shocks one into the recognition of some essential truth and offers the possibility of a transformation into a new mode of being in the world in the light of that truth, and it offers the possibility of a certain newness born of a relationship to its revelation. In this, the classic as a "realized experience"[20] of some essential aspect of truth carries with it a certain normative but also liberating character. It carries with it an offer and demand for self-transcendence not only into the world of the classic itself but also into the possible transformative mode of being which it offers. Furthermore, the classic, while rooted in its own particular history, contains within it an essential timeliness which transcends time. It is, in a sense, ever new. Created in a historied past, it invites a relationship of participative interpretation in the present and offers the possibility of a new perspective on the future – and all within the world, within history. In this sense, the classic as classic holds time in a tension of past, present, and future, what Tracy has called a "philosophical notion of time" wherein "man's con-sciousness-in-process…reveals to man (in his self-consciousness) the ultimate ontological reality of every present moment as including the past in memory and open to the future both by way of one's own projections into it and by way of the future's transcendent demands upon one now." Time is not "atomized' into separate spheres for Tracy.[21]

Moreover, that ever-newness is not just guaranteed by the fact that human beings constantly interpret pluralistically but, quite importantly, by the very nature of the classic itself in that it is always an event of, to use Tracy's language, "disclosure and concealment."[22] Thus, when Tracy speaks of the truth of the classic, he speaks of truth as manifestation, as *aletheia*, as "at once a disclosure and a concealment."[23] This fundamental sense of the classic as that which bears a transformative truth – dialectical in that it is both disclosure and conceal-ment – rises from the basic notion that the classic carries with it the character of both permanence and excess. Thus, the classic always carries within it a certain "otherness," an interruptive distance and excess even as it invites participation, relationship. Therefore and in summary form, Tracy claims:

> When we deliver ourselves over to the subject matter produced through form in a clas-sic text, we discover what is other than and beyond ourselves. In the final moments of all interpretation, beyond but through explanation into some appropriated understand-ing, we discover ourselves as a finite part, as participatory in, belonging to yet distanced from some essential aspect of the whole. In the paradigmatic expressions of the human spirit – in those texts, events, persons, actions, images, rituals, symbols which bear within them a classic as authoritative status, we find in our experienced recognition of their claim to attention the presence of what we cannot but name as "truth." The truth we find there may not be adequately expressible in the propositions of objective consciousness. Yet that truth as at once a disclosure and a concealment of what, at our best and most self-transcending in interpreting the classics, we cannot but name "reality." In some matters, only the paradigmatic is real.[24]

We recall from previous discussions that for Tracy the eschatological refers to the final as ultimate, to a power not merely under human control which offers transcendence as a real newness and superabundance and which interrupts – even reverses – ordinary and mundane understandings, including that of time. The classic "echoes" the eschatological dimensions of Tracy's thought. Tracy claims that the classic bears "a certain kind of timelessness – namely the timeliness of a classic expression radically rooted in its own historical time and calling to my historicity."[25] Once created, shared, and interpreted in history, the classic transcends time and carries with it a potentially liberating power of its own. The essential truth disclosed and yet concealed by the secular classic may not be the ultimate truth; yet the essential may indeed echo or point to an aspect of the ultimate, the whole, while it offers new, rich and potentially transformative understandings.

The Religious Classic: Manifestation of the Whole by the Power of the Whole

David Tracy's exposition of the classic in *The Analogical Imagination* is a step on a journey of intensification into greater concrete particularity. In his exposition, Tracy moves by way of particularity from the secular to the religious as Christian classic, that classic which affords him entrée into the whole as ultimately final, in an eschatological "journey of intensification." Tracy's importantly informative statement about God, the Final and thus Eschatological Reality, reflects that very movement:

> Who, in this perspective, is God? God is the power not our own disclosing itself in philosophy as the one necessary individual, the power disclosing itself in all religious experience as the graced reality of the whole manifested by the power of the whole and in the Christian experience of the Christ event as the personlike yet transpersonal power of pure, unbounded love, that ultimate reality which grounds and pervades all reality, the reality with which we must ultimately all deal.[26]

This is the theological conclusion derived from Tracy's journey of intensification and particularity via the classics in *The Analogical Imagination*. To be sure, the above statement with its language of ultimacy clearly resonates with Tracy's fundamental systematic claims about Christian eschatology. What is also important to note is that Tracy makes strong and progressively more concrete claims in this summary statement.[27] The progressive movement claims ultimately that "wholeness" is the keyword or animating character of the religious classic. "Wholeness" takes on the concrete and particular (historical and incarnate) shape of love in the finality of the revelation of the Christian classic, in the person and event of Jesus as the Christ, and in a life lived in love. Much as "limit" serves as a revisionist entry point for the discovery of the religious as eschatological in *Blessed Rage for Order*, the "whole" serves as the gateway for the properly religious as eschatological in *The Analogical Imagination*. Therefore, investigating what Tracy means by the "whole" is essential for understanding the eschatological in his thought in *The Analogical Imagination*, Tracy's text on Christian systematics.

In Tracy's analysis, the secular classic "will intensify the need for the self's intensification into a liberation to and by a reality greater than the self."[28] Furthermore, it invites participation in that greater reality but not exhaustion of its fullness. Both the secular and religious classics share the same structural characteristics.[29] They point to the essential. They are ever timely as they transcend time insofar as their meaning is, in important aspects, timeless. They are both events of disclosure and concealment, participation and distanciation, and enveloping and developing understanding. One is captured, encompassed by, and invited into relationship with the power of the secular and religious classics in spite of their otherness.

However, Tracy notes that "in the religious classics, the subject matter, as yet more intense, complex and ambiguous (as a manifestation not of some essential aspect of the whole but of the whole itself by the power of the whole), cannot but take over the entire process more intensively yet."[30] This is the case because:

> Like all classics, religious classics will involve a claim to meaning and truth as one event of disclosure and concealment of the reality of lived existence. Unlike the classics of art, morality, science and politics, explicitly religious classic expressions will involve a claim to truth as the event of a disclosure-concealment of the whole of reality *by the power of the whole* – as, in some sense, a radical and finally gracious mystery.[31]

Given this perspective on the relationship between the secular and religious classic as a relationship of part to the whole and thus also of the move to greater intensification in both its particularity and universal significance, one can see the "echoes of the eschatological" in the notion of the classic. As in the case of Tracy's analysis of limit, the secular world and the world of religion are not set over and against each other; the eschatological need not be relegated to another alien world. Yet Tracy's emphasis on the whole as the distinguishing concept of the religious classic lends to it an intensity that moves the eschatological dimension further to the forefront in Tracy's thought. The very concept of wholeness manifest by its own power contains within it that sense of a power which is final, ultimate, total, and complete in its "radical and finally gracious mystery."[32]

It is perhaps for this reason that Tracy embarks on his discussion of the religious classic with a reiteration of his claims from *Blessed Rage* for the religious dimension of human existence as the dimension of limit. The religious classic as religious is a manifestation of limit because limit is inherent in the religious dimension of existence. However, rather than focusing primary attention on the "limit-to," as Tracy does in *Blessed Rage for Order*, *The Analogical Imagination* shifts greater attention to the "limit-of" aspect of religious existence.[33] The power of the whole revealed in the religious classic is then the power of the ultimate mystery of "limit-of." Furthermore, the wholeness manifested in the religious classic has within it the power of eliciting a holistic human response. Thus, Tracy states: "...that sense of...the power of the whole pervades a religious classic to such an extent that there ethos and worldview are inextricably intertwined."[34] In other words, the wholeness of the manifested religious classic itself fosters a sense of the wholeness of reality wherein what one comes to believe finally in the light of the religious classic also impels one to a certain way of living. Worldview and ethos, understanding and right action, are inextricably linked by the power of the religious classic in its revelation of the whole.[35]

It is an appropriate reading of Tracy to make the claim that what he means by the whole manifested in the religious classic is God. Ultimately, Tracy asserts this claim in his discussion of the religious classic as a classic event of proclamation.[36] This is another naming of God as the eschatological reality. The Final as Ultimate Reality is the Whole of all reality.[37] Such a naming deepens and enriches our understanding of the eschatological by speaking about God's ultimacy in terms of totality, completeness, or wholeness.

What then does Tracy say about this intriguing but complicated keyword, the "whole," in his exposition of the religious classic? Tracy speaks of religion as the experience and language of the whole. Attempting to interpret the religious classic, the classic in which the whole is disclosed yet also hidden is an exercise in risk[38] precisely because the whole is "in some sense, a radical and finally gracious mystery,"[39] a gift. And as mystery and gift, the whole offers no "certainty but [promises]...some realized experience of the whole by the power of the whole."[40] Both history and finitude on the human side and permanence within excess on the side of the religious classic serve as the real basis for this claim. Both past (realized experience) and future (promise) are offered in the present mystery and power of the whole. The concept of the whole thus interrupts and breaks the barriers of ordinary time. It is for this reason that Tracy contends that the religious classic must necessarily make use of both the genres of "proclamation" with its primarily future orientation and "manifestation" with its primarily present orientation to reflect this temporal unity-in-tension revealed in the whole of religious classics.[41] Furthermore, the whole is revealed, made manifest, by its own power and liberates one to trust that "how we ought to live and how things in reality are, are finally one."[42] The revelation of the whole of the religious classic then offers the possibility of eliciting the human response of a present faith as trust and of hope in future.

This language of the whole serves to reinforce the claim that the whole, for Tracy, is God who is the Ultimate as Final and thus eschatological reality who graces humanity with some realized and realizable experience of liberation. Thus Tracy can later say, "The present experience of grace [gift] is acknowledged in Christian faith as the final reality with which we must all deal – the incomprehensible reality of the ultimate mystery named God."[43] But the whole is also the object of "human instinctual desire." Tracy names this desire as "the instinct of the human spirit for some relationship to the whole."[44] This is an important insight because it points up that the whole entails relationship, the grace or gift of relationship. The very structure of the religious classic as disclosure and concealment accompanied by participation with distanciation implies relationship. Indeed, one can make the further assertion that, for Tracy, the whole finally reveals itself as the gift or grace of relationship. Note how Tracy says at one point in his discussion of the whole and of the religious classic, "that reality is finally gracious, that the deepest longings of our minds and hearts for wholeness in ourselves, with others, with history and nature, is the case – the case granted as gift by the whole."[45] In other words, the wholeness revealed by the whole in the religious classic is the manifestation that reality, finally and ultimately, is the gift of a relationship to Otherness as Ultimate Mystery, to God, and to all creation. This is the gift which stimulates that human yearning for wholeness, for relationship. And this gift itself offers an intense participation in tension with non-participation precisely because of the otherness of Ultimate Reality as Mystery. Tracy notes:

> For the authentically religious impetus is one where the intensification process is itself abandoned into a letting go of one's own effort at intensity. One lets go because one has experienced some disclosure of the whole which cannot be denied as from the whole. One is actually, finally related to the whole because one participates in, belongs to, is caught up in some disclosure of the whole. That disclosure is simply given, recognized, accepted. The self acknowledges a power not one's own while also recognizing that this radical "belonging-to" posits itself as gift only by implying the contrary.[46]

Embedded then in the experience of the wholeness of the religious classic is some beckoning relationship, a relationship of tensive and unsettling participation in and distanciation from the whole, but a relationship nonetheless which reveals that all is relationship. It is no wonder then that Tracy will finally claim that the "analogical imagination," that gift which is also a possibly authentic response to the religious as Christian classic manifesting the whole, is a matter of "ordered relationships" of "God-Self-World."[47] Note also how, finally, Tracy makes the connection between the religious and Christian classic via this concept of wholeness as relationship, further intensified as love, in this powerful Christian faith statement:

> For the Christian belief in Jesus Christ as the decisive self-manifestation of God is also the decisive disclosure for Christians of all existence – the self, history, nature, the whole. All are internally related by that engifted and commanded love to the power who is Love.[48]

Therefore, Tracy speaks of "wholeness," his revisionist eschatological keyword or naming in *The Analogical Imagination*, in two ways: God as the Ultimate and Final Reality is the whole of reality, and relationship is the whole as final reality. What unifies these two interpretations of wholeness is Tracy's final claim that God as the Whole, the very Limit-of all existence, is Pure, Unbounded Love. For love, the agapic love of the Judeo-Christian tradition, is first and foremost a relationship, a relationship of other regard, of love without condition, which God as Love is, reveals, and offers. Thus Tracy will say that "the always-already presence of…love is the final key to reality."[49] This offer of love demands of humanity a related response which unites both ultimate meaning and ethical responsibility. This is the eschatological truth which becomes the final as whole truth in Tracy's continued journey of intensification from the religious to the Christian classic where wholeness takes concrete and particular (historical and incarnate) shape in the person and event of Jesus Christ.[50]

The Christian Classic: Eschatological Wholeness Manifested Finally and Decisively

The closing pages of Tracy's discussion of the religious classic in *The Analogical Imagination* serve as an introduction to his unique systematic christological exposition on the person and event of Jesus as the Christ. Tracy's journey into the concrete particularity of the Christian tradition leads him to explore what he considers to be the core question of Christianity,[51] the fundamental christological question wherein not only concrete and particular but also universal and final Christian claims surface. In this journey, Tracy asks: "Is not the whole symbol system [of Christianity] grounded in the radical Christian faith that Jesus Christ is both the decisive word and the decisive manifestation of God and

ourselves?"[52] Tracy answers this question affirmatively. The Christian classic
is the revelation, the "word" and "manifestation" of God as the Whole, the
Ultimate and Final Reality, offered in and through the concrete and historical
Christ event. This person and event reveals finally and decisively that God is
indeed Pure, Unbounded Love inviting the response of loving relationship.
Therefore, Tracy embarks on the final steps of his journey of intensification
with the following lengthy but important assertion, an assertion which both
locates the Christian classic within the framework of the religious classic and
also contains within itself Tracy's christological "working canon"[53]:

> Every classic is the result of a particular journey of intensification and distanciation.
> Every religious classic recognizes itself not as its own but as a gift and command from
> and by the power of the whole. For the Jewish, Christian, and Islamic traditions, this
> experience of the whole is an experience of a who: a loving and jealous, living, active,
> covenanting God, a God who discloses who God is, who we are, what history and
> nature, reality itself ultimately are. For the Christian community from New Testament
> communities to the present there is one single expression from God proclaimed to be,
> manifested and represented in a myriad of symbols, images, genres, concepts, doctrines
> as God's own self-manifestation and thereby – only thereby – as beyond all relative
> adequacy: the decisive event named Jesus Christ.... The classic event for the Christian
> is the religious event of God's self-manifestation in the person Jesus the Christ: an event
> that happened, happens, and will happen.[54]

Tracy's fundamental christological question and "canonical" response serve
not only as an entrée to his unique form of christological reflection,[55] but also
to highlight the direction of his christological and eschatological reflection via
carefully selected wording within that working christological canon.

The christological question and response stated above disclose the wholeness which characterizes the Christian religious classic as eschatological in three
significant ways. First, the eschatological wholeness of the Christian classic is
revealed in its "decisiveness," in its "full adequacy," to manifest God, the Ultimate Reality. Secondly, that wholeness is also revealed in the tensive temporal
nature of the Christian classic, in that it is an event which "happened, happens,
and will happen," and therefore interrupts, transforms, and illuminates the
ordinary understanding of time as it relates past, present, and future in a new
manner. Tracy's working christological canon exhibits classical permanence in
its decisiveness,[56] and its excess is exhibited in its tensive temporal character.
Finally and most importantly for the Christian living in the world, that Christian
classic proclaims and tells a story, a narrative of a life lived in eschatological
wholeness: the life, death, and resurrection of Jesus as the Christ manifest

concretely in the Gospel narratives and in such symbols as "cross-resurrection-incarnation."[57] This is the life which calls for the holistic unity of ethos and worldview in the concrete form of Christian as eschatological existence. The story discloses an eschatological way of living, of acting in the world.

Expanding on the first notion then, one might note that Tracy's canon rests on the Christian faith claim that in the whole of the classic Christian symbol system we find God, the Eschatological Reality, and God's relationship to humanity decisively manifest in Jesus as the Christ. Thus, the christological entails the eschatological because the christological reveals decisively and thus finally the whole of all reality. Tracy will then later say that:

> ...the Christian believer senses that here in the event of Jesus Christ the primal word and manifestation of God and thereby of ourselves, of history, nature, the whole is decisively revealed as an event not of our own making yet confirming our deepest longings for wholeness in the whole.[58]

Jesus Christ is the "primal" word and manifestation of the "primal" Reality, that is, God. This is a crucial eschatological claim. The person and event of Jesus as the Christ bespeaks and manifests the Whole as Ultimate Reality and humanity's relationship to that Whole of reality. Thus, in the tradition of von Balthasar, Daniélou, Rahner, and Sauter but within the language and methodological structure of the classic, Tracy claims that Jesus as the Christ is the *Eschatos*, the final and decisive event of God's self-disclosure.[59] This theme continually runs through all of Tracy's christological reflections in *The Analogical Imagination* and, for that matter, in later texts. When Tracy speaks about the person and event of Jesus the Christ, he does so with such eschatological descriptors as "ultimacy" and "full adequacy" in contrast to human interpretations of the Christ event as "relatively adequate." Tracy describes the Christ event in terms of "...God's own self-manifestation where full adequacy, no longer relative, decisively happened, happens, and will happen," as the "...one event of full, decisive adequacy: the event of God's own self-manifestation through and in Jesus Christ."[60] Therefore, Tracy makes the same eschatological as christological claim which echoes throughout the Christian tradition in a variety of interpretive forms – but again – within a revisionist methodological structure, within the hermeneutic of the classic.

Secondly, Tracy's christological canon also rests on the notion that the religious classic as revelation of the whole necessarily entails a certain wholeness or unity-in-tension in the temporal tension of past, present, and future, and this unity-in-tension comes to human expression in both manifestation (presence as gift) and proclamation or word (future as command).[61] This is a tension which as eschatological calls into question the ordinary understanding of time as atomistic. It highlights the fact that the time of the religious classic, eschatological time as time from the whole, presents one with a new understanding of time in that it relates past, present, and future in a dynamic tension because the religious classic reveals the whole, the whole which carries with it both permanence and excess of meaning in its truth as *aletheia.* Thus, as eschatological, this tensive sense of time both interrupts ordinary notions of time and yet offers an alternative sense of time. The Christ event as an already-not-yet concrete reality manifests this very eschatological sense of time. Thus, Tracy can say of the Christ event in explicit eschatological terms:

> To speak Christian eschatological language is to speak a language where the religious power of the whole has entered time and history in the decisive proclamation of this particular word and event, where that power has freed the "profane" to become the "secular" and has liberated the present *and* the future from the exclusive hold of the sacred time of past origins by empowering history and ethical action with religious power. That Christian religious dialectic continues to occur in the empowering of Christians to enter the struggle of history and time, to search for, work for, think for the *new* of a future which is an empowered *adventum* and a hoped-for, paradigmatic *promissio* in the always-already, not-yet reality of the present.[62]

The above reference further underscores the claim that the explicitly eschatological dimension of Tracy's project can – indeed, must for the Christian – be discovered by way of the concrete particularity and universality of christology.[63] Tracy asks the pointed christological question regarding Christian faith in the decisiveness of the Christ event. He then makes specific claims, eschatological claims, about the finality of that classic event. The Christ event is not only one which is eschatological in that it reveals who God is finally and decisively; that event also interrupts and re-interprets the ordinary understanding of time and brings to it a real and illuminating newness. Such newness merges the sacred with the secular and also impels ethical action in the world as it promises the possibility of a positive future born of that ethical action empowered and directed by the Christ event.

Tracy contends that the Christ event is a "re-presentative" event, a "realized experience." In terms of the category of time, the eschatological event of Jesus the Christ is then a "tensive" event which is disclosed as an "already and not yet" reality. Indeed, if one were to look for a unifying theme running throughout Tracy's christology – other than his working canon that the person and event of Jesus Christ manifests God as Pure, Unbounded Love[64] and, therefore is the *Eschatos* – then one would have to conclude that this temporally tensive eschatological character of the Christ event is such a theme.[65] To Tracy, this tensive event as both already and not yet informs the whole Christian symbol system rooted in the Christ event.[66] It is even disclosed in the tensive character of complementary New Testament interpretations of the Christ event, in the multiplicity of its genres.

Moreover, it is genuine faith in this always-already-and-not-yet eschatological character of the person and event of Jesus Christ which serves as the basis for the eschatological hope that we hear echoed in 1 Peter 3:15, not only because of the classic nature of this event, i.e., in its permanence and excess, but also because of its concrete historical character, its power of revelation in history, in the world, in time. The reality of the suffering of the Christ and of the Christian world of the Apostle engenders hope through the vindication of resurrection as it underlines the tensive nature of eschatological time. Thus Tracy will note at one point: "The recognition of suffering and the suffering Messiah leads to a heightened recognition of our not-yet state – personally, societally, and historically – and the not-yet reality of Messianic times [eschatological times] and, in that sense, to a heightened recognition of the cross, suffering and rejection in christology."[67] The concrete reality of the interruption of suffering in the life of the Christ, still present to the world in the Christ event, requires Tracy to make the claim that the Christ event as eschatological entails both a present and future orientation. Thus, while sympathetic to the Bultmann's existential reading of christology as verified by his referencing of the Bultmannian stance,[68] Tracy is not at all willing to collapse eschatology into the present.[69] He would agree with Zachary Hayes's claim that "history is open to a future held out to it by God."[70]

Tracy's consistent identification of the Christ event with eschatological time – decisively disclosive of the reality of God but always in the mode of already-and-not-yet – clearly surfaces in his genre analyses of the New Testament texts.[71] The christologically disclosive genres of the New Testament texts serve to "re-present" the past/present/future orientation which stands as one of the grounding principles of Tracy's eschatological assertions and of his hermeneutical notion of the Christian as religious classic. Tracy's particular discussion of the genres of "apocalyptic" and "early Catholicism" in the New Testament texts bears the greatest and most explicit force in balancing the already-not-yet character of the person and event of Jesus Christ.[72] Referring to the "corrective" genres of apocalyptic and early Catholicism, Tracy maintains that:

> Apocalyptic pervades the entire New Testament: sometimes explosively in Mark 13, 1 Thessalonians and the Book of Revelation; sometimes transformatively, as in the context of Jesus' proclamation of the reign of God in the parables and the ministry narrated in the synoptics; sometimes as disclosive of the cross, as in Mark's Son of Man christology or Paul's theology of the cross; at still other times dimly, as in 2 Peter's somewhat routine yet real reminder of the presence of apocalyptic hopes in the world of "early Catholicism."[73]

Apocalyptic hope is hope for a *novum*, a really new future in the face of suffering, in the light of the pain of the negation of Christ and humanity's cross. In contrast to a present-oriented early Catholicism with its focus on doctrine, the New Testament apocalyptic understanding of the Christ event serves as a balance for the focus on presence. In other words, the corrective disclosures of the genres of apocalyptic and early Catholicism in the New Testament texts highlight the already-not-yet eschatological nature of the Christ event. Christology as construed from a hermeneutic of genre analysis points to the very eschatological nature of the person and event of Jesus Christ and of humanity in tensive temporality.[74]

Tracy also observes this same sense of the eschatological nature of the Christ event as already-not-yet in the disclosures of the other central genres of the New Testament texts: in "proclamation," "narrative," and in the "symbolic and reflective thought" of both Paul and John. At first glance, one might conclude that proclamation and narrative and Paul and John are set over against each other in Tracy's discussion. That is, one might be tempted to conclude that Gospel proclamation and Paul as disclosive genres are more concerned with the future. For example, a key kerygmatic proclamation in Mark is future oriented. "This is the time of fulfillment. The Kingdom of God is at hand. Repent and believe in the Gospel" (Mk. 1: 15). Moreover, Paul's lengthy discussion of the nature of resurrection in 1 Corinthians is future oriented. "Christ has been raised from the dead, the first fruits of those who have fallen asleep.... When everything is subjected to him, then the Son himself will also be subjected to the One who subjected everything to him, so that God may be all in all" (1 Cor. 15: 20, 28). On the other hand, in the Lucan narrative we hear Jesus state that "But if it is by the finger of God that I cast out demons, then the Kingdom of God has come upon you" (Lk. 11: 20). Furthermore, in John we read, "Whoever believes in the Son has eternal life" (Jn. 3:36).[75]

However, such a dichotomy is too simplistic and not reflective of the sense of temporal wholeness embedded in the Christ event. Rather, Tracy's reading of the various genres as classic disclosures not only supports his claim that the christological interpretations of the person and event of Jesus the Christ are richly pluralistic but also supports the sense that the Christ event is eschatological in the very fact that it is an already-not-yet event of decisive divine manifestation. The differentiation between proclamation and narrative, to Tracy, entails not only future as set over against presence but also direct address/confrontation (proclamation) complemented by subtlety (narrative). Tracy makes the point: "Where proclamation confronts us directly with its word of address and its powerful appeal to respond to the nearness of God disclosed in the event of Jesus Christ, the gospels prefer to tell the story of this Jesus and allow that narrative's disclosive power to work its event-ful disclosure and transformation of the same truth."[76] Indeed, to Tracy, proclamation itself contains within it a tensive unity of past, present, and future. Speaking of the event character of the Christian proclamation, Tracy thus notes: "The gift of the spirit of that Lord [Jesus the Christ] to the present is also a promise for the future and a disclosure of the true meaning of the past."[77] Moreover, the narratives, for all their subtlety, do also disclose the temporal tensiveness of the Christ event. "A tension pervades these narratives between some fulfillment of the eschatological reign of God in the ministry, passion, and resurrection of Jesus and the yet unfulfilled hope for the end time and for all, the living and the dead, in that reign of the Coming God."[78] Both proclamation and narrative then disclose the temporal tensive nature of the christological as eschatological Christ event. Hence, in proclamation and narrative, the christological as eschatological carries with it a newness for human time, a newness which relates past, present, and future into a unity, a whole, while still preserving difference.

Furthermore, Tracy sees a similar differentiation between direct address as confrontation and subtlety in manifestation reflected in the symbolic and reflective theological thought of Paul and John, a differentiation which also reveals the already-not-yet eschatological tension in the very nature of the Christ event. For instance, Paul confronts his faith communities with the cross; yet his key symbols are the dialectical symbols of both cross and resurrection. Tracy notes:

> Paul's theology forces the reader again and again to face the "scandal," the "folly" of the cross of Christ: an event where all our lies, fears, anxieties, compulsions, illusions and distortions, our thousand strategies to justify ourselves are decentered and defamiliarized as they are brought to recognize the power of God on the cross as seeming weakness, suffering, forgiveness. Paul's texts will not let loose his grip on his exposure of both our pathetic and our heroic-tragic attempts at self-justification. At the same

time the Pauline texts disclose and conceal the reality of a new self in Christ enabled, empowered, commanded, freed to become a transformed [resurrected] self who is even now caught up in that power and lives even now through that gift...a self involved in the dialectic of a constant decentering self-recognition of the never-ending "not yet" in every "even now."[79]

Note how in Tracy's interpretation of Paul the Pauline dialectic of cross and resurrection as the "realized experience" of Jesus as the Christ offers the possibility of a "realizable experience" not only of cross/suffering but also of resurrection/transformation to humanity. This is all within the context of an eschatological temporality both within the Christ event and within the already-not-yet historicity of humanity.

Tracy contends that John's thought takes on a more contemplative tone. "In John thought itself has found a mode of meditative, manifestory expression for this reality of unfolding, encompassing exaltation. The shock of beauty in that glory manifests the need for a meditative, a contemplative mode of thought" focused on "incarnation."[80] Yet, resonant with Paul, John too points out that glory and exaltation come by way of dialectic; humiliation/exaltation takes shape in suffering and self-surrendering love. John too recognizes the already-not-yet character of the Christ event in that dialectic. As Tracy notes, John particularly reveals this dialectic within his final and ultimate, concrete and particular claim that "God is Love" (1 John: 8), the claim which the incarnation of Jesus as the Christ reveals in its particularity. Tracy thus says:

> Love's strength, for John, lies in its ability to let go; to sacrifice itself for the other; to let go into a manifestation of the love of Jesus Christ – the love disclosing God's own self as Love and disclosing the gift of a new self-understanding as a self in love without restriction.[81]

In a summary statement, Tracy relates the eschatological temporal tensiveness of the Christ event with the dialectical and meditative styles of Pauline and Johannine thought in the following assertion: "The full complexity of those symbols and those modes of thinking – cross-resurrection-incarnation, dialectic and meditative thought – disclose the reality of an event which is here even now, which has always already been here, which is still not yet here. The dialectic of these symbols is the adverbial dialectic of an always-already which is yet a not-yet."[82] While apocalyptic and early Catholicism explicitly point up the tensive eschatological temporality of the Christ event, the other genres – proclamation, narrative, and symbolic and reflective thought – also manifest the already-not-yet character of the person and event of Jesus the Christ.

The Eschatological Shape That a Life of Wholeness Can Take

In the previous section, the claim was made that the Christian classic, precisely as christological, manifests eschatological wholeness in two ways. First, it manifests the decisive and thus final revelation of who God as the Ultimate Reality is. God is Love – Pure, Unbounded, Love. God is loving relationality lying at the heart of all reality. Tracy notes: "Love, and love alone, is the surest clue to who God is and to what reality…finally always-already is."[83] This is the "whole" truth informing and directing the shape of Christian existence. Secondly, the claim was made that the Christian classic in its excess, in its historical but also trans-historical nature, is an already-not-yet reality, a non-ending story which not only preserves the real distinction of past, present, and future but also relates those temporal dimensions in a timely and yet timeless fashion. Again Tracy notes: the "non-end" of the Christian classic "…discloses that all, in one sense, has already happened. And yet the story does not end."[84] The Christ event, the very manifestation of who God is, has happened, does happen, and will happen. Eschatological wholeness is revealed then in these two dimensions of the Christian as religious classic, in a christology dramatically disclosing an eschatology. In both cases, relationality rises to the surface as a characterizing feature of the eschatological wholeness disclosed in the Christ event. God as Love and God's very loving of humanity and all creation most clearly is a matter of relationship. So too the eschatological sense of time manifested in that very revelatory event, the "already-not-yet," "that which has happened, happens, and will happen," connects past, present, and future in a relationship of temporal unity-in-tension. In this view as Christian, love has been, continues to be, and will always be at the very heart of all reality.

Moreover, the eschatological wholeness of the Christian classic precisely as classic does more than disclose the wholeness of love in tensive temporality for Christian eschatological reflection. It invites related action, participation, the appropriation of that disclosure into lived eschatological existence. The Christian classic points to, offers as gift, and indeed demands of humanity a life lived in eschatological wholeness because the concrete and particular nature of the Christ event as whole "tells the whole story." As such, it not only makes manifest who God is in a manner which transcends ordinary time, in the already-not-yet; it also reveals who we are and are to become in the light of that revelation. Why is this the case? This is the case precisely because Love, the Final as Ultimate Reality, is both "gift and command."[85] It is the always-already given gift of relationship inviting a response of the same nature and calling for a unity of worldview and ethos, of thought and action, animated by that relationship. In a word, this event also reveals what shape Christian existence as authentic and eschatological can and must take in history, in the world. To reiterate, the Christ event is the final eschatological event for the Christian because it reveals fully, wholly, decisively, and concretely who God is in a manner which is both timely and yet timeless. Concomitantly it also reveals what authentic Christians living in the world are to become in relation to that revelation. Tracy's following lengthy but significant commentary not only reiterates the eschatological nature of the Christ event but also, quite importantly, clarifies and particularizes the shape that an authentic relationship to that eschatological event must take:

> For the Christian to affirm "I believe in Jesus Christ" is to affirm the reality of God's own self-manifestation in the person Jesus Christ.... The christological affirmation is a religious-existential one: an affirmation that bears the character of a response. That response of trust in its disclosure of all reality is named faith. To state "I believe *in* Jesus Christ" is to affirm that, in whatever form of mediation I have experienced this event, the event itself as the decisive event of God's self-manifestation in Jesus Christ takes primacy. The event happens as a realized experience of the truth of life bearing its own shock of recognition of who we are and who God is, bearing as well its own defamiliarizing confrontation of our usual performance, even our ordinary expectations and questions by its disclosure that "something else may be the case"...a profound confirmation that our deepest yearnings for wholeness in ourselves, in history, in nature, in the whole are grounded in the structure of reality itself. We may now dare to let go of our other, usual "gods" – success, fame, security, self-justification – by letting go into the final reality with which we must all ultimately deal: the power of that pure, unbounded love who is God, the knowledge that reality itself is finally gracious, that existence – ourselves, history, nature – in spite of all is not absurd.[86]

For Tracy, authentic Christian existence in the light of the Christ event first and foremost takes shape in faith as trust in the eschatological Christ event. It is a "religious existential" response to the shocking recognition that "God's own self-manifestation" takes place in the reality of the Christ and that this manifestation reveals that God, the Final Reality, is "the power of pure unbounded love" warranting that "reality itself is finally gracious, and that existence...is not absurd." Faith then as both a shock of recognition about the nature of the eschatological core of all reality and a trust in that recognition characterizes authentic Christian as eschatological existence. Furthermore, that faith believes and trusts in love and loving as the final power, the whole which both grounds all reality and answers "our deepest yearnings for wholeness."[87] Moreover, the promissory nature of eschatological Christ event as already-not-yet wherein the power of love has been vindicated and assured in the person and event of Jesus as the Christ warrants eschatological hope for the authentic Christian living in a history, in a world of finitude and suffering. It makes hope directed by a life of loving plausible.

Within these key assertions, therefore, there lies a praxis oriented dimension to the eschatological wholeness of the Christian as religious classic, praxis-oriented in that it calls for living a life of "virtued" existence. The Christian yearning and hope for concrete holistic existence exists only by way of a Christian faith in the power of the Whole Who is Love, the pure loving relationality at the very core of existence. Ultimately in *The Analogical Imagination*, David Tracy names human beings as those rational creatures whose existence is characterized by the deepest yearnings for wholeness. This naming even lies at the heart of Tracy's complex phenomenological analysis of the pluralistic, postmodern situation in *The Analogical Imagination*; for there he summons up the support of the postmodern "masters of suspicion," i.e., Marx, Freud, Nietzsche, and Heidegger, to make the claim for contemporary humanity's "not-at-homeness."[88] Tracy characterizes our "not-at-homeness" as our "fragmentation,"[89] the interruption of our lack of wholeness.

For Tracy as Christian systematic theologian, that interruptive lack of wholeness can be overcome – can free us for the Whole – by the concrete "religious-existential response" of a present faith in that prior but always offered and always to be offered gift of the Christ event, the event of Pure, Unbounded Love, the final and thus eschatological event. It is this gift which promises and gives rise to Christian hope for a future, the predominant interest of eschatology. Resurrection within the whole of the Christ event warrants that hope.[90] It makes hope plausible. In other words, Christian existence – eschatological existence precisely as Christian – is existence in Christ,[91] in the faithful and hopeful discipleship which takes shape as an imitation of a decisive and thus universally significant yet concrete and particular classic life lived in love. Herein then lies another dimension of the wholeness of relationality which characterizes all reality. It is the relational response to the eschatological Christ event by way of an active life of virtued discipleship lived concretely and historically in faith and hope in the final power of love. Recognition of the classic event as gift stimulates a certain way of acting.

Tracy has spoken of Christian theology as necessarily "christomorphic" as revelational of a "form" of authentic existence. The concrete life of Jesus the Christ is the decisive and final form of an authentic eschatological existence in the world.[92] It is a life of love, suffering but free love, to which Christians are invited to respond in kind and in faith and hope. Perhaps the following quotation can serve as a summary statement for Tracy's final concrete and decisive step in the journey from the religious to the Christian classic, to the eschatological classic event of the Christ. This is the step that takes on the shape or character of a "religious-existential" response, in authentic active relationship to the eschatological Christ event:

> To live a life based on a fundamental trust in the power of love as God's own reality and God's own gift and command to human beings bears its own kind of verification. As even a day's attempt to live that kind of life can disclose to any person, any Christian attempting to become a Christian will learn swiftly the harsh truth in the narratives about this Jesus: rejections, conflict, suffering, cross. To follow the path of that kind of life of trusting, other-regarding love is to trust in that vision and accept that fate in a hope embraced for the sake of the hopeless and a faith grounded in his resurrection. The final test of that vision will always be the risk of a life. The final test is in the future. In the present, there exists the Christ event to elicit, enable and command that risk by its presencing of the Christian tradition and its dangerous memory of this Jesus who is the Christ. The shock of recognition and confrontation in that event commands Christians to risk a life on that always-already, not-yet vision of what reality ultimately is. For the Christian truly believes in Jesus Christ only by risking the kind of life narrated as Jesus' own. The Christian believes in Jesus Christ as God's ownmost self-manifestation by trusting that the risk is grounded in the nature of reality itself and by living that trust. The Christian believes with Paul and all other classic persons of the tradition, the saints and witnesses who actually took that risk, that "all is yours and you are Christ's and Christ is God's." The rest is commentary.[93]

This powerful statement characterizes the shape that an authentic Christian eschatological existence must take, the shape of a life lived in faith, love, and hope; it also exemplifies not only the inter-relationship of faith, love, and hope in the whole of authentic Christian as eschatological existence but also connects that sense of inter-relationship to the other two eschatological dimensions of Tracy's christological reflection: the final claim that God, the Ultimate and thus Eschatological Reality, is revealed finally and decisively, wholly, in the classic Christ event as Love and that such a revelation bears within it the tensive but unifying eschatological sense of temporality. Such an ever timely revelation also unifies worldview and ethos by offering and commanding the Christian to "risk a life" of virtued discipleship, of faith, love, and hope in this world. For such a life is a matter of risk precisely because it rests first and foremost on faith and hope in the final power of love in and in spite of tensive temporality, human suffering, and finitude. Yet it is not a foolish, senseless risk because it is a risk warranted by the eschatological manifestation of the Christ event. It is a plausible risk. And thus for Tracy, this Christian as religious classic which reveals the whole finally and decisively is an event of eschatological liberation via a life of faith, love, and hope towards the wholeness for which humanity yearns. For in the Christ event "we are finally freed to embrace a fundamental trust in the whole, to demand of ourselves, by that trust, a hope for the sake of the hopeless, to risk a life in the impossible gospel possibility of a faith and hope working through love given as pure gift and stark command."[94] In a word, Christ as eschatological person and event frees one for a life of virtued discipleship in this our world, in our now sacred secularity wherein Christian faith and hope are animated by and worked out through the power of love.

Concluding Remarks

As William Shea noted, David Tracy's theological project in *The Analogical Imagination* is an exercise in method as applied to Christian systematic theology. It is a revisionist exercise in that it applies the hermeneutic of the classic to what Tracy considers to be the eschatological focal meaning of Christianity: the person and event of Jesus as the Christ. In this sense, Tracy's revisionist spirit and methodology are primarily focused on retrieving and reinterpreting the core of the Christian tradition for a modern/postmodern world by way of the hermeneutic of the classic. Yet this very exercise has served to disclose further revisionist namings of both God and of the contemporary human situation that have eschatological dimensions. In the previous chapter, I demonstrated that "limit" discloses the eschatological dimension of Tracy's project in *Blessed Rage for Order*. In this present chapter, I have demonstrated that the "whole" provides a similar service in *The Analogical Imagination*, the "whole" as the relationship of love and loving lying at the very heart of all reality and providing the clue and direction for overcoming the interruptive fragmentation of the human condition. Furthermore, I contend that the same pattern of eschatological thinking that surfaced in *Blessed Rage* appears in Tracy's revisionist foray into Christian systematics. Just as the disclosure of an eschatological reality in a naming (limit in *Blessed Rage*) evokes at the same time an appropriate action or response (transcendence in faith), the whole and thus eschatological story of existence, the story of love in the decisive and final Christ event, beckons engagement in loving relationship as the only and final way in which to overcome fragmentation. Worldview and ethos are intimately related; understanding of the eschatological reality directs one towards a plausible way of living in the present and into the future. In this sense, Tracy again moves his readers beyond the confines of a chosen theological genre, i.e., systematics as an exercise in speculative ordering per se, to a form of theological discourse that entails both speculation and practice, and I contend that the eschatological dimensions of Tracy's project are precisely what fuel that movement. Systematics is an essential building block for Christian eschatology, but systematics alone may not be adequate to the task of constructing a Christian eschatology. For the insight that the wholeness of loving relationship lies at the heart of all reality demands that loving relationship as an offer calls for the same response, the reciprocal act of loving.

Tracy concludes his systematic text with a methodological proposal for the engagement of an "analogical imagination." This method itself is based upon the recognition or sense that reality is ultimately a matter of relationship as it seeks to discover similarities in differences, relationships of similarity, if not identity. In this sense, the analogical imagination is a strategy born of a fundamental insight into a reality already present, a gift already given. On an existentially religious level then, the analogical imagination is much more than a method; it is itself a grace, an event of faith, a gift of recognition – however fragile, incomplete, and sometimes fleeting – of the whole of all reality. Admittedly on one level, the methodological, the revelation of the eschatological person and event of Jesus Christ stimulates in the theologian an analogical imagination as a fruitful strategy with which to deal with plural interpretations of this Christian "focal meaning."[95] However and existentially, that person and event also has the power to engender within the Christian in lived religious existence the possibility of recognizing in faith and appropriating via an analogical imagination that final gift/revelation which lies at the heart of the whole of reality. The analogical imagination is an imagination that can live with and have faith and hope in a classic story as powerful and mysterious as the Christian classic, the classic that reveals finally that all is relationship and that all authentic relationship is ordered and fired by the power of active loving. That timeless, classic, and eschatological story can thus be remembered in the present and, in that remembering, stimulate action on behalf of love in whatever trying and interruptive historical situations awaiting the believing and hoping Christian's future, in whatever situations of fragmentation that may arise.

Therefore, the gift of the analogical imagination in concert with the hermeneutic of the Christian eschatological classic is, for Tracy, the gift of seeing, recognizing, appropriating, and acting upon – indeed, of trusting in and risking a life for – the "ordered relationship"[96] at the heart or at the radical core of the whole of reality. What concretely characterizes this ordered relationship at the heart, and thus at the eschatological core, of all reality? Love characterizes this ordered relationship. The "classical" life, death, and resurrection of Jesus as the Christ reveals this with finality and wholeness and points to the order of love as the only authentic mode of Christian as eschatological existence. Tracy notes in his concluding comments about the analogical imagination "that grace [the gift of the revelation of Jesus as the Christ], when reflected upon [by the analogical imagination] unfolds its fuller meaning into the ordered relationships of the God who is love, the world that is beloved and a self gifted and commanded to become loving,"[97] for "every human understanding of God is at the same time an understanding of oneself and visa versa. Every proper understanding of the self is never an understanding of some unreal, isolated self but an understanding of the self in internal relationships, in intrinsic coexistence with the reality of the 'world'....It is impossible to separate these realities God-self-world."[98]

The language of basic faith in the worthwhileness of existence disclosed via Tracy's analysis of limit and transcendence dominates in *Blessed Rage for Order*. Yet, the language of wholeness in relationship as love dominates in *The Analogical Imagination*. Love is at the eschatological core of all reality, and loving is the preferred pattern for eschatological existence. Love is recognized in a basic faith and stimulates hope for a humanity facing the future while caught in the historicity and interruptive ongoing suffering of this present world. The final as decisively whole of reality is classically revealed by way of the concrete and particular (historical and incarnate) Christ event as the analogically ordered relationship of love, a relationship which invites participation yet preserves difference. It is from the revelation of this event that one can, in faith and hope, name God finally, decisively, and wholly. It allows Tracy to claim: "the only God there is is the God who is Love...that ultimate reality which grounds all and pervades all reality, the reality with which we must ultimately all deal."[99] And we can deal with that ultimate reality best by the reciprocal acts of faith and hope in loving relationship.

Thus the Christian as religious classic, for Tracy, reveals the eschatological by way of a revisionist methodology, a hermeneutic of that very classic to discover anew and appropriate its disclosive and directive power. This classic reveals the ultimate and final whole of reality, and the Whole is Love and wholeness is characterized by the relationship of love. This love is both gift and command, a present reality promising and relating past and present to a future of wholeness only by demanding the ethical human acts of faith and hope in the power of love. The gift of the analogical imagination is the gift of seeing the eschatological finality of this relationship in and in spite of human interruptive temporality and finitude. Tracy's revisionist treatment of the Christ event discovers a final reality that is an "unending story," always available to give direction towards living into the future. Thus and in sum:

> Whatever classical route of spirituality any individual Christian takes in trying to live a life like the life of Jesus of Nazareth narrated in the gospels, no one can forget that the story must finally be remembered in its entirety: as a narrative of real negation and real exaltation, of real suffering and active love, as a proclamation and manifestation of the Crucified and Risen One who lived, lives, and will live, as an unsettling, disorienting narrative which disclose the judging, healing truth that the final power with which we must all deal is neither the coercive power of this world nor our own tortured memories, but the power of that pure, unbounded, compassionate, judging love which *is* the final reality, who *is* God. The Christian story has not ended and will not end until all the living and the dead are touched – how we know not.[100]

A revisionist theological perspective critically attends to both tradition and present conditions. A revisionist theological perspective that takes the shape of a hermeneutic of the classic and final story of Christianity must do the same. David Tracy's revisionist treatment of the Christian story names who God is and who we are to become as we risk entering an unknown future from an interruptive, fragmented present. It critically attends to both tradition and the present condition while, at the same time, it offers a schema or pattern for living that is eschatological. In this, Tracy's treatment soberly recognizes that this very story places an enduring action-oriented demand on humanity. We are commanded to touch and be touched by the final power of love, the eschatological power of love, in spite of the uncertainties of the future. Once again then, eschatological insight entails the responsibility for action and points to a pattern of eschatological discourse that must properly encompass both reflection and action, a form of discourse that will finally be claimed as best taking shape as a rhetoric. Analysis of Tracy's thought in *Plurality and Ambiguity* will only serve to reinforce this constructive claim by way of further revisionist and more postmodern namings. For in *Plurality and Ambiguity,* Tracy fully recognizes that relationship is at the heart of all reality, but he does so with an intensified and sober realization of the radical difference and otherness inherent in relationship. And dealing with difference and otherness, key postmodern themes and Tracy's eschatological namings in *Plurality and Ambiguity*, makes living in the present and into the future all the more uncertain, threatening, ambiguous, interruptive, and ultimately in need of the persuasive power of the rhetorical word if hope for a future can remain alive.

Notes

1. William M. Shea, "Review Symposium," *Horizons* 8/2 (Fall, 1981), p. 315. Perhaps Tracy would agree with Shea on this point. In concluding *AI*, Tracy notes: "In an already lengthy work, it would be inappropriate and impossible to attempt a full systematics. And yet an outline of what the arguments and interpretations of this work suggest for the basic form of a Christian systematics seems in order." See p. 421.

2. *AI*, p. 449.

3. The following "presumption" on the part of Tracy should be reiterated and kept in mind in the discussion of the Christian classic in *AI*. As has been noted previously, very early in his career, Tracy made explicit eschatological claims. They were that God, the Ultimate as Final Reality, has acted decisively, finally, in the person and event of Jesus as the Christ, that this event bears with it the temporal tensiveness of the "already-not-yet," and that Christian existence is eschatological existence. See again Tracy's "Horizon Analysis and Eschatology" in *Continuum* 6 (Summer, 1968), p. 177. These are claims from a specific, i.e., Christian, tradition, from an "explicit religion." They are systematic claims. The analysis of Tracy's systematic text, *AI*, then should help to fill out those very claims.

4. *AI*, p. 129.

5. *AI*, p. 126.

6. The methodological turn to critical correlation serves as the organizing structure for *Blessed Rage*. One can, however, make the claim that although the classic becomes the predominant methodological organizing structure for Tracy's move into systematic theology in *The Analogical Imagination*, Tracy also engages in a method of correlation in that text, albeit in reverse order. In *BRO*, Tracy moves from the human situation to the theological/Christian tradition; he moves from the Christian tradition (via the Christian classic) to the postmodern human situation of "uncanny not-at-homeness" in *AI*. See the move from the Christian classic in Chapters 6 and 7 to the "situation" in Chapter 8.

7. *AI*, p. 64. Note that the correlation of the two general poles of theological reflection is still present here in the definition of the systematic theologian's task – the correlation of the tradition and the present situation, that is, in the manner of re-interpretation.

8. *AI*, p. 130.

9. *AI*, p. 99.

10. See Chapter 1 beginning on p. 3.

11. See again p. 111 of *AI*.

12. *AI*, p. 116. Note that Tracy does not limit the classic to the structure of a text alone in a more traditional understanding of the classic. Tracy's understanding of the classic as capable of being presented in a multiplicity of forms demonstrates a broader understanding of the classic. Indeed in this very text, Tracy defines the "Christian classic" as an event and not a text, the event of Jesus Christ. See Part II of *AI* beginning on p. 233. Here Tracy stands with Paul Ricoeur in claiming that the classic may be more than a text; it may be an action of significance, an event. In *Theology After Ricoeur: New Directions in Hermeneutical Theology*, (Louisville: Westminster John Knox Press, 2001), Dan R. Stiver points out that, for Ricoeur, the classic can include both "texts and nontexts," actions, events. Stiver bases this claim on his reading of Ricoeur's "The Model of the Text: Meaningful Action Considered as a

Text" and of Ricoeur's *Time and Narrative*. See pp. 97ff of Stiver's work. As an aside, the event character of such a classic as the Christ event reinforces the historical, in-the-world nature of this paradigmatic classic.

13. *AI*, p. 102.

14. Tracy refuses to allow the classic as authentically classic to remain a "period piece," curiously interesting but fixed in the past. Thus, on p. 106 of *AI*, Tracy appropriates William Faulkner's claim that "the past is not really dead; it is not even past." Thus also, Tracy finds a purely "historical critical" approach to the classic resting on an analysis of the "mind of the author, the social circumstances, the life-world of the text, or the reception of the text by its original addressees" as necessary but insufficient for the interpretation of the classic. Such an approach, for Tracy, leaves the classic in the past and thus fails to do justice to the classic's ability to transcend time and offer the possibility of a transformative mode of being in the present world and into the future. See p. 105 of *AI*.

15. *AI*, p. 126.

16. Here again, Tracy is indebted to Ricoeur and Gadamer (and perhaps Plato) in his appropriation of knowledge/understanding as a matter of "participation" or "belonging to" as well as "distanciation." See, for instance, Ricoeur's classic essay, "Toward a Hermeneutic of the Idea of Revelation" in *Harvard Theological Review* 70/1-2 (January – April, 1977) beginning on p. 1 where Ricoeur speaks of poetic discourse as "belonging-to amid the ruins of descriptive discourse" (see p. 24) and his discussion of "participation" in relation to "distanciation" beginning on p. 28. These very same concepts form the basis of Tracy's own discussion of the production of the classic beginning on p. 124 of *AI*.

17. This is Ricoeur's term. See *AI*, pp. 118ff. The concept of "enveloping/developing," for Ricoeur, describes the interpretation of the classic as understanding-explanation-understanding.

18. *AI*, p. 119.

19. *AI*, p. 114.

20. Note how the concept of "realized experience" in the case of the classic resonates fully with Tracy's earlier (in *BRO*) appropriation and interpretation of Ogden's "re-presentational" fact as real possibility.

21. Interestingly, Tracy makes this assertion in the course of his discussion of Christian eschatology in "Horizon Analysis and Eschatology." See p. 177. There is thus a resonance between this philosophical understanding of time, the nature and functioning of the classic, and the "already-not-yet" character of the Christian classic Christ event, for Tracy, the eschatological event.

22. See the above quote as well as his discussion of the production of the classic as a matter of radical participation or intensification and, dialectically, distanciation. Indeed, the production of the classic as both intensification and distanciation as well as the interpretation of the classic as understanding-explanation-understanding contain within themselves a tensive temporality which is born of the prior claim that the classic is an event of the disclosure and concealment of the truth or some essential aspect of the truth. See particularly p. 130 of *AI*.

23. See again *AI*, p. 130 and later *PA*, p. 28.

24. *AI*, p. 130.

25. See again *AI*, p. 102.
26. *AI*, pp. 430–431. The perspective is that of the religious classic and finally that of the Christian classic.
27. That is, from statements about God as the final reality named from the perspective of fundamental theology as the one necessary existent grounding all existence to the systematic perspective on God as the power of the Whole Who is Love.
28. *AI*, p. 200.
29. See Tracy's claim to this effect on p. 199 of *AI*. "Any classic will produce its meaning through the related strategies of intensification of particularity and intensification of distanciation in expressions." This is the case because all classics bear within themselves a permanence and surplus of meaning; they both disclose and conceal truth. They also both transcend the ordinary notion of time.
30. *AI*, p. 200.
31. *AI*, p. 163.
32. *AI*, p. 163.
33. Thus Tracy notes: "On present terms, a religious classic may be viewed as an event of disclosure, expressive of the 'limit-of,' 'horizon-to,' 'ground-to' side of 'religion'...a self-manifestation by the power of ultimate mystery itself." See *AI*, pp. 162–163.
34. *AI*, p. 163.
35. Hence, later Tracy will identify the Christian classic as that which is both "gift and command." See, for instance, p. 269 of *AI*.
36. See Tracy's concluding comments on the relationship of manifestation and proclamation as dimensions of the religious classic where he notes that what the religious classic proclaims is that the "reality of the whole [is] now disclosed as God." See *AI*, p. 209. See also p. 331 where Tracy identified God as manifest in the Christ event as "the power who is Love." In this sense, Tracy anticipates his discussion of the Christian classic in his discussion of the religious classic itself in his systematic progression into greater particularity.
37. One must be cautious in attempting to understand Tracy at this point however. Tracy speaks of religion and of the religious classic in terms of the whole. Religion as religion deals with the whole of reality and not a part or particular aspect of reality. That is, to Tracy, what makes religion religion. Tracy, however, does not wish to identify the whole with what he calls a "right wing" Hegelian understanding of totality where, finally, God takes on the character of the Absolute Spirit into which all is folded. He seems to be suspicious of an *Aufhebung* where perhaps the individual is lost in the totality. See his discussion in note 21 on pp. 182–183 of *AI*. Yet, the religious classic, to Tracy, really does "catch one up" into a participation with the greater reality.
38. *AI*, p. 155.
39. *AI*, p. 163.
40. *AI*, p. 177.
41. Hence, Tracy's appreciation of Mircea Eliade's contribution to the study of religion as manifestation as well as his appreciation for Barth and Bonhoeffer's contribution to the study of religion as proclamation. See the discussion of the religious classic as the revelation of the whole both as "manifestation" and "proclamation" beginning on p. 202 of *AI*. In this lengthy exposition, Tracy makes the claim that the religious classic, precisely as

a mysterious disclosure/concealment, as a truth as *aletheia,* is a dialectical event of "two main dialectical moments – an existential intensification of participation, expressing itself through distanciation in shareable form" (p. 203). And through history, religion itself may take on the shape of either a "mystical-priestly-metaphysical aesthetic emphasis" or a "prophetic-ethical-historical emphasis" (p. 203). Tracy's claim is that both dimensions are indicative of authentic religion. What is also important to note is that inherent in those two major emphases is the notion of religious or sacred time as encompassing past, present, and future. While, for instance, manifestation is present-oriented, proclamation is future-oriented, but not exclusively so.

42. *AI*, p. 164.

43. *AI*, p. 375. A son of Rahner, Tracy often tends to name God in this fashion. Tracy sees this naming of God as "ultimate mystery" as an apt descriptor which does service to both the Catholic and Protestant traditions of naming God. See, for instance, his article "The Hermeneutics of Naming God" where he states: "The Reformed tradition focuses that mystery on the notion of the Hidden-Revealed God. The Catholic tradition focuses its attention on the notion of the Comprehensible-Incomprehensible God. Both address their major attention and their central energy to the hiddenness as revealed or the incomprehensibility as positive; in sum the mystery of God as the Ultimate Mystery." See *Irish Theological Quarterly* 57/4 (1991), p. 253. Tracy applies this same theme in his discussion, "God of History, God of Psychology" in ONP, beginning on p. 47.

44. *AI*, p. 194.

45. *AI*, p. 177.

46. *AI*, p. 201.

47. See *AI*, beginning on p. 429.

48. *AI*, p. 331.

49. *AI*, p. 331.

50. As an aside, Tracy's journey of intensification in *The Analogical Imagination,* i.e., the movement into greater particularity via the exposition of the secular classic, the religious classic, and finally the Christian classic, mirrors a similar global movement across the two major texts (BRO and AI). There is a similar journey into particularity taking place in both texts. Thus, Tracy will make the argument for neo-classical theism (panentheism) in BRO by referencing the process view of reality as ultimately relational and temporal and then make an analogical/transcendental claim that the dipolar (process) God of Pure, Unbounded, Love is the only God who bears meaning and meaningfulness for humanity in the light of this prior claim about the fundamental (metaphysical) nature of reality. See his argument in BRO, pp. 172ff. When Tracy ultimately makes the same claims about God and relationality as love at the very heart of all reality in AI, he does so not via abstract (transcendental) analysis but within the framework of an analysis/interpretation of the particularity of religious/Christian classical revelations. All of this reinforces a claim that Tracy's theological project with its theological insights coheres across texts and the claim that Tracy is on a journey of intensification wherein the same insights into the ultimate (the eschatological) are warranted from both abstract and concrete starting points.

51. See p. 233 of AI where Tracy notes: "...there is one classic event and person which normatively judges and informs all other Christian classics, and which also serves as the classic

Christian focus for understanding God, self, others, society, history, nature and the whole Christianly: the event and person of Jesus Christ."

52. *AI*, p. 215.

53. This is Tracy's own term to describe some "rule of thumb" or "final horizonal discrimen which seems relatively adequate" to the diverse and plural christological interpretations of the apostolic tradition. See his comments to that effect on p. 254 of *AI* and in a lengthy note on p. 290. See note 29. Tracy recognizes and appreciates the diversity of the New Testament texts. He finds such diversity enriching and not confounding. He states on p. 254, "The reality of diversity must be affirmed as fact in the New Testament, in the entire Christian tradition, in the contemporary Christian community.... The reality of pluralism is a value: a value to enrich each by impelling new journeys into both particularity and ecumenicity." Yet Tracy also contends that there is a universal whole in spite of the diversity, the "working canon" that God in God's very self is revealed decisively and finally in the person and event of Jesus the Christ. The reality of diversity is what impels him to adopt a hermeneutical stance towards christological reflection wherein "relative adequacy" on the side of human interpretation arises from the faith claim for the full adequacy of the final and decisive revelation of God in Jesus the Christ.

54. *AI*, pp. 248–249.

55. That is, through the hermeneutical approach of genre analysis of New Testament texts rather than the more traditional approach of historical-critical quests for the "historical Jesus." Tracy makes the case for his own approach in his "Introduction to Part II: A Methodological Preface" beginning on p. 234 of *AI*. Born of his recognition of the limitations of historical-critical studies as well as of the pluralities of interpretations within the New Testament, this approach is critically sympathetic to that of Rudolf Bultmann and Martin Kähler. See Tracy's note to that effect on p. 245, note 23 and again on p. 300, note 97. Tracy's argument in support of his own hermeneutical approach to christology fundamentally rests on the claim that historical quests are just that – historical – and not theological! Yet, Tracy does not dismiss the role of historical-critical study out of hand. As he notes on p. 260 of *AI*, historical-critical studies, along with "social-scientific" studies, perform a "functional" service. They permit analyses of the "realities of...religion in its contemporary setting." However, the hermeneutical approach making use of literary analysis gets at the "substantive," the "whole." Thus, Tracy notes in the later text, *Plurality and Ambiguity*, "...history, as Adolf von Harnack insisted, must have the first but not the last word in all interpretation." See *PA*, p. 39. One might note, as an aside, that Tracy was criticized for adopting what has been called this "christology from above" stance in *AI*. To attempt to cover this controversy would go beyond the scope of the present study. Yet, a valuable reference in this matter would be Elizabeth Johnson's critique of Tracy (or perhaps of Tracy via Bultmann) in "The Theological Relevance of the Historical Jesus: A Debate and a Thesis" in *The Thomist* 48/1 (January, 1984), pp. 1–43. Ironically, Johnson's own christological interpretation of Jesus Christ as the one who brings to humanity "wholeness" (her term) and "human liberation" resonates finally with Tracy's own interpretation. See p. 39 of her article. It seems that a "christology from below" and a "christology from above" can find a converging center.

56. That is, in spite of the fact of the plurality and relative adequacy of interpretations of that working canon.

57. *AI*, p. 249.
58. *AI*, pp. 330.
59. See again the discussion of Jesus Christ as the *Eschatos* in the first chapter. Recall along this line of thought, for instance, that Rahner has claimed that the "assertions of Christology" are "at the base of eschatology" precisely because Jesus the Christ is the *Eschatos*. See Rahner's "The Hermeneutics of Eschatological Assertions" in *Theological Investigations* (Baltimore: Helicon, 1966), Volume IV, p. 345. See also von Balthasar's classic referencing of this claim in the light of Jean Daniélou's thought in "Some Points on Eschatology," *Explorations in Theology* (San Francisco: Ignatius Press, 1989). See note 8 on p. 261. "According to [Daniélou's] viewpoint, Christ in the hypostatic union of the two natures is the *Eschaton* which governs both the time of promise and fulfillment, and essentially, as he who has come, is the one coming and the one who fulfills all things." As person, Christ is the *Eschatos*; as event, Christ is the *Eschaton*. Thus, von Balthasar himself claims "Jesus Christ, who is the revelation of God, [is] the whole essence of the last things." See pp. 260–26. Note how both finality and tensive temporality are also blended in von Balthasar's comments. This notion of Jesus the Christ as the *Eschatos* is also echoed in the contemporary Protestant tradition – at least as portrayed by Gerhard Sauter in his discussion of "radical" eschatology in *What Dare We Hope? Reconsidering Eschatology.* See p. 48. "Understanding eschatology depends heavily on not dealing merely with some kind of *eschaton* (end) [in terms of 'time'] or *eschata* (last things) existing on the horizon of theology – whether that horizon appears to be near or far – but on treating Jesus Christ as the *eschatos*, and ultimately, on a consideration of God."
60. See p. 259 of *AI*. See also p. 309.
61. See again Tracy's discussion of such beginning on p. 202. Both forms of expression are necessary because, in conjunction, they serve to express better, more fully, the wholeness of the Christian classic. Later in *AI* Tracy adds the historical and liberating praxis expression of the liberation theologians to manifestation and proclamation. See his discussion of all three valid and related forms of expression in Chapter 9, beginning on p. 371. In this, genres and forms of expression not only serve to point up the plurality inherent in Christian understandings of the Christ event but also allow the temporal unity-in-tension of the Christ event to surface.
62. *AI*, p. 216. Note the explicitly eschatological language of hope for liberation in advent and promise, eschatological language that echoes through the Christian tradition. See again Moltmann's discussion of a *novum* and *adventum* in *The Coming of God: Christian Eschatology* beginning on p. 25. See also von Rad's claim that the eschatological prophets of the Hebrew Scriptures preached the coming of a "new state" in their "message of the new thing" in his *Old Testament Theology*, Volume II. See p. 119. Tracy sees this newness – uniquely as Jewish and Christian interpretation – as the newness which brings the sacred to the world and history, to the secular. Thus, to Tracy, the "sacred and profane" dichotomy discussed by Eliade in *The Sacred and the Profane: The Nature of Religion* (New York: Harcourt, Brace, and World, 1959) gives way in the Jewish and (finally) Christian tradition to the "sacred in the secular" impelling ethical action in the world and into the future and not in a return to the "sacred time of origins." See Eliade's discussion beginning on p. 68 of his classic text. See also Tracy's comments on p. 216 of *AI* where he states: "The sacred time of origins

(*Urzeit*) is reformulated and transformed as the proclaimed and promised time of the end-time, hoped for as really new." It is the Christ event as both "already and not yet" which warrants that Christian eschatological claim.

63. That is, in *The Analogical Imagination*, although the same case can be made for the movement of his thought in *Blessed Rage* wherein Tracy moves from the philosophical to the more explicitly hermeneutical analysis of New Testament texts and the "christological fact."

64. This is summarized again on p. 317 of *AI*. "The New Testament from beginning to end confesses that this Jesus of Nazareth is none other than the Christ, the Lord, true and saving word, decisive manifestation of the whole as the 'who' named God: the pure self-giving, self-exposing unbounded Love which is the whole encompassing us, who is the reality meeting us in the event of divine self-manifestation proclaimed and manifested in Jesus Christ." Note again – Christ is the *Eschatos*, the decisive manifestation of the Whole who is God, who is Love – and this within Tracy's christological reflection.

65. Textual references in *AI* are too numerous to cite completely. A few citations will suffice. See p. 249 as quoted above; see also Tracy's retrieval of Bultmann's sense of the eschatological Christ event as "ever happening event" on p. 261 and 269; see his claim that the christological symbols of cross, resurrection, and incarnation are symbols which carry this already-not-yet character of eschatological time on p. 282; see again Tracy's claim that the Christ event is one that "de-centers" the self-satisfaction and complacency of the post-modern ego because that event is a "never ending" event of the "not yet in every now" on p. 284; and note how Tracy sees the tensive character of the eschatological Christ event as that which "frees us for the whole" on p. 312.

66. One can see this, for instance, in the case of word (proclamation and future) and sacrament (manifestation and presence). It also informs what Tracy considers to be the two major christological trajectories in the tradition, i.e., *logos* and *kerygma* christologies. See his lengthy discussion to that effect beginning on p. 303 of *AI*. At this point of the text, Tracy makes the case for a plurality of christological reflections in the Christian tradition, a plurality which is correlative with the very christological pluralities within the New Testament texts themselves. These New Testament pluralities serve as the central content of Tracy's discussion in Chapter 6 of *AI*.

67. *AI*, p. 243, note 8.

68. See, for instance, p. 261 and 269.

69. Kevin Daugherty in "The Eschatology of David Tracy," *Southwestern Journal of Theology* 36 (Spring, 1994), pp. 27–28, states that "Tracy does not deny a future redemption from death and sin, but he focuses on the eschatological hope of transforming the present." See p. 28. This is perhaps an over-generalization. In his christology as disclosive of eschatology, Tracy works to maintain the tensive balance between the present and the future as his christological characterizations in *AI* attest. Yet eschatological hope is released in transformative praxis in the appropriation of the focal meaning of the Christ event for Tracy. Refer to Tracy's "credo" in *PA* on pp. 113–114. "... my own hope is grounded in a Christian faith that revelations from God have occurred and that there are ways to authentic liberation...." While Tracy does not necessarily focus his christology and eschatology on the eternal or on the *eschata* (or, for that matter, on the end-time itself), he does hold present and future in a tension.

70. Zachary Hayes, *Visions of a Future: A Study of Christian Eschatology*, p. 38. This sense of eschatological time which holds present and future in tension is also echoed in Joseph Ratzinger's *Death and Eternal Life* where Ratzinger notes: "In many faceted parables, Jesus proclaimed the good news of the Kingdom of God as a reality which is both present and still to come.... By gazing on the risen Christ, Christianity knew that a most significant coming had already taken place. It no longer proclaimed a pure theology of hope, living from mere expectation of the future, but pointed to a 'now' in which the promise had already become present." See p. 44. The same theme appears in Rahner's classic, "The Hermeneutics of Eschatological Assertions," See *Theological Investigations*, Volume IV, pp. 332–333 in particular.

71. Tracy's primary goal in exploring the diverse theological and literary genres of the New Testament texts is to point up the enriching christological pluralities in evidence in the Christian tradition. Yet these pluralities also point up this tensive temporality inherent in the very classical nature of the Christ event. Disclosure and concealment, permanence and excess of meaning, participation and distanciation are concepts which necessarily carry with them this tensive temporality.

72. *AI* pp. 265ff.

73. *AI*, p. 266.

74. This is not to say that the tensive temporality of the already-not-yet Christ event should be a theological or eschatological mystification to human beings. To be sure, on the face of it, this phrase, "already-not-yet," appears to be a logical contradiction. However, Tracy is suspect of any great division between the natural and the supernatural and of any other worldly (and other-timely) theological mystifications. As eschatological, this tensive sense of temporality brings to the ordinary understanding of time a new understanding of time as a relationship, an interpenetration of past, present, and future. As he has noted in other writings, Tracy understands human time as "philosophical/theological" time, as time-in-process. In "Horizon Analysis and Eschatology," Tracy makes the claim that human time should not be construed in "any kind of naïve way as a series (linear or otherwise) of atomistic moments." See p. 177.

75. *NAB* Version.

76. *AI*, p. 276.

77. *AI*, p. 269.

78. *AI*, p. 279.

79. *AI*, pp. 283–284.

80. *AI*, p. 285.

81. *AI*, p. 285.

82. *AI*, p. 308.

83. See again *AI*, p. 431.

84. *AI*, p. 307. This theme, that in the incarnation the whole eschatological story has already happened and yet is non-ending, is echoed in the eschatological "thought experiment" of Kathryn Tanner in her response to contemporary scientific claims that the future of the cosmos itself holds little room for hope. That is, Tanner claims – like Tracy – that eschatological existence is one of relationship, of love with the God of Love. This is a relationship that already exists through the grace of creation and redemption in incarnation, and will

exist in spite of the eventual demise of the cosmos as we know it. See her essay: "Eschatology without a Future!" in *The End of the World and the Ends of God* edited by John Polkinghorne and Michael Welker (Harrisburg, PA: Trinity Press International, 2000). See pp. 222–237. However, Tanner uses this claim to dismiss concern for the future – at least an ultimate future of cosmos.

85. *AI*, p. 269.

86. *AI*, p. 329.

87. See again, *AI*, p. 329.

88. See this lengthy discussion of our "not-at-homeness" manifest and exposed in class struggle (Marx), in infrapersonal conflict (Freud), in the exposure of the Enlightenment myth of cultural progress (Nietzsche), and in the ultimate failure of *techne* (Heidegger). See also Tracy's claim for our "uncanny" sense of a gracious mystery which lies at the base of all reality giving rise to a variety of forms which hope may yet take for humanity wherein "we may yet be coming home" because "we recognize that uncanny affirmation only because we finally sense some reality, vague yet important, which we cannot name but which is, we sense, not of our own making." See *AI*, pp 345ff. and especially, pp. 363–364. See also Tracy's discussion of those secular and religious forms of hope beginning on p. 358, e.g., hope in a future utopia, hope in sheer "wonder of existence," hope in a retrieval of a tradition history, etc. The sense of the uncanny releases all of these hopes. Of course, Tracy as Christian systematic theologian and not as cultural analyst alone will name that Uncanny (Mystery), God.

89. *AI*, p. 356.

90. As Tracy notes, "the resurrection of the crucified one liberates our hope for all of history," and for a future freed from the suffering, alienation, and oppression of our "not-yet" actuality. See *AI*, p. 426.

91. See Tracy's clear claim to this effect when he speaks of "the radical discipleship of an *imitatio Christi*" on p. 435 of *AI*.

92. Thus, Tracy will say in "Theology and the Many Faces of Postmodernity" in *Theology Today* 51/1 (April, 1994) "Christian theology should always be determined in its understanding of God and humanity by its belief in the form-of-forms, the divine-human form, Jesus Christ – the form that must inform all Christian understanding of God and transform all Christian understanding of human possibility for thought and, above all, action." See p. 111.

93. *AI*, pp. 331–332. The "commentary," for Tracy, takes the shape of the various christological expressions of the Christian tradition which he treats in the ninth chapter of *AI*, beginning on p. 371, i.e., the "Catholic" manifestation orientation, the "Protestant" proclamation orientation, and the liberation/action/praxis orientation which spans Christian denominations. Again for Tracy, such orientations need not – indeed must not – be set over against each other; rather such orientations, taken in concert, reveal the fullness, the wholeness, the depth of the person and event of Jesus as the Christ. Thus, analogy (manifestation) and dialectic (proclamation) as christological orientations in the tradition are all "relatively adequate" expressions in need of each other to "tell the whole story" just as the various New Testament genres are needed. Tracy notes on p. 420 of *AI*, "Each of these traditions – the religious traditions of manifestation, proclamation and action, the theological language traditions of analogy and dialectics, the experiential situational

traditions of fundamental trust and suffering – posit themselves as theologies within an uncanny journey through and in the event-gift-grace disclosed in the entire Christian symbol system."

94. *AI*, p. 430.
95. *AI*, p. 408.
96. *AI*, pp. 429ff.
97. *AI*, p. 446.
98. *AI*, p. 430.
99. *AI*, p. 431.
100. *AI*, pp. 280–281.

· 4 ·

ESCHATOLOGICAL DIMENSIONS IN DAVID TRACY'S *PLURALITY AND AMBIGUITY*

David Tracy's third major text, *Plurality and Ambiguity: Hermeneutics, Religion, Hope*, appeared in 1987, some six years after *The Analogical Imagination* was published. As one can note from the title of this third text, Tracy's theological project continued to be one that wrestled with the challenges of pluralism in modernity/postmodernity, although at this point in his career the postmodern critiques of modernity tended to occupy the greater part of his thought.[1] Gaspar Martinez characterizes Tracy's greater willingness to wrestle with postmodernity at this point in his career with the following informative comment:

> Tracy's own thinking undergoes a journey of intensification into the experience of the radical plurality and ambiguity that are the main features of the postmodern situation. Although his understanding of plurality was already acute and radical, that understanding took an even more decisive turn in the 1980s.[2]

In *Plurality and Ambiguity*, Tracy clearly joins with contemporary thinkers in making the claim that "today's philosophical climate is distinguished by postmodern terms such as incommensurability, historicity, fissure, otherness and difference"[3] and in dealing with that climate, in the words of Richard Bernstein, in a "sensitive, judicious, and humane" manner.[4] Moreover, Tracy's writings after the publication of *Plurality and Ambiguity* continue to echo the postmodern themes of difference, otherness, and interruption, what Thomas Guarino calls "fissure." Thus, in an article appearing in *Cross Currents* in 1996 entitled "The Hidden God: The Divine Other of Liberation," Tracy asserts that "the real face of our period...is the face of the other....The other and the different come forward now as the central intellectual categories across all major disciplines, including theology."[5] Thus, Tracy comes to name God as the Other, as the "eschatological God who disrupts all continuity and confidence."[6] In this sense perhaps, Tracy's own "analogical imagination" has begun to take on the features of a more "eschatological imagination" in the sense that his theological project has become fired more by the recognition of interruptive radical difference and otherness than by similarities and yet also by hope in and in spite of that radically interruptive difference and otherness. For Tracy, such interruption does not diminish eschatological hope. It intensifies hope into more than sentiment; it makes hope action.

Continuities But Also Radical Intensifications

In any ongoing analysis of Tracy's theological reflections over time and across major texts, one must recognize that there are still many continuities to Tracy's thinking. Tracy always strives to devise adequate and appropriate methods or strategies for reasonable and responsible theological reflection in the face of pluralism. In *Plurality and Ambiguity*, Tracy focuses his attention on the pluralisms in society and culture at large. He again suggests a method with which to approach the classics of both religion and culture: the "hermeneutic of critique, retrieval, and suspicion."[7] Indeed, Tracy stills holds cultural and religious classics as valuable; they are still "exemplary examples" which "have the possibility of being universal in their effect."[8] Religious and cultural classics alike can afford the postmodern world "some enlightenment" and "some Utopian possibility of emancipation."[9] But in this postmodern world, indeed in all times of "cultural crisis,"[10] the classics themselves must not only be retrieved for new interpretations, but must also be held up to a certain measure of suspicion; they must be questioned concerning their real ability to afford enlightenment and, most especially, some element of emancipation, for emancipatory action or liberation figures quite largely in Tracy's most recent writings.[11] Thus, Tracy will conclude *Plurality and Ambiguity* with the claim that "my own hope is grounded in a Christian faith that revelations from God have occurred and that there are ways to authentic liberation."[12]

At first glance, one might assume that this third text would concern itself with devising a method for carrying out a practical theology as part of a logical progression in his theological project from fundamental to systematic to practical theology, and all in the face of pluralism. To be sure, in *Plurality and Ambiguity* there is a pragmatic shift in Tracy's language from method to that of "strategy"[13] in the face of radical postmodern plurality and ambiguity in the world. The language of strategy accompanied by resistance implies a more active, practical orientation to Tracy's project – in short, a concern with praxis.[14] He praises Aristotle in *Plurality and Ambiguity* for, among other things, Aristotle's notion of *phronesis* or practical wisdom.[15] Tracy's audience in *Plurality and Ambiguity* is not confined only to academy or church. The audience is broader; it is the whole postmodern world of secular history and culture[16] to which both academy and church belong. Most importantly, it is a world where differences not only give rise to conflict of interpretations (as, at times, in the case of systematic theology) but also to the interruptions of actual historical violence, to evil played out in history as a result of conflicting interpretations. To Tracy, such interruptions/evils demand action, resistance, and finally solidarity. Tracy contends that "we are in dire need of a new strategy for facing the interruptions of radical evil in our history."[17]

Yet *Plurality and Ambiguity* is perhaps only a prolegomenon to a full blown practical theology in the face of radical plurality and ambiguity. It is a prolegomenon because, while in the text Tracy sustains a clear and methodical analysis of the human condition in its radical plurality and ambiguity, he only suggests an adequate concrete theological model of response to that very plurality and ambiguity in his final discussion of religion. This is the model of the "mystical-political" revealed best perhaps in the "texts of the prophets, Exodus, and the apocalypses,"[18] in proclamations of judgment and hope for liberations. In this sense, *Plurality and Ambiguity* turns back toward a greater emphasis on the "limit-to" of the human condition without exploring fully the nature of the "Limit-of" all existence.[19] Thus, the text is a first step towards a practical theology. In this first step, and in spite of the intensification of his postmodern concern with otherness, difference, and interruption, Tracy continues to occupy himself with the question of reasonable and responsible method. Yet one must note that the postmodern recognition of radical interruption compels Tracy to place a strong emphasis on critique and suspicion without ever abandoning the retrieval of enlightening and emancipatory classics. Thus, he prefaces *Plurality and Ambiguity* with the twofold claim that "the theme of this small book is conversation,"[20] critical and – appropriately at times – suspicious conversation, and that "a central theme of this book is memory,"[21] that is, memory as retrieval of religious classics.

What Tracy also clearly retrieves from his previous texts are two dense namings or conceptualizations: the identification of the religious dimension of human existence with the keyword limit[22] and the call for an analogical imagination with which to confront and live with difference, albeit now radical difference.[23] The case was made in the discussion of *Blessed Rage for Order* that the religious notion of limit has an eschatological dimension to it wherein the eschatological is viewed as finality in terms of ultimacy. Such a claim remains inherent in Tracy's discussion of the limit/religious questions of human existence in *Plurality and Ambiguity*. Those questions cut to the very core of human existence (the limit-to in the face of Limit-of). They are existential questions of ultimacy and thus are eschatological questions, albeit eschatological questions which are in the world existential questions. Furthermore, Tracy's proposal of the engagement of an analogical imagination in the face of radical religious plurality, while admitting the possibility of similarity, now focuses greater attention on the problem of difference, radical (and thus eschatological) difference. Tracy thus claims in *Plurality and Ambiguity*:

> Authentic analogical language is a rare achievement, since it attempts the nearly impossible: an articulation of real differences as genuinely different but also similar to what we already know. On a more existential level, an analogical imagination suggests a willingness to enter the conversation, that unnerving place where one is willing to risk all one's present self-understanding by facing the claims to attention of the other.[24]

Yet the very fact that Tracy still calls for risking a life on the possibility of (and with hope in) an analogical imagination in the face of the radical interruptions of difference and otherness confronting the postmodern human being provides an entry point into what is perhaps the most intense eschatological shift in Tracy's thought at this juncture of his theological career. In the face of the intensifications of radical interruptions, in the face of radical difference and otherness, Tracy calls for the "need to reformulate the question of religion as a question of hope."[25] This is an important turn in the discussion of the eschatological dimension of Tracy's theological project. Hope, that primary eschatological virtue,[26] becomes the "central category"[27] for Tracy's postmodern theological reflection. In this sense, then, and with a recognition of the radical, ultimate, and thus eschatological plurality and ambiguity of our postmodern world, *Plurality and Ambiguity: Hermeneutics, Religion, Hope,* can be viewed as an ecumenically sensitive essay in response to the command in

1 Peter 3: 15: "Always be ready to give an explanation to anyone who asks you for a reason for your hope."

Plurality and Ambiguity is not only a credo[28] about the enlightening and emancipating values of religious and thus eschatological classics; it is also a sustained reflection on religion as a strategy, as an act of eschatological hope within this postmodern, interruptive world. Religious existence is eschatological existence. That point was made quite clearly in the analysis of both *Blessed Rage* and *The Analogical Imagination*. Yet in the face of what Tracy perceives as the radical interruptions with which postmodernity confronts us, that religious as eschatological existence must now be lived primarily as an exercise of hope, a life of hope exercised in and through plurality and ambiguity. The goal of the discussion of the succeeding pages will then be to support this claim by way of analysis of what Tracy perceives to be the radical interruptions – the radical as ultimate and thus eschatological interruptions – confronting human existence in this world as well as the authentic as hopeful eschatological response to those interruptions. This would be in clear contrast to various inauthentic, presumptive or despairing responses to radical plurality and ambiguity, and, most especially, in contrast to the "presentism" inherent in what Tracy calls the modern subject's illusory confidence in "more of the same."[29] For the radical interruptions which Tracy names are indeed interruptions which belie any over-confidence in human control and mastery and yet still contain within themselves the promise of future possibilities, possibilities of enlightenment and emancipation.

The Eschatological in Radical Interruptions

The subtitle of Tracy's *Plurality and Ambiguity* is "*Hermeneutics, Religion, Hope.*" The title and subtitle synthesize three key themes which Tracy develops in *Plurality and Ambiguity*: first, that existence is ultimately, finally, and thus eschatologically riddled with radical plurality and ambiguity at its very heart, i.e., in the nature of truth as primordial truth or *aletheia*, in the very structure of language, in ambiguous history, and, most importantly, in the very foundation or ground for all existence which he names "Ultimate Reality."[30] Tracy relates plurality to difference and ambiguity to otherness. Both are disclosed in existence in the interplay of language and history and both are ultimately not of our control.[31] This recognition on Tracy's part leads to two other related sub-themes: first, his understanding of the human being as "interpreter," as the one ever engaged in the task of hermeneutics precisely because of radical difference and otherness at the very core of existence,[32] and secondly his own radical assertion, finally, that religion, "the most pluralistic, ambiguous, and important reality of all,"[33] must be an exercise of hope as the most authentic human response to the naming of this world as radically plural and ambiguous.

Tracy thus connects the interruption of radical plurality and ambiguity as recognized[34] by postmodern consciousness to "hermeneutics, religion, and hope." In a word, the interruptive nature of radical plurality and ambiguity necessarily presents us with an anthropology: a picture of the human being as necessarily an interpreter and a critical and suspicious interpreter in the light of that interruption. This is the case precisely because the ultimate uncontrollable realities of difference and otherness and of the plurality and ambiguity born of such difference and otherness invite – indeed, often demand – of human beings a plurality of critical and sometimes suspicious interpretations. Furthermore, the authentically religious as eschatological response to that fundamental recognition is, for Tracy, the response of hope, that primarily eschatological way of dealing with radically plural and ambiguous existence.[35]

It is not surprising that Tracy begins his discussion of hermeneutics, religion, and hope by once again retrieving the notion of the classic. To Tracy, classics not only have the benefit of providing some insight of universal and compelling significance; they are also the "best examples for testing any theory of interpretation,"[36] and implicitly any anthropology because "to interact with classic texts is to converse with difference and otherness"[37] inherent in the "complex process of interpretation itself,"[38] with their compelling truth(s), and with the plurality and ambiguity with which classics confront us and which demand our interpretation. Tracy's discussion of the nature and role of the classic in culture(s) in *Plurality and Ambiguity* can be viewed as illustrative not only of their potential truth value for a culture but also of a fundamental and radical anthropological claim. This is the claim that the human being as critical interpreter must wrestle with the interruptive difference and otherness inherent in reality. The plurality and ambiguity of classics are themselves not only "structured expressions of the human spirit"[39] but also reflections on or interpretations of ultimately plural and ambiguous realities,[40] realities which "have the possibility of being universal in effect" and claim our attention because they are "difficult to ignore."[41]

For Tracy, the French Revolution serves as a telling example of the nature of the classic as well as of the nature of the human being as interpreter. As that event which inaugurated modernity and engendered a multiplicity of interpretations,[42] it not only reveals the plurality (difference) of human interpretations of classic events of history but also – and quite importantly for him – the ambiguity of classic historical and cultural events, ambiguity of such a radical nature as to support Walter Benjamin's claim that "every great work of civilization is, at the same time, a work of barbarism."[43] Indeed, the interruptive nature of this classic yet barbarous event throws into sharp relief the radical ambiguity of history and particularly the ambiguous history of Western European "modern" culture. For this revolution gave birth not only to a renewed appreciation for democracy and for the dignity of the rational human subject but also to barbarous violence – reigns of terror – in presumptive service to those very enlightened appreciations.

The French Revolution is then not just a telling example of how a classic event invites a plurality of interpretations by the human being as interpreter. Perhaps more importantly for Tracy, the French Revolution is also the ambiguous modern classic event *par excellence.*[44] This is the case because to Tracy and to postmoderns the recognition of the power of human reason, that hallmark of a revolutionary modern consciousness, was and is an ambiguous recognition precisely because it has tended to glorify the autonomy of the rational human subject, indeed, to claim an autonomy (with an accompanying history of dominating and violating superiority) that modern and postmodern history has called into question as illusory.[45] Thus in his discussion of the French Revolution and the modern Western European Enlightenment tradition of "purely autonomous consciousness"[46] which fueled it, Tracy indicts that autonomous rational ego so glorified by the classic event of the French Revolution with the words: "Autonomy is a mirrored mask that, ripped away, reveals Narcissus peering at an indecipherable code, believing all the while that he has at last found his true self."[47] The very history of effects of that Revolution with its conscious and presumptive "turn to the rational subject," when viewed honestly and critically, radically calls into question the optimistic assumption that there is indeed such a thing as the purely autonomous rational ego.[48]

With this assertion on Tracy's part in mind, the assertion that the purely autonomous rational ego is a presumptive illusion on the part of modern self-consciousness, we are also confronted with another way of identifying a non-transcendental or secular eschatological dimension inherent in Tracy's thought in *Plurality and Ambiguity.* Tracy asserts that postmodern critical consciousness demands a recognition and acceptance of death, that primordial, final, and thus eschatological interrupter of presence. This is not the "private" personal death of the individual that traditional tracts on Christian eschatology have discussed through the ages as part of the general exposition on such last things as death, judgment, heaven, and hell. This is the public death of the purely autonomous rational ego of Western Enlightenment modernity, that ego which has in modern history and thought presumptively laid claim to the belief that "humans are the measure of all things"[49] and that the scientific worldview born of that claim can make for unlimited human progress and mastery of the world. The radical plurality and ambiguity of language and history as recognized and analyzed by postmodern consciousness – sometimes in a genuine humility and sometimes unfortunately in despair – has, for Tracy, proclaimed with finality that:

> Prevailing notions of a purely autonomous ego must go. It matters little whether that ego takes on the studied smile of reason of the Enlightenment, the volcanic passion of the romantic, or arid self-satisfaction of the positivist, or the mature complacency of much modern psychology. Whether we know it or not, we are all de-centered egos now.[50]

The interruptive plurality and ambiguity of reality as recognized by postmodern consciousness has come to view modern Western history – influenced as it was so strongly by the French Revolution and its anthropological assumptions – with such suspicion as to, in Tracy's words, call for a "de-centering" of the purely rational ego. This would be a de-centering that is of such a decided nature as to radically interrupt and claim for dead that ego. It must of course be admitted that Tracy is speaking of this death, this radical and thus eschatological interruption, in a metaphorical way. Yet for Tracy, this metaphor reflects a cultural and historical reality, the death of a certain collective cultural consciousness which has proven to give rise to an ambiguous or even violent history. In this sense, Tracy's assertion reinforces the claim that the eschatological dimensions of Tracy's theological project – in this case, a cultural death as an aspect of the eschatological reality – are dimensions which need not be found in a dualism positing two warring worlds in eschatological mystification: the profane and the sacred above and beyond the profane. The death of the post-Enlightenment purely autonomous ego is an eschatological finality played out in this world, oftentimes in historical violence and enslavement.

Thus the French Revolution and its history of effects reveal plurality and ambiguity in our modern history. Yet at the same time, this classic event of modernity, when analyzed in all of its complexity and in its "conflictual history of reception,"[51] serves to demonstrate as a telling example Tracy's naming of the human being as critical interpreter at her/his very core. The interpretive claim for the death of the modern autonomous rational ego is a profoundly significant case in point. Therefore, Tracy asserts: "To be human is to be a skilled interpreter" and "to understand at all is to interpret."[52] To Tracy, human understanding is always a process of interpretation, of interpretive engagement or conversation with the "other" and the "different" whether otherness and difference come to one in the form of a tradition, a cultural consciousness, a text, a person, or a classic event. This is a core fundamental human reality for Tracy, demonstrating in difference and otherness the interruptive dimension of existence. Furthermore, since this process of understanding as interpretation of otherness and difference takes place in conversation in its variety of forms, it is also – to retrieve but one more of Tracy's ongoing themes – always "public."[53] It is public precisely because, once again, understanding as interpretation is *the* human task, that human effort to deal with difference and otherness, with plurality and ambiguity at the heart of reality. Tracy thus claims:

> But we humans must reason discursively, inquire communally, converse and argue with ourselves and one another. Human knowledge could be other than it is. But this is the way it is: embodied, communal, finite, discursive.[54]

Recalling that in *Blessed Rage for Order* Tracy's transcendental and phenomenological analysis of human limitation allowed us to characterize eschatological finality in terms of an ultimacy through limit and that in *The Analogical Imagination* a hermeneutic of the Christian classic served as a response to the fundamental human yearning for wholeness disclosing the possibility of its authentic achievement, we came to see that dimensions of eschatological finality and authentic human responses to eschatological finality have clearly emerged. However, in *Plurality and Ambiguity* with its language of interruption, of difference and otherness at the very core of reality, what invests plurality and ambiguity with eschatological finality as ultimacy? What is it about the plurality and ambiguity that Tracy sees at every turn which makes it a final as ultimate and thus eschatological reality? And, most importantly, how can such fissure offer any real and truly authentic hope?

The Interruption of Truth

The starting point for answering these questions lies in Tracy's claim that the plurality and ambiguity which confronts the human being (and thus demands that she/he be defined primarily as interpreter) is of a radical nature; it results from a recognition of a radical difference and otherness, interruption to

sameness, at the very core of existence. Much as "limit" and "the whole" served
to unfold the eschatological dimension of Tracy's theological project in his first
two major texts, the intense interruption to modern consciousness of radical
plurality and ambiguity performs a similar service in *Plurality and Ambiguity*. To
the limit and wholeness dimensions of the ultimate, the final, the eschatological, we add "radical," radical and interruptive plurality and ambiguity born of
difference and otherness.

Tracy's most important claim for interruptive difference and otherness at
the very heart of reality lies in his fundamental understanding of the nature of
truth, for truth is, to Tracy, that which human beings find themselves compelled
to seek finally and ultimately in order to make sense out of their own existence,
indeed, out of all existence.[55] Truth as truth has a certain finality about it, and
yet Tracy's hermeneutical sense of truth, truth as *aletheia*, contains within it a
sense of otherness that defers full and final presence and that implicitly posits
the promise of future.

Tracy makes the claim that understanding is interpretation in conversation in the first pages of *Plurality and Ambiguity* by way of analysis of the classic
as that phenomenon which always invites new interpretation because of its
"excess of meaning."[56] In that process and quite importantly, Tracy makes a
case for radical difference and otherness both in classics and at the core of
reality by retrieving and according "primacy to one largely unforgotten notion
of truth,"[57] the fundamental hermeneutical notion of "truth as manifestation in
both disclosure and concealment." This is a notion that is and has been crucial
to Tracy's project.[58] Tracy makes his case for truth as *aletheia* in the course of
his discussions of the classic because classics manifest significant truths, and
religious classics reveal ultimate truths.[59] As the classic bears within it a certain
permanent and challenging excess of meaning, so too it manifests its truth as a
disclosure and yet a concealment as it invites the human response of recognition, interpretation, and re-interpretation over time.[60] Concealment lies inherent in the excess and thus ambiguous nature of the truth of the classic, and it
demands reinterpretations. Presence and future are inherent in this notion of
primordial truth as both disclosure and concealment.

For Tracy, this primordial notion of truth is not the truth of scientific and
empirical verification;[61] nor is it to be reduced to the notion of correspondence.
"Truth, in its primordial sense, is manifestation.... truth as manifestation is
real...," Tracy claims quite strongly, "and it does suffice."[62] As manifestation in
both disclosure and concealment, primordial truth is not under human control.
Rather, it is recognized, not created. Moreover, this primordial and ultimate

truth revealed in the classic is potentially dialogical in nature because it invites human interpretation. Thus, the nature of truth as manifested through the classic event, text, symbol, ritual, etc. received and interpreted through human conversation again serves to reinforce Tracy's notion that human understanding is never private. Interpretation as conversation is a dialogue that is triangular in that it is comprised of the phenomenon such as the truth of a classic text, event, and/or persons, the interpreter(s) of the phenomenon, and the interaction between these two poles.[63] Tracy summarizes his understanding of truth as *aletheia* and its relationship to the dialogical interpreter in the following:

> Truth manifests itself, and we recognize its rightness. More technically stated, truth is here understood, on the side of the object, as the power of disclosure and concealment in the object itself; and that disclosure is related to truth as an experience of recognition on the side of the subject. There is, in every true manifestation, an intrinsic, that is, dialogical, interaction between the object's disclosure and concealment and the subject's recognition. That interaction is conversation.[64]

For Tracy, primordial truth is self-legitimizing and thus not dependent on "communal critical practices of validating claims to truth."[65] Such practices are, for Tracy, a "second order" testing of the relative adequacy of the interpretation of manifested truth revealed under its own power.[66] They become theories and methods for processing the more primordial recognition of truth as *aletheia*.[67]

Why is truth as manifestation self-legitimizing? This is the case because this truth as manifestation in disclosure/concealment is what Heidegger would call the "truth of Being" which traditional metaphysics in its focus upon the essences of beings has tended to obscure.[68] In his essay on "The Origins of the Work of Art," Heidegger calls upon philosophers to let the truth of the Being of beings be with this exhortation: "We ought to turn toward the being [a particular being], think about it in regard to its being, but by means of this thinking at the same time let it rest upon itself in its very own being."[69] Thus Heidegger notes in another essay: "To metaphysics the nature of truth always appears only in the derivative form of the truth of knowledge and the truth of propositions which formulate our knowledge. Unconcealedness, however, might be prior to all truth in the sense of *veritas*. *Aletheia* might be the word that offers a hithero unnoticed hint concerning the nature of *esse* which has not yet been recalled."[70] It is this sense of truth as disclosed/concealed in engaged conversations with the classics and prior to truth as *veritas* that primarily informs Tracy's work at this point.[71] Moreover, this is the same sense of truth which Gadamer espouses and which Tracy appropriates in his own hermeneutical analysis of the nature of language and of human participation in it. Joel Weinsheimer captures Gadamer's sense of *aletheia* as insight disclosed in language thus:

> Insight cannot be controlled or produced at will because it is not something that we do, an activity of the knowing subject, but rather an event; in an insight something occurs to us. Something that is prior to knowledge speaks to us. When things suddenly become clear, manifest, and evident – when we see them truly for the first time – then their very visibility discloses the light that makes insight possible. The event of understanding reflects and responds to the continuing self-presentation of being in tradition.[72]

This is what the truth of Tracy's classic and of all authentic conversation does. It discloses its own primordial truth which the human being recognizes but does not create in the process of interaction and interpretation. Recognition is a response to the claim of the truth of the classic, to what Ricoeur calls its "non-violent appeal."[73] Moreover, appropriation of the truth manifested in the classic is also a participation, "a belonging-to (*appurtenance*)."[74] Here we see Tracy's appropriation of Gadamer and Ricoeur, for to Tracy, "to converse with any classic text is to find oneself caught up in the questions and answers worthy of a free mind."[75] It is for this reason that Tracy likens the interpretive interaction or conversation with the truth of the classic to a "game" in which we are "caught up" and not in control precisely because of the otherness and difference that is both disclosed and concealed in classic truths.[76] Moreover, it is for this reason that Tracy can state that "we belong to history and language; they do not belong to us"[77] because truth as primordial manifestation is disclosed in our history and our language and is not subject to full human mastery.

What is most important about Tracy's understanding of the nature of truth as *aletheia* in the present argument is the fact that Tracy names this truth as manifestation in both disclosure and concealment as primordial truth. Primordial truth is the kind of truth which interrupts complacency by cutting to the very heart of existence and human understanding thereof. If indeed primordial truth is truth which conceals its final meaning as it reveals, then this truth bears within itself a certain measure of "otherness," deferral of full presence,[78] and thus ambiguity for the finite, historical, interpreting human being. In this vein, Heidegger notes in the matter of truth as *aletheia*: "There belongs to it the reservoir of the not-yet-uncovered, the un-uncovered, in the sense of concealment."[79] The very nature of primordial truth then, for Tracy, serves to illustrate the interruptive difference and otherness which lies at the heart of all reality. Yet, its "not-yet-uncovered" nature implies at least the possibility of greater "unconcealedness" in a future as yet unavailable and fuels hope.

The Interruption of Language

Moreover, and joining in the twentieth century "linguistic turn" of such thinkers as Wittgenstein, Heidegger, de Saussure, and the deconstructionist Derrida,[80] Tracy makes a second claim for difference and plurality in another fundamental dimension of human existence: the dimension of human language. Tracy contends that the very nature of human language, that essential agency by which human beings communicate about truth and that "world" in which human beings necessarily live,[81] is also characterized in its very structure by difference and otherness. Tracy takes that linguistic turn quite seriously because of his postmodern claim that language, knowledge (the positive result of the search for truth), and reality are intimately related. The linguistic turn of the twentieth century has "become an uncanny interruptive exploration of the radical plurality in language, knowledge, and reality alike."[82]

Tracy credits both Wittgenstein and Heidegger, each in his own way, for bringing to postmodern attention the essential but interruptive and plural nature of the human world of language. In sum, Tracy notes:

> The analysis of the ineradicable plurality of languages and forms of life was the singular contribution of Wittgenstein. The insistence that every disclosure is at the same time a disclosure and a concealment, since Being always both reveals and withdraws itself in every manifestation: this was the unique achievement of the late Heidegger....Both thinkers concentrated on the inescapable reality of language as well as our plural uses of it and its uses of us.[83]

Tracy's retrieval of the structuralist linguistic analysis of Ferdinand de Saussure and later poststructuralist linguistic analyses can serve to highlight further Tracy's claim that human language, so integral to human existence in the world, is structured at its very core by way of difference and thus gives rise to radical plurality. Much as primordial truth is both a disclosure and a concealment and therefore interruptive to complacency with sameness, language in its very structure[84] is built upon difference. Tracy thus joins with de Saussure in making the claim that "in the linguistic system, there are only differences,"[85] where presence is only affirmed through absence in language. Furthermore, recognizing the contribution of linguists such as de Saussure and deconstructionists such as Derrida to the postmodern realization of the interruptive nature of reality through the analysis of language, Tracy notes:

> Deconstructionists challenge all claims to uncovering the fully systematic character of any language by insisting upon the implications of the fact that no system can adequately account for its own ineradicable differential nature....for poststructuralists, meanings function along a whole chain of signifiers. We never in fact reach a unitary meaning present to itself as a sign freed from all the differences needed to produce the meaning. No sign, on Saussure's own analysis, is free from the traces of other officially absent signifiers. The traces of those absent signifiers must operate through the whole differential system ad infinitum for any sign to have meaning at all.[86]

Tracy's appropriation of the notion of primordial truth calling for interpretive understanding always open to new understandings,[87] finds a certain parallel in the linguists' radical understanding of the very nature of language as significa-tion through difference and otherness, presence and yet also absence.[88] What is also essential to continue to emphasize in Tracy's discussion of the radical dif-ference inherent in the very nature of language is his over-arching claim for the ontological status of language. If language enjoys such an essential status, and if it is in its very structure interruptive, then such claims continue to support Tracy's firm belief that reality is interruptive in key essential elements, i.e., in both the nature of truth as well as in discourse in search of truth. The interrup-tions of disclosure/concealment and signification through difference are radical interruptions threatening easy complacency with sameness.

The Interruptions of History and the Other as Mystery

Along with primordial truth and language, history is necessarily a place of inter-ruption. "History is not only contingent; history is interruptive."[89] On one level, the human desire to master truth and interpret it by way of language will always be problematic precisely because of the radical and interruptive difference and otherness at the very core of those two dimensions of human existence. Yet on another more intense and interruptive level, the human will to assert interpreta-tions in spite of the radically interruptive nature of truth and language, to make the claim for full presence in spite of presence/absence, disclosure/concealment, may lead not only to further ambiguity but also to the presumptuous and willful assertion of a dominating interpretation even in ways that can take on violent and barbarous form within history. And indeed this is and has been the case.

Tracy's litany of modern, radically violent interruptions in history in support of "favored" interpretations of reality, claims to full presence and mastery of truth, serves as proof of this human move to self-assertion. He thus notes by way of example in his own language of radical intensification:

> The genocide of six million Jews by the Nazis is – is what? *Shocking* seems an altogether inadequate adjective to apply to that enormity, Then what was it? Madness? Aberration? Sin? Or all these, and something more, something demonic and more radically interruptive of our history than we can imagine? The Holocaust is a searing interruption of all the traditions in Western culture....And our century includes that and more. Witness the following litany of terrifying events: the Armenian massacres, the Gulag, Hiroshima, Uganda, and Cambodia.[90]

The self-asserting drive to claim as exclusively true a favored interpretation of reality from a particular, historical, and thus contingent perspective is ultimately for Tracy a human failure to recognize, as postmoderns have, that reality itself is interruptive in its plurality and ambiguity. This drive towards the assertion of "more of the same" stands opposed to a recognition of difference and otherness. Such self-assertions not only refuse to recognize the viability and possibility of different interpretations; such self-assertions also tend to deny the very fact that there are "others" of any value at all – other persons, other voices. Indeed, such interpretations and actions are, religiously speaking, not merely the interruptions of error but the interruptions of human sin wherein "the self keeps turning in upon itself (*curvatus in se*)[91] in an ever subtler dialectic of self-delusion."[92] This sense of sin as *curvatus in* se plays out, to Tracy's way of thinking, not only in private and personal illusory interpretation but also quite publicly, that is, in ideology formation and its propagation into "systemic distortions."[93] It is a presumptive and willful turn to the subject and collective subjects who is/are the predominant and predominating elite rather than a turn to the other, the person (and culture) who is different and, as different, truly other.[94]

Most importantly, this assertion of the self at the expense of the other sinfully denies the difference and otherness of that final, ultimate, eschatological Reality whom we call God. To Tracy in *Plurality and Ambiguity* and in his later writings, God is the Ultimate Reality,[95] the eschatological reality, indeed in the words of Marion, "*Dieu sans l'être.*"[96] As such, God is the Other as Mystery, at once a tremendous and fascinating Mystery, that locus of ultimate truth that is indeed both disclosed in revelations and yet still concealed precisely as Mystery. As such, this God can never be fully controlled or mastered by human speech or interpretation. When he speaks about God as Ultimate Reality, Tracy states:

> In and through even the best speech for Ultimate Reality, greater obscurity eventually emerges to manifest a religious sense of that Reality as ultimate mystery.... There is no classic discourse on Ultimate Reality that can be understood as mastering its own speech. If any human discourse gives true testimony to Ultimate Reality, it must necessarily prove uncontrollable and unmasterable.[97]

For Tracy, the unmasterable truth of God is the truth of *aletheia* in its most primordial, most ultimate and final, most eschatological sense. This is the God who is both disclosed and concealed: in Protestant thought, revealed yet hidden; and in Catholic thought, comprehensible yet incomprehensible;[98] in both interpretations "the eschatological God disrupting all continuity and confidence."[99] In this sense, and speaking about not human existence alone but about divine existence as the very ground of all existence, Tracy sees the Final and Ultimate Reality – the Eschatological Reality – in a parallel yet eminent intensification: as interruptive Otherness and Difference, as Mystery which both discloses and conceals precisely as Mystery. This naming of God in *Plurality and Ambiguity* is reflected and summarized in Tracy's later writing:

> The re-thinking of God's reality...that divine reality, in our postmodern period, may be found, above all, in the otherness and difference through which God manifests Godself anew with an interruptive, othering power....[100]

Therefore, David Tracy truly makes the case for the radical interruption of difference and otherness at the very heart of all reality. Plurality and ambiguity in human interpretation devolving from the disturbing radical difference and otherness at essential levels of human existence such as thought, language, and history are ultimate realities that necessarily interrupt any human sense of full presence, mastery, and control. This recognition of plurality and ambiguity brings to death the presumptuous optimism of full presence and mastery of the purely autonomous rational ego of modernity. Moreover, to Tracy, a refusal to recognize and deal with the radical realities of difference and otherness can lead human beings down the path of yet another interruption and this one of human origin: the reactionary interruption not of error but of sin. Sin occurs when human beings refuse to recognize the humbling truth that there is and will always be radical difference and otherness in thought, language, and history, and – most importantly – in the Ultimate Reality of God "in whose image human beings were formed"[101] and who is the very ground of this world of difference and otherness. This is the Ultimate Reality who then calls us to recognize that the "modern ego is built on quicksand... [and as such is in need of] something sturdier that either optimism or pessimism."[102] And that "something sturdier" is hope. The authentic religious – and Christian – human being must draw strength from hope, "modest"[103] hope, but real hope nevertheless.

The Shape of Hope Finally in and in Spite of Radical Interruptions

David Tracy concludes his analysis of the postmodern world and condition in *Plurality and Ambiguity: Hermeneutics, Religion, Hope* with a retrieval of two short but profound classical aphorisms, one from Socrates and the philosophical tradition and the other from classic Buddhist religious thought. Both are in service to what he perceives to be the essential goals of a life lived neither in optimism/presumption nor in pessimism/despair but in the "sturdiness" of hope, a truly authentic hope. From Socrates, Tracy retrieves the maxim: "The unreflective life is not worth living," and from Buddhism he appropriates the maxim: "The unlived life is not worth reflecting upon."[104] Authentic life is a risk critically reflected upon and lived out in the light of that critical reflection. These aphorisms articulate for Tracy what truly authentic hope is at both the secular and religious levels.[105] Truly authentic hope hopes for some understanding or enlightenment and some emancipation or liberation for a humanity that is "finite, estranged, and needing of liberation by a power not its own."[106] As such, it is an active religious hope that finds consolation and strength in understandings compelling public efforts towards human emancipations. In an ecumenically sensitive way, Tracy voices his own hope in this manner:

> We can continue to give ourselves over to the hopes alive in all the great religions: a trust in Ultimate Reality, a hope for the ability to resist what must be resisted, a hope in hope itself, a hope that fights against our exhausted notions of what hope might be. For most religious believers, that hope arises from the belief that Ultimate Reality is grace-ful. For nonbelieving interpreters of the religious classics, that hope may be glimpsed in the religious classics by sensing some enlightenment, however tentative, and some Utopian possibility of emancipation, however modest.[107]

David Tracy's concerted effort to make the case for hope as the final and definitive religious strategy in order to deal authentically with the interruptions of plurality and ambiguity, difference and otherness, truly then enlivens his growing eschatological spirit. This is a spirit which is hopeful as it recognizes in faith as a trust or confidence the possibility of real enlightenment and emancipations in this our secular but religious world, and this in spite of radical interruption. By contrast, the human failure to reflect and act on those enlightening possibilities of emancipation results in an inauthentic and sinful response to radical plurality and ambiguity, the response of presumptive certainty about the future or a despair that finds no positive value in future. Worse yet, to presume that radical plurality and ambiguity does not exist, to presume that essential truths and ultimate truth can be captured, tamed, controlled by autonomous human reason becomes a real danger, the danger of accepting the tyranny of a "more of the same" mentality.

Yet two questions still remain. First, how is it that Tracy can claim that "we can continue to give ourselves over to hope" in the face of the radical and disturbing interruptions of difference and otherness at the core of all reality? How can Tracy find real hope in fissure, in radical interruption? Secondly, what concrete "in this world" eschatological shape does Tracy's hope finally take? How does Tracy come to characterize authentic and true hope? Perhaps a clue as to the answer to the first question, the question of envisioning hope in the face of radical fissures, lies in Tracy's final characterization of the self in *Plurality and Ambiguity* where Tracy asserts that the modern subject or self, the purely autonomous ego, is finally dead. Yet Tracy also makes the claim that "the subject, however chastened and transformed, has not been erased."[108] The death of modern Western Enlightenment self-consciousness, metaphorical yet real in a concrete history, leads not to extinction but to a chastened transformation into "a more fragile self…" yet still "open to epiphanies,"[109] or manifestations of truth as *aletheia*.

For the transformed and chastened self, there are "echoes of hope" which fortify hope even in the interruptions inherent in primordial truth and human language and history. Tracy intimates as much when he claims: "And yet I write this book, and you read it,"[110] and this after his lengthy exposition on the radically interruptive nature of primordial truth, language, and history bringing to death the purely autonomous modern rational subject. While primordial truth and truths are truths which contain within themselves concealedness and thus point to an element of futurity, they also contain a presence, albeit not full presence. Primordial truth is a manifestation in disclosure, the rightness of which we as human beings can recognize and interpret with relative if not full adequacy. In other words, truth as *aletheia* does disturb and interrupt in its concealedness; yet it gives hope for understanding in its disclosure, however incomplete that disclosure may be. Relative adequacy as the finite but authentic human response to primordial truth is itself an act of a true and authentic hope both in the disclosive power of primordial truth and in the ability of the human being to deal with that truth by interpreting it. Tracy speaks of relative adequacy as the authentic and hopeful interpretive response to the primordial truth(s) of classics in the following:

> To give an interpretation is to make a claim. To make a claim is to be willing to defend that claim if challenged by others or by the further process of questioning itself. When there are no further relevant questions either from the text or from myself or from the interaction that is questioning, then I find relative adequacy. I then present my interpretations to the community of inquiry to see if they have further relevant questions.[111]

Relative adequacy as a disciplined exercise of human interpretation of primordial truth does authentic justice to primordial truth in two very important senses. As adequate it critically recognizes a presence, a manifestation; as relative it remains open to future questioning and fuller understandings and humbly never claims the power to capture a full presence. The chastened and transformed self can then exercise hope by authentically dealing with interruptive primordial truth by way of relatively adequate interpretations.

Moreover, while Tracy sees human language as interruptive in its very structure, as absence always present to presence precisely as absence, he refuses to let such absence extinguish authentic communication. Again, "And yet I write this book, and you read it." This is a reality. While appreciative of Derrida's postmodern insights, Tracy does not fully surrender to the deconstructionist claims of Derrida where "any claims to full presence, especially claims to full self-presence in conscious thought, are illusions that cannot survive a study of language as a system of differential relations" and therefore where the "abyss of indeterminacy...is our situation."[112] Such a surrender would contain within itself an admission of despair rather than hope. Indeed, the illusions with which Tracy is primarily concerned in *Plurality and Ambiguity* (and which he decries as presumptive rather than despairing) are the illusions of systemic distortions born of prevailing elitist interpretations by the modern autonomous subject and foisted upon others in an interruptive history.[113]

While Tracy accepts the provisional and differential structure of language, he also carries the linguistic turn beyond merely structural difference towards interpretive conversation leading to some understanding. That is to say, Tracy as engaged in twentieth century hermeneutics himself fully accepts the ontological but pluralistic nature of language. However, he points out that the analysis of language "moves past words to sentences and eventually to texts" and "insists that language is neither system alone [de Saussure] nor use alone [Wittgenstein], but discourse [Ricoeur]"[114] wherein truth is revealed in the participative engagement of discourse or conversation. Thus, and in response to any wholesale deconstructionist despair of any presence, Tracy gently reminds deconstructionists that "at its best, deconstructive criticism is also discourse"[115] which itself makes truth claims. Tracy fully appreciates the deconstructionist caveat against any presumptive claims to full presence and in doing so makes room for deferral and future; Tracy also, however, sees future in the promise born of sometimes tentative disclosures as he refuses to despair of presence alto-gether. Such presence/absence demands continued conversation wherein hope in the power of relative adequacy fuels a willingness to continue conversation, dialogue. Tracy notes in the matter of the possibility of knowing truth at all:

> To lose any belief in pure self-presence as well as any claims to certainty or to apodictic knowledge is not to deny the possibility of knowledge itself. What we know, we know with relative adequacy, and we know it bounded by the realities of language, society, and history. On any particular issue, we can know when we have no further relevant questions. It is possible, therefore, to know when we know enough.[116]

Tracy's truly authentic hope then at this essentially interruptive level of human language lies in the possibility and reality of discourse, of authentic conversa-tion leading to some enlightenment.[117] Such a hope necessarily then requires a stance towards the other of history and the otherness of the classic not as a threat but as a conversation partner. Such a stance seeks neither to dominate nor to dismiss the other as of no value and thus as non-person. Indeed, such a stance obliges one to seek out and listen to the voice of the "non-person."[118] In other words, the open recognition of primordial truth as a manifestation which both discloses and conceals is a recognition of the power of hope inherent in primordial truth, a power which offers further hope in the concrete practice of authentic and open conversation in solidarity with the others of the classics and of history. Hope offers and at the same time demands discourse, conversation, and in doing so confronts the chastened and transformed self with the inter-ruptive reality of the voice of the other and the different, be that the other and different voice of classics or of persons. And precisely as open and authentic, such conversation gives rise not to the despair of alienation and isolation where, in the words of one of Tracy's favored poets T. S. Eliot, "...you live dispersed on ribbon roads, and no man knows or cares who is his neighbor,"[119] but to the hopeful possibility of some real enlightenment and some real solidarity with the other in sharing enlightenment and communally acting upon that enlightenment for the sake of present and future emancipations of the human spirit. The hope then inherent in the very nature of primordial truths, the truths which in their own otherness will not permit themselves to be captured by an easy coherence, demands the authentic human and hope-filled practical strategies of both conversation and solidarity, solidarity as a standing-with the different and the other in the manner of conversation. In sum, the fundamental interruption of radical difference gives rise to plurality, and plurality can be dealt with by way of authentic conversation hoping for some enlightenment, some understanding. Furthermore, radically interruptive otherness gives rise to ambiguity, and ambiguity can be dealt with by way of solidarity with the other hoping for some emancipation, some liberation.

What serves as final and ultimate warrant for Tracy's hope, hope in and in spite of the interruptive nature of primordial truths, language, and history, is yet again Tracy's basic faith in an analogical imagination. This is the case because Tracy's hope is ultimately grounded in a faith in an Ultimate Reality which is characterized pre-eminently by difference and otherness, those characteristics which give rise to the plurality and ambiguity of human and religious existence. We recall Tracy's claim that religion is the "most pluralistic, ambiguous, and important reality of all."[120] It is pluralistic and ambiguous on two levels. On one hand, as Tracy notes, "any religion, whether past or present, in a position of power surely demonstrates that religious movements, like secular movements, are open to corruption, . . . religious fanaticism and its demonic history."[121] Thus Tracy reminds us of Pascal's famous aphorism that "men never do evil so completely and cheerfully as when they do it from religious conviction."[122] But such plurality and ambiguity – indeed, such violent interruption in the name of religion – operates from an illusory perspective and sinful refusal to reckon with the fundamental reality that radical difference and otherness is at the heart of all existence.

On the other hand, the religious human being ultimately – and thus eschatologically – must finally be liberated by the recognition, in the words of Wittgenstein, that "that the world is, is the mystical," that the Ground of that mystical sense is an Ultimate Mystery which affords "consolations without a cause," and that such a Ground also demands of the authentic religious human being a humble stance of "learned ignorance."[123] This is the authentic religious human being of postmodernity who, chastened and transformed by the fissure and interruption of difference and otherness at every turn, finally comes to recognize that "hope is granted by the one Reality that, as Ultimate, must be radically other and different, however that Reality is named – Emptiness, the

One, God, Suchness."[124] In other words, a sobering realization has once again come upon the postmodern human being, a sobering realization confronted by the fundamental and chastening question: if indeed the Ultimate and Eschatological Ground of all humanity[125] and of all existence is radically and finally unmasterable Difference and Otherness, can we – dare we – assert human mastery and domination over the essential truths of existence and, in doing so, refuse authentic and open conversation and solidarity with the other? If indeed the primordial Truth of all existence, and to retrieve Tracy's language in *Blessed Rage* and *The Analogical Imagination,* the very Limit-of or Ground-to all existence, must be named not only as the Whole but the Whole precisely as radically Different and Other, how is it that the human being can presume full presence and mastery over fundamental realities not ultimately of human control such as truth, language, and history? Such realities in their difference and otherness mirror the Difference and Otherness which grounds them. There is analogy – similarity respecting difference – operating here. An analogical imagination still remains at work in Tracy's thought. And this analogical imagination also affords, once again, a coherence between the secular and the religious dimensions of human as eschatological existence. Authentic secular existence is, for Tracy, all of a piece with authentic religious existence.

Ultimately, then, Richard Bernstein is correct in characterizing David Tracy's text *Plurality and Ambiguity* as a "credo." For Tracy's affirmation of the possibility of hope in some enlightenment and some liberation in and through plurality and ambiguity rests on a basic faith in the power of a gracious Ultimate Reality which offers to humanity Its Truth as both revelation/disclosure and mystery/concealment, in presence but also absence which yet promises future. It also rests on a faith in analogy where the Primordial Truth of all existence as Disclosure/Concealment is mirrored in classical disclosures/concealments of primordial truths affording hopeful understanding and liberation. Tracy admits his grounding in faith finally in the closing pages of *Plurality and Ambiguity:*

> As I suspect is clear by now, I do believe in belief. I believe that faith in Ultimate Reality can make all the difference for a life of resistance, hope, and action. I believe in God. It is, I confess, that belief which gives me hope.[126]

For Tracy then, faith in the manifest, liberating power of an Ultimate and thus Eschatological Reality gives hope, a hope that sees promise and future neither in the optimistic presumption of full presence nor in the despair of absence. Rather hope lives in the real tension between presence and absence, between the present and the future, and between the interruptive disclosures and concealments which Mystery grounding all history affords. It is no wonder then that Tracy characterizes religious existence, eschatological existence in this postmodern world, as hopeful precisely as resistance, attention, and solidarity with the other. Resistance is a necessary ingredient in the risking of a life of hope in the face of the tensions of radical difference and otherness. Resistance is necessary to countermand human strivings for easy coherences. Hope as resistance becomes action as it remains open to future as promise.[127]

In his own classic study of eschatological hope, *Theology of Hope,*[128] Jürgen Moltmann identifies three key enemies of hope by retrieving two classical literary tropes and a philosophical perspective. Such retrievals parallel what has come to be known in the Christian religious tradition as sins against hope. Moltmann notes that the "presumption" of Prometheus, the "despair" of Sisyphus, and the "presentism" of Parmenides all militate against the exercise of authentic religious (and Christian) hope. They all rob hope of any real future. Tracy shares the very same concerns as Moltmann when he speaks about religion as the final, ultimate, and hopeful strategy with which to face radical plurality and ambiguity. David Tracy's characterization of authentic religion as an exercise of hope by way of resistance, attention, and solidarity provides his eschatological hope with a certain sturdiness in that it guards against the very sins of hopelessness which Moltmann and the Christian tradition identify.

Religion, that eschatological enterprise, is first and foremost hope as resistance, for Tracy sees sturdy hope in resistance to "more of the same"[129] religious and secular interpretations which assume mastery and control over primordial truths and the Primordial Truth at the heart of religion. This is a resistance to the complacency inherent in a Parmenides-like faith in full and eternal presence. This is a resistance on behalf of concealment that hopes for the promise of future and further enlightenment spurring on liberations. Such resistance also demands critical "attention"[130] to any and all presumptions of full mastery and presence, to an optimistic assumption of control over that which, in its very difference, can never be fully controlled. Such resistance also demands "solidarity" with and not isolation from the others who would question any domineering attempts to assert as finally true elitist interpretations. Such solidarity recognizes and embraces otherness not as a threat to mastery and control but as a hopeful response to the eventually debilitating despair of isolationism. And such solidarity also recognizes and appropriates relatively adequate interpretations – shared in conversation – that lead to emancipations and liberations.

Concluding Remarks

Concluding then, I contend that in *Plurality and Ambiguity: Hermeneutics, Religion, Hope,* David Tracy has further intensified his theological project by disclosing and reflecting critically upon the radically interruptive nature of all reality and of the very God or Ultimate Reality who grounds that reality. Tracy names both God, the Ultimate Reality, and the human situation by way of the interruptive language of difference and otherness giving rise to plurality and ambiguity in this worldly existence. There is clearly an eschatological dimension to this naming process, for radical claims, both for the human situation and for the reality of God, are ultimate claims, final claims, and in this world eschatological claims.

Moreover, I also contend that the eschatological dimensions/namings of Tracy's thought in *Plurality and Ambiguity* – much like in *Blessed Rage for Order* and in *The Analogical Imagination* but more intensively so in the face of post-modernity – are revisionist dimensions/namings that point in the direction of action. This is reflected in Tracy's profoundly intense assertion that the *praxis* of religious hope grounded in faith in the enlightening and liberating power of Ultimate Reality and exercised in solidarity with the other is not a preferred strategy for dealing with radical interruptions. Rather, Tracy sees religion as the praxis of hope born of faith and exercised in solidarity with the other as the final in this world strategy for dealing with – living with – radical interruptions. Tracy's sober and critical recognition of the radical nature of interruptions to existence, interruptions inherent in the very nature of primordial truth and of human language, in historical action, and in the very character of God, the Ultimate Other and Different One, not only underlines his revisionist fidelity to the morality of scientific knowledge but also draws him towards religion finally as the exercise of a faith-based and active hope. This is a sturdy hope, an intense hope, an active hope that "fights on behalf of all of us"[131] and that does not retreat from this world into mystifying certainty claims about a world and time beyond human comprehension. This is a hope that recognizes the ambiguity of the future as it takes concrete shape in this world in the form of resistance to "more of the same" presentist interpretations dismissing the promise of any future. This is a religious hope that gives critical attention and suspicion to presumptive, overly optimistic certainty claims about final realities. This is a religious hope that does not isolate the self, either personally or collectively, in a world of captured truths or in silence but a hope that finds hope itself in listening to the voice of the other. This is a hope that believes in the manifestory power of primordial truth, in a real presence to that brand of truth. However, it is also a hope in the promise of future inherent in the concealedness of that same truth. This is a hope which declares that understanding leading to and compelling action towards real human emancipations is possible only if exercised in conversation and solidarity with the others of our history and in faith in the Other grounding that history. And this is a hope which finds enlightenment and emancipation in grace-filled moments of "prayer, discipline, conversation, and actions of solidarity-in-hope."[132] This is a hope that, above all, is a revisionist hope in that it accepts the sober realities of the present situation and history, the ambiguities and unavailability of the future, and yet retrieves the Mystery of God in conversation with human realities and ambiguities to stimulate courage to live into the future.

Finally then, we recall that in 1 Peter 3:15, the biblical author exhorts his readers to be ready always to account for their hope, their Christian as religious and eschatological hope. That particular religious community accounted for that hope by way of faith in the manifestory power of Jesus as the Christ, as the incarnate revelation of the Ultimate Reality named God. While it is true that David Tracy's audience in *Plurality and Ambiguity* is broader than that of Peter's particular Christian community, he too accounts for his hope, that predominant eschatological virtue – and in an ecumenically sensitive manner – by way of a faith in the power of that same Ultimate Reality[133] (however named). Religious faith then warrants hope, active hope, the hope of solidarity in and in the face of radical interruptions. As such, this hope countermands the interruptive and sinful hopelessness of presentism, presumption, and despair. If Tracy's revisionist namings "limit/transcendence" evoking faith disclose the eschatological dimension of his project in *Blessed Rage for Order*, and if his revisionist namings "fragmentation/wholeness" manifesting the power of the relationality of love perform the same service in *The Analogical Imagination*, then the interruption of "radical difference and otherness" giving rise to hope discloses yet another eschatological dimension to David Tracy's theological project. For to Tracy, "neither optimism nor pessimism but hope is at the heart of the Christian vision of both nature and history."[134] And once again, this eschatological dimension takes shape in risking a life in this world, a life animated by faith, engaged in hope, and finding enlightenment and emancipation in acts of solidarity, in acts, finally, of other regard, respect, and love.

Therefore, drawing to a close this lengthy investigation of the eschatological dimensions of David Tracy's theological project, I make the claim that patterns of eschatological thinking have surfaced in that very project and in his major writings. Tracy's namings of both God and the contemporary human situation are revisionist namings. Limit, the Whole, and Difference and Otherness as Mystery are all namings and revised and coherent ways of dealing with the two poles of a revisionist theological position: the tradition and the contemporary human condition. These namings have eschatological dimensions to them, eschatological dimensions in terms of ultimacy, decisive finality, and radicality that interrupt present complacencies. What is most important to note is that these very namings in their eschatological dimensions are directive. They all move understanding of eschatological disclosure or discovery beyond discovery per se and towards action, in Tracy's words towards "risking a life" in this interruptive present and for a yet objectively unavailable future.

What ultimately surfaces in this analysis of the eschatological dimensions of Tracy's project is a notion about eschatology that the review of twentieth century research on Christian eschatology only hinted at: the claim that eschatological reflection must find a way of marrying thought to action, speculation to practice. This is a pattern of eschatological thinking that consistently surfaces in Tracy's project as he faces the ambiguity of the future. Revisionist Christian eschatology in recognition of that ambiguous future must therefore find a form of discourse, a theological genre, which does service to this pattern of thinking as it deals with a future that is objectively unavailable yet still of deep human concern. As I have noted, Richard Bernstein characterized Tracy's *Plurality and Ambiguity* as a "credo." It is both a critical naming of the modern/postmodern situation accompanied by a testimony to the power of hope as action. Indeed, *Plurality and Ambiguity* is a call to hope as action, an exhortation on behalf of a credo. *Plurality and Ambiguity* itself – precisely as a credo – begins to take on the shape of rhetorical discourse.

In the final chapter of this study then, I will identify the general features or components of a revisionist Christian eschatology with David Tracy's revisionist perspective, namings, and pattern of thinking as building blocks or foundational pieces. With these foundational pieces, I will claim that a revisionist Christian eschatology for this present world can be constructed as an "eschatological imagination" within a form of discourse that does service to both the speculative and practice dimensions of eschatological thinking. The form of this discourse will be that of a rhetoric, discovery directing action in the face of the interruptive nature of the future. The notions of radical interruption, of future as interruptively unavailable, and of hope that finds its truth value in action on behalf of the Christian story will all figure as key components of a revisionist eschatological imagination as a rhetoric of virtue, a rhetoric of hope.

Notes

1. This is not, however, to say that Tracy has become so postmodern in his thinking as to altogether abandon the project of modernity. He prefers to come to postmodernity through modernity. Tracy is loath to – indeed, will not – abandon the "morality of scientific knowledge" which so motivated his efforts in *Blessed Rage for Order*. Thus Tracy will conclude *Plurality and Ambiguity* with the claim: "We can continue to give ourselves over to the great hope of Western reason." See p. 113 of *Plurality and Ambiguity*. Furthermore, Tracy's 1990 article "On Naming the Present" which serves as the lead article in his collection of articles published under the same title *On Naming the Present: God, Hermeneutics, and Church* (New York: Orbis Books, 1994), pp. 3–24, makes the same claim. He sees value in the emancipations of modernity, in the retrievals of neo-orthodoxy, and in the suspicions of postmodernity. All are essential and contributory conversation partners to the effort to "name the present" theologically.

2. Gaspar Martinez, *Confronting the Mystery of God: Political, Liberation, and Public Theologies* (New York: Continuum, 2001), p. 206.

3. Thomas Guarino, "Revelation and Foundationalism: Toward Hermeneutical and Ontological Appropriateness," *Modern Theology* 6/3 (April, 1990), p. 221.

4. See Richard Bernstein's claim to that effect in his characterization of Tracy's *Plurality and Ambiguity* as a "credo" which "exhibits the classical virtue he [Tracy] so admires, *phronesis* (practical wisdom)." See p. 85 of Bernstein's review of *Plurality and Ambiguity* in *The Journal of Religion* 69 (1989) entitled "Radical Plurality, Fearful Ambiguity, and Engaged Hope."

5. David Tracy, "The Hidden God: The Divine Other of Liberation," *Cross Currents* 46/1 (Spring, 1996), p. 5.

6. See again "The Hidden God," p. 7.

7. *PA*, p. 84.

8. *PA*, p. 12.

9. *PA*, p. 113.

10. *PA*, p. 7. Tracy views the postmodern present as one of "cultural crisis;" as such, it calls into question the "Enlightenment version of the autonomous ego." See *PA*, p. 16.

11. It is for this reason that Tracy claims in "The Hidden God" that "genuine thought today begins in ethical resistance," a resistance that leads to liberation. See p. 5 of "The Hidden God: The Divine Other of Liberation." See also how this theme of liberation carries over into Tracy's systematic christological reflections at the same time in which *PA* was published. See, for instance, Tracy's claims that "Jesus Christ, Liberator is an appropriate model for contemporary christology" in "The Christian Understanding of Salvation-Liberation" in *Buddhist Christian Studies* 7 (1987), p. 138.

12. *PA*, p. 113.

13. See for instance his claim: "Optimism and pessimism do not help us reach a true understanding of the plurality and ambiguity of our history. Resistance, attention, and hope are more plausible strategies." See *PA*, pp. 71–72. See also p. 84 where Tracy states that "above all, the religions are exercises in resistance."

14. See for instance Tracy's reference to praxis in the opening pages of *PA* on p. 10. See also his claim in the final pages of *PA* that "every interpretation, as interpretation, is an

exercise in practical application." See p. 101. Note also Tracy's reference to William James's criteria for authentic religious experience as entailing "possibility and openness," cognitive "coherence," and "ethical-political criteria," action-oriented criteria, in PA, p. 91. Tracy's admiration for James's fusion of personal religious experience with ethical action also surfaces in Tracy's later publication, *Dialogue with the Other: The Inter-Religious Dialogue*. See Tracy's appropriation of James's criteria for authentic religious experience as "live," "forced," and "momentous" as that which can "guide one's conduct" on pp. 35ff. It is this concern with emancipatory ethical practice as an essential criterion for the validity of the claims of religious classics which Thomas Guarino sees as Tracy's improvement over Gadamer's interpretation of the nature of the classic. See p. 232 of Guarino's "Revelation and Foundationalism."

15. PA, p. 80.

16. This postmodern secular culture is, for the most part, that of Western post-Enlightenment modernity/postmodernity. Yet, at the same time, Tracy also demonstrates a sensitivity to global cultures as evidenced by his periodic references to non-Western religious experiences. Note his determined effort to provide for non-Western understandings of God as the Ultimate Reality in his namings of that Reality on p. 85 of PA and his admiration for neo-Confucianism, Taoism, and Chan Buddhism for their ability to integrate religious insight/illumination with lived practice on p. 102.

17. PA, p. 71. On p. 67 of PA, Tracy provides a brief litany of contemporary "terrifying events" disclosive of this radical evil in history: the Armenian massacres, the Gulag, Hiroshima, Uganda, Cambodia, and "the Holocaust [that] searing interruption of all the traditions in Western culture."

18. See p. 104 of PA. This theological model as the authentic human as Christian response to radical postmodernity continues to echo in Tracy's thought to this present day. However, in an appropriation of the thought of the liberation theologian, Gustavo Gutierrez, Tracy renames that model the "mystical-prophetic." See Tracy's discussion of "mystical-prophetic resistance and hope" in *On Naming the Present* on pp. 18ff. See also his reference to the prophetic and the "meditative" (i.e., mystical) as appropriate Christian responses to the "many faces of postmodernity" in his 1994 article in *Theology Today* 51/1 (April, 1994) entitled "Theology and the Many Faces of Postmodernity," beginning on p. 104. This theme also appears in Tracy's 1991 article in the *Irish Theological Quarterly* 57/4 entitled "The Hermeneutics of Naming God." See especially pp. 260ff.

19. It should be pointed out that Tracy's unwillingness to focus on the more particular nature of systematic claims on the nature of the "Limit-of" all existence, i.e., the one Christian theologians name God, reflects both Tracy's fidelity to the claim for radical pluralism in all of reality, including the realm of religion, as well his greater ecumenical sensitivity. Such sensitivity is quite evident in Tracy's succeeding text, *Dialogue with the Other: The Inter-Religious Dialogue*.

20. PA, p. ix of the preface.

21. PA, p. xii of the preface.

22. See Tracy's retrieval of the keyword limit in his final discussion of religion as the most appropriate strategy for confronting radical plurality and ambiguity in this our postmodern world beginning on p. 86 of *Plurality and Ambiguity*. He retrieves the very same "fundamental

[limit] questions" which he raised in *BRO* in his claim for religion as the answer to "radical contingency and mortality," to "suffering, that contrast experience par excellence," to "a pervasive anxiety, even terror, in the face of some unnameable other that seems to bear down upon us at certain moments," to "why we sense some ethical responsibility to live an ethical life when we cannot rationally prove why we should be ethical at all," and to "why we need to affirm a belief that there is some fundamental order in reality."

23. See Tracy's discussion of the analogical imagination in relationship to the active resistance essential to the postmodern human subject on pp. 92–93 of *Plurality and Ambiguity*. In the matter of the pluralities of contemporary religious expression, he claims that "that there are profound similarities between them (religions) is obvious, but those similarities are, at best, analogies, that is, similarities-in-difference."

24. *PA*, p. 93.

25. *PA*, p. ix.

26. It is important to note that, given Tracy's focus on the question of religion in the postmodern world as a focus on the question of hope, *Plurality and Ambiguity* is perhaps his most eschatological text. Such a claim is based upon the prior claim from the Judeo-Christian tradition that hope figures predominantly in any theological reflection on the eschatological, and this book is all about hope. Yet, ironically, Tracy makes use of the term "eschatological" only once in *PA*, i.e., in his reference to Bloch's "Utopian and eschatological visions." See *PA*, p. 88.

27. *ONP*, p. 81.

28. As Richard Bernstein noted. See the reference in note 4 of this present chapter.

29. *PA*, p. 84.

30. Hence, Tracy will conclude *Plurality and Ambiguity* with a claim for Ultimate Reality, i.e., God, "as ultimate mystery," that most profound "Other," that demands a return to and appreciation for the apophatic theology of one such as Meister Eckhart. See p. 108.

31. Thus in *Plurality and Ambiguity*, Tracy notes that "we do belong to language and history more than they belong to us" on p. 67. Moreover, Tracy discusses plurality in terms of "difference" inherent in all authentic speech in Chapter 3 and ambiguity in terms of "otherness" in history in Chapter 4. For example, and in reference to Heidegger's analysis of "authentic" speech, Tracy notes on p. 52, "For Heidegger...plurality and difference are always present in all authentic speech." Furthermore, in discussing the radical ambiguities of history in Chapter 4, Tracy notes that the voices of the "others" interpret history differently from us. Quite importantly, this points up the ambiguity inherent in all interpretation. See for instance, p. 79 where Tracy claims that "there is no innocent interpretation, no innocent interpreter, no innocent text" and where he notes that "the voices of the other multiply.... Their voices can seem strident and uncivil – in a word, other. And they are." They are so precisely because they call into question the ambiguity of a history content with "more of the same" interpretations by the dominant and dominating voices of the elite.

32. This claim on Tracy's part that the human being can be described as interpreter is not a new claim. Tracy took a hermeneutical turn early in his career as both *BRO* and *AI* demonstrate. What is perhaps most significant about Tracy's claim for the human being as interpreter in *PA* is his additional greater emphasis on the role of suspicion and critique as essential

elements of interpretation, an emphasis which was hinted at in *AI* but which has grown significantly in *PA*.

33. *PA*, p. x. This is the case for Tracy not only because of the many forms or interpretations of "religion" made by human beings but also, most importantly, because the final focus of religious existence is on "Ultimate Reality," the Mystery of God. See p. 108 of *Plurality and Ambiguity*.

34. This term "as recognized" is most important. Postmodern consciousness – in Tracy's view – does not posit radical plurality and ambiguity; it recognizes a reality beyond human control.

35. In this sense then, Tracy has made a subtle change in his organizational structure or patterning of his major texts. In *BRO* and *AI*, Tracy presented and defended method and then applied such to material theological questions/issues. He employed the literary structure of what he calls "mixed genres." In *Plurality and Ambiguity*, Tracy's organizational structure is more "linear;" he defines the fundamental nature of the human being in the light of what he perceives to be ultimate reality and then offers a possible religious strategy to deal with that reality.

36. In this case, the theoretical claim that the human being is, at her/his very core, an interpreter of the radical plurality and ambiguity of all reality. See *PA*, p. 14.

37. *PA*, p. 20.

38. *PA*, p. 14.

39. As Tracy claimed in *AI*, p. 116.

40. It should be noted that one of Tracy's primary goals in *Plurality and Ambiguity* is to make the claim that even in times of cultural crisis, classics, including religious classics, can still be retrieved and re-appropriated critically as potentially enlightening and emancipatory. See pp. 106–107 of *PA*. Yet in making that claim, Tracy also makes the fundamental anthropological claim that the human being is, at core, an interpreter of plurality and ambiguity, of difference and otherness.

41. *PA*, pp. 13, 15.

42. Tracy demonstrates the plurality and variability of interpretations of the classic of the French Revolution beginning on p. 2 of *Plurality and Ambiguity* by asking a series of questions which can give rise to a variety of interpretive responses. For instance, he asks: "The French Revolution – what was it? The beginning of the modern age or merely the continuation of traditional power politics by other means?" He further asks how best can we interpret this classic event: as event, in and through texts, by way of symbol analysis or ideological analysis, by interpretation of the actions of individuals or the rituals they inaugurated?

43. As quoted by Tracy in *PA* on p. 69.

44. As such, it clearly meets Tracy's criteria of ambiguity as identified in note 15 of *PA* on p. 131. "Ambiguity can mean, cognitively, the true and the false; morally, the good and the evil; religiously, the holy and the demonic."

45. And that Tracy will, in his later discussion of religion, "intensify" into the language not of mere illusion but to that of sin. See *PA*, p. 74 where he notes that "sin is not mere error. Sin is understood as inauthentic existence...a perverse denial of one's finitude and a willful rejection of any dependence on Ultimate Reality."

46. *PA*, p. 16.
47. *PA*, p. 16.
48. Thus will Tracy reference the "feast of Reason in Notre Dame" wherein the French Revolutionaries replaced a sober and modest view of the power of human reason with its very deification along with the effect of such deification: "the procession of the tumbrels to the guillotine." See p. 5 of *PA*. The glorification – indeed, deification by way of symbolic action – of autonomous human reason can lead to an illusory confidence in the power and majesty of that autonomous human reason, a power played out, however, in the "destruction of the royal tombs at Saint-Denis and of much else now judged feudal, gothic, oppressive" and the "seemingly endless parade of pitiable individuals undergoing the new public ritual of death." Tracy's series of questions as to the proper interpretation of the classic event of the French Revolution beginning on p. 4 of *PA*, i.e., questions about the proper interpretation of that Revolution as event, in its texts, symbols, ideologies, etc., not only illustrates the reality of plural interpretations of classics but also the illusory nature of this particular inaugurating classic of modernity.
49. *PA*, p. 50.
50. *PA*, p. 50.
51. *PA*, p.14. See at this point where Tracy claims that "there is no classic text that has not occasioned the same kind of puzzling history of reception."
52. *PA*, p. 9.
53. In speaking of Tracy in relation to intelligibility or understandability, Ted Peters has noted that, for Tracy, such implies publicness. See Ted Peters, "David Tracy: Theologian to an Age of Pluralism" in *Dialog* 26 (1987), p. 300.
54. *PA*, p. 27.
55. This concern for truth and the truth value of religious/theological claims looms large in both of Tracy's previous texts. Hence, Tracy made the case for the truth of religious claims in *BRO* with such criteria as meaning, meaningfulness, and transcendental verification and for systematic religious claims in *AI* in terms of the classic's power of manifestation and in the relative adequacy of its interpretation. It is this very human drive to seek truth which also, for Tracy, can lead to the development of theory and method. See his discussion of the role of theory, method, and even the necessity for timely argument in Chapter 2 of *Plurality and Ambiguity*, beginning on p. 28. See his caveat against method hardening into closed methodologisms on p. 46.
56. *PA*, pp. 12ff.
57. *PA*, p. 28.
58. The foundational nature of this notion for Tracy's thought is evidenced by his retrieval of that notion at every turn. See, for instance, note 92 on page 118 of *BRO* and page 564 of "The Uneasy Alliance Reconceived: Catholic Theological Method, Modernity, and Postmodernity" in *Theological Studies*, 50, 1989. See also p. 115 of *AI* where Tracy retrieves this notion of truth as both a disclosure and concealment in classic works of art, indeed in all classic texts and events.
59. In this sense, Tracy's discussion of the nature of the human being as interpreter and of the role of classics in *Plurality and Ambiguity* is a retrieval of a similar discussion in *The Analogical Imagination*. What is different in *Plurality and Ambiguity* is that Tracy's emphasis is on the intensification of difference rather than on similarity.

60. In this claim, Tracy operates as a retriever from the philosophical as hermeneutical tradition, as his lengthy notes on pp. 120–121 of *Plurality and Ambiguity* bespeak. Truth as manifestation, as disclosure/concealment, is one of Heidegger's philosophical contributions to Tracy's discussion. Interestingly, Tracy prefers the Heideggerian notion of truth as manifestation in disclosure/concealment over Gadamer's truth as manifestation in disclosure alone. This serves Tracy's argument better. Classics invite continuing interpretation because their truth value is both disclosed and concealed. This twofold nature of truth as manifestation in disclosure/concealment serves as warrant for Tracy's claim for the interruptive nature of existence. For every disclosure, there is the interruption of concealment.

61. Hence, Tracy rejects the overly optimistic claims of truth mastery by way of scientific positivism. On p. 48 of *Plurality and Ambiguity*, Tracy makes the strong statement that "positivism as an intellectual interpretation of science is intellectually bankrupt." This is the case because such a perspective fails to recognize the hermeneutical nature of the scientist herself/himself. As Tracy notes in relation to the scientific enterprise: "... 'fact' means not an uninterpreted 'already-out-there-now real' but a verified possibility" and he contends that we must acknowledge "...that all data are theory-laden and all inquiry is interested."

62. PA, p. 29.

63. PA, p. 10. Tracy's debt to Gadamer for this understanding is acknowledged in note 6, pp. 115–116. The dialogical nature of conversation as interpretation in interaction is underscored by Gadamer's notion of the "fusion of horizons," "the paradigm of hermeneutic experience by which, without leaving the old one, we acquire a new horizon that allows an expansion of what is possible to see, learn, understand." See Joel Weinsheimer's discussion in *Gadamer's Hermeneutics: A Reading of Truth and Method* (New Haven: Yale University Press, 1985), p. 244.

64. PA, p. 28.

65. As Richard Bernstein would have it. See Bernstein in "Radical Plurality, Fearful Ambiguity, and Engaged Hope," p. 89.

66. It is at this point that intersubjective argument enters into the process of understanding. Note Tracy's explanation of such in *Plurality and Ambiguity*, p. 29. Note also Tracy's warning that such second order warranting of truth as manifestation through conversation can lead to the loss of the "primary importance of manifestation (more fully disclosure-concealment-recognition)...as the demands of argument take over." This is precisely what Heidegger critiqued in traditional metaphysics.

67. As, for example, the methods of historical and literary criticism of classic texts. See Tracy's discussion of the "second order" nature of such methods and their limitations beginning on p. 35 of *Plurality and Ambiguity*.

68. Heidegger made this significant claim in his classic essay, "The Origin of the Work of Art." See the essay beginning on p. 17 of Heidegger's text, *Poetry, Language, Thought*, Albert Hofstadter, translator (New York: Harper and Row, 1971). See particularly, Heidegger's claim – in his discussion of the "thingliness" of the work of art – that this loss of the sense of the "Being of beings" began when "Roman thought took over the Greek words without a corresponding, equally authentic experience of what they said, without the Greek word." See p. 23.

69. See Heidegger's "The Origin of the Work of Art," p. 31.

70. Quoted from Martin Heidegger's "The Way Back into the Ground of Being" in *Primary Readings in Philosophy for Understanding Theology*, Diogenes Allen and Eric O. Springsted, eds. (Louisville: Westminster/John Knox Press, 1992), p. 252.

71. Again, Tracy's lengthy notes identifying this warrant for his understanding of truth as manifestation appear on pages 120–121 of *Plurality and Ambiguity*. There he attributes this understanding of truth first to Heidegger but then also, with nuances, to Gadamer and Ricoeur.

72. Joel C. Weinsheimer, *Gadamer's Hermeneutics*, p. 258. Note that for Gadamer (and Tracy) this insight comes prior to knowledge but not prior to language. For both, language has the ontological status of "already always being there." See p. 50 of *Plurality and Ambiguity*.

73. Paul Ricoeur, "Toward a Hermeneutic of the Idea of Revelation," p. 37.

74. Paul Ricoeur, "Toward a Hermeneutic of the Idea of Revelation," p. 28. Ricoeur "borrows" this concept from Gadamer's *Truth and Method*. See Weinsheimer's comments regarding Gadamer's *Zugehorigkeit* or belonging-to in *Gadamer's Hermeneutics*, p. 249; Weinsheimer notes "we come to realize that belonging is an ontological way of talking about the condition achieved by the fusion of horizons," Gadamer's fusion of horizons. See page 251.

75. *PA*, p. 20.

76. See Tracy's discussion to that effect beginning on p. 17 of *Plurality and Ambiguity*. He notes on pp. 18–19: "We learn to play the game of conversation when we allow questioning to take over. We learn when we allow the question to impose its logic, its demands, and ultimately its own rhythm upon us...." And "Whenever we allow the text to have some claim upon our attention, we find that we are never pure creators of meaning. In conversation we find ourselves by losing ourselves in the questioning provoked by the text."

77. *PA*, p. 29.

78. And thus implies a future in that deferral; its disclosure may also imply the promise of a future glimpse at a fuller presence.

79. Martin Heidegger, "The Origin of the Work of Art," p. 60.

80. See *PA*, Chapter 3 beginning on p. 47.

81. This ontological connection of world and language and the human being is a key element in the hermeneutics of Gadamer, which clearly influenced the thought of Tracy as noted above. Weinsheimer's insight into Gadamer is to the point here. "For Gadamer ... the coincidence of language with the human world is not merely chronological but essential. It implies that language is not one among many human possessions, for it is not a possession at all but rather constitutive of what it means to be human. Language is not one among other things in the world, for the relation of language and world is reciprocal. [quoting Gadamer in *Truth and Method*, p. 419] 'The world is world only insofar as it comes to language, but also language has its own real existence in that the world is presented to it.'" *Gadamer's Hermeneutics*, p. 254.

82. *PA*, p. 47.

83. *PA*, p. 51.

84. Tracy here claims that language is not plural in a merely diachronic fashion, i.e., as giving rise to plural meanings of words over time, in its "use" or as *parole* in the words of Benveniste. See pp. 52–53 of *PA*. It is also synchronically different, as system or *langue*.

85. PA, p. 54. See Tracy's language "examples" of such difference, of presence in tension with absence on pp. 56–57 of *Plurality and Ambiguity*. "*Tree* means 'tree' by *not* being *free, three, be, thee, she,* and so forth."

86. PA, pp. 56–57.

87. It is for this reason that Jennifer Rike has characterized Tracy's understanding of truth as a "moving viewpoint," a term adapted from Tracy's mentor Bernard Lonergan. In "Introduction: Radical Pluralism and Truth in the Thought of David Tracy," Rike states: "…no absolute viewpoint upon the whole is possible, only a moving viewpoint, always in the process of reevaluating its past judgments in the light of new evidence, always alert to the possible inadequacies in its determinations and evaluations of the real." See p. xiv in *Radical Pluralism and Truth: David Tracy and the Hermeneutics of Religion*, Jennifer Rike and Werner Jeanrond, eds. (New York: Crossroad, 1991). This is not, however, to identify Tracy with "relativism" in spite of the use of the term "moving viewpoint." He fully recognizes along with Luther that there are times when one must say: "Here I stand; I can do no other." See PA, p. 91.

88. Derrida's famous "neologism" is informative here. Derrida sees in *différance* the conflation of two verbs: to differ and to defer. Michael Scanlon interprets this Derridian insight as an example of the differential and future oriented nature of language. Because language is understood only in relation to difference, in the difference of one signifier with another, it carries with it a quality of the concealed; as such it defers meaning and makes, necessarily, a place for future in presence/absence. See Michael J, Scanlon, O.S.A., "The Postmodern Debate" in *The Twentieth Century: A Theological Overview*, Gregory Baum, ed. (New York: Orbis, 1999), p. 234.

89. PA, p. 68.

90. PA, p. 67.

91. Note Tracy's reference to Augustine's classical notion of sin here.

92. PA, p. 74.

93. PA, p. 80.

94. Such as "the hysterics and mystics speaking through Lacan; the mad and the criminals allowed to speak by Foucault; the primal peoples, once misnamed the primitives, defended and interpreted by Eliade; the dead whose story the victors still presume to tell; the repressed suffering of peoples cheated of their own experience by modern mass media; the poor, the oppressed, the marginalized – all those considered "nonpersons" by the powerful but declared by the great prophets to be God's own privileged ones." See PA, p. 79. Furthermore, by appropriating the findings of modern psychological analysis, Tracy even recognizes otherness within the self itself. See PA, p. 78.

95. That is, in whatever language form Ultimate Reality takes in diverse cultures. See PA, p. 85.

96. See Tracy's appropriation of Jean-Luc Marion at this point in "The Hermeneutics of Naming God" in *The Irish Theological Quarterly* 57/4 (1991), p. 261. Marion's characterization of God as "God without being" correlates well with the Heideggerian caveat against the classical effort to define beings into categorical essences. God as God without being cannot be captured and defined.

97. PA, pp. 108–109.

98. "The Hermeneutics of Naming God," p. 253.

99. ONP, p. 43.

100. "The Hermeneutics of Naming God," p. 263.

101. *PA*, p. 114. Note that Tracy's eschatological imagination, an imagination born of hope in and in spite of radical interruption, never abandons his notion of an analogical imagination. Indeed, an analogical imagination itself affords the promise of future and thus hope.

102. *PA*, p. 76.

103. *PA*, p. 113.

104. *PA*, p. 113.

105. It should be noted that Tracy's very selection of these two aphorisms with which to conclude his discussion again implicitly reinforces the claim that Tracy refuses to set one world up against the other. His concerted effort to dismiss religious mystifications as played out in separating the secular and the religious and in deferring the religious to another realm is reflected here in his selecting and connecting enduring philosophical and religious truths of existence. Furthermore, the very fact that Tracy speaks about risking a life in religious faith, hope, and love within the context of describing the "historied" and "discoursing" efforts of human beings to "become human beings" on p. 107 of *PA* continues to reinforce that overarching claim on Tracy's part. It also implicitly reinforces Tracy's belief in the power of *praxis*.

106. *PA*, p. 89. As such, this postmodern humanity cannot then rest in the illusory complacency of the purely autonomous modern rational ego.

107. *PA*, p. 113.

108. *PA*, p. 82.

109. *PA*, p. 83.

110. *PA*, p. 82.

111. *PA*, p. 25. Here recall that classic can be text or event.

112. *PA*, p. 59.

113. Such are the illusions of such "isms" as scientism, positivism, and romanticism on the purely secular and cultural level and totalizing theological elitism and reductionism on the religious level. See Tracy's caveats against such presumptiveness on pp. 33, 48, 50–51, and 100ff of *Plurality and Ambiguity*.

114. *PA*, p. 61. It is at this point, Tracy's limited acceptance of Derrida on the one hand and his return to Ricoeur's "discourse" on the other hand, where Nathan A. Scott, Jr. sees Tracy as inconsistent and too much of an "irenicist." In other words, Scott maintains that Tracy's "great natural courtesy of spirit" leads him to "listen" and attend to all interpretations, even that of Derrida where the self is little more than a speaking pronoun, and where nothingness is always lurking, and "where, under the influence of the new *mystique* of deconstruction, confidence in the very idea of selfhood begins to be shaken." In this, Scott maintains that Tracy "makes some very crucial concessions – that meaning is dispersed along the interminable chain of signifiers and that the ego is, therefore, without any center, that the autonomous self is, to be sure, an illusion." In defense of Tracy however, a de-centered self is, for Tracy, a chastened self and not a lost self. Tracy attends to Derrida and deconstructionism because they have something of intellectual significance to say, insights to share in the conversation, and not because they have captured *the* truth. We must remember that truth is a moving viewpoint in need of testing for Tracy and that Tracy's greater inconsistency would be his refusal to engage in conversation with the other, i.e., Derrida. See Scott's argument in "Hermeneutics and the Question of the Self" in *Radical Pluralism and Truth: David Tracy and the Hermeneutics of Religion*, Jennifer Rike and Werner Jeanrond, eds. (New York: Crossroad, 1991), pp. 81–94.

115. *PA*, p. 62.

116. *PA*, p. 61. That is, until such a time when we come to recognize that further and future questioning of truth claims is demanded by the concealedness of those truth claims.

117. It is at this juncture that Tracy points out that authentic conversation, discourse as a hope in spite of the interruptive nature of human language, must follow some "hard rules" in order to insure authenticity and respect for the other's interpretation. On p. 19 of *PA*, Tracy notes: "Conversation is a game with some hard rules: say only what you mean; say it as accurately as you can; listen to and respect what the other says, however different or other; be willing to correct or defend your opinions if challenged by the conversation partner; be willing to argue if necessary, to confront if demanded, to endure necessary conflict, to change your mind if the evidence suggests it." Tracy notes – as an aside – that such hard rules are merely a variation on his mentor Bernard Lonergan's "transcendental imperatives:" "Be attentive, be intelligent, be responsible, be loving, and, if necessary, change."

118. Such as the poor and the marginalized. See Tracy's claim to that effect on p. 103 of *Plurality and Ambiguity*. Yet Tracy also contends that a willingness to risk one's favored interpretation by way of exposure to the interpretation of others demands attention to many voices and not just the voices of the poor and marginalized. No one class can have an exclusive certainty in a world where truth remains both disclosure and concealment.

119. See T. S. Eliot's "Choruses from the 'Rock'" in *Collected Poems, 1909–1962* (New York: Harcourt, Brace, Jovanovich, Inc., 1936, 1963).

120. *PA*, p. x.

121. *PA*, p. 85.

122. Quoted in *PA*, p. 86.

123. *PA*, p. 8.

124. *PA*, p. 85.

125. That is, the "God in whose image human beings were formed." *PA*, p. 114.

126. *PA*, p. 110.

127. As an aside, this sense of hope as a resistance open to future resonates with Karl Rahner's sense that hope as a "theological virtue" is a "process of constantly eliminating the provisional [and thus is resistance to complacency with more of the same] in order to make room for the radical and pure uncontrollability of God." See Rahner's "On the Theology of Hope" in *Theological Investigations*, Vol. X (London: Darton, Longman, and Todd Ltd, 1973), pp. 245–259.

128. Jürgen Moltmann, *Theology of Hope* (Minneapolis, MN: Fortress Press, 1993). See pp. 8–36.

129. *PA*, p. 84.

130. This is attention as a certain suspicion. Recall that Tracy espouses a hermeneutic of retrieval, suspicion, and critique with which to conduct interpretation in this our interruptive postmodern world.

131. *PA*, p. 114.

132. *PA*, p. 114.

133. This is the Ultimate Reality which Christians have come to name with "their central metaphor 'God is love.'" See the reference in *PA*, p. 108.

134. *ONP*, p. 81.

· 5 ·

AN ESCHATOLOGICAL IMAGINATION: A REVISIONIST CHRISTIAN ESCHATOLOGY IN THE LIGHT OF DAVID TRACY'S THEOLOGICAL PROJECT

As I bring this study to conclusion, I reiterate my claim that eschatological dimensions pervade all of Tracy's major theological writings, and they give direction to his thought. These dimensions have emerged from an analysis of his "namings" of God, the human situation, and what he considers to be the authentic response to those namings across major texts and over time. Tracy's theological namings such as "limit," the "whole," and the "different and other as mystery" all have clear eschatological dimensions and evoke the active Christian responses of faith, love, and hope. The namings then are directed towards action. Furthermore, these dimensions have been disclosed within the framework of a revisionist theological position with its commitment to the morality of scientific knowledge and to the public nature of theological reflection. David Tracy is committed to and operates out of a revisionist position that allows a given religious tradition and the contemporary human situation to inform, challenge, and, in doing so, enrich each other in mutual and public conversation.

In these final pages then, I will briefly reiterate the general contours of the field of Christian eschatology today and summarize what I have gleaned from analysis of the eschatological dimensions of Tracy's revisionist theological project. Tracy's project, in its eschatological namings, in its direction toward action, and in its critical revisionist perspective, functions foundationally for this revisionist Christian eschatology and undergirds the constructive thesis of this study. This is the thesis that a revisionist Christian eschatology – what I name an *eschatological imagination* – is best constructed as a rhetoric of virtue, a rhetoric of hope as action in and for a world that has passed from modernity to postmodernity.[1] An eschatological imagination as rhetoric seeks to persuade or exhort – in critically reasonable testimony or witness to the Christian story – towards authentic Christian eschatological living in what Tracy himself has named "interesting times,"[2] a postmodernity of plurality and ambiguity passing through and disenchanted with the claims of modernity.

The Contemporary Situation

As noted at the very beginning of this study, there are a variety of ways to approach this complicated topic of Christian eschatology, complicated because it seeks, properly and finally, to make assertions about something not objectively available yet subjectively of great human concern: the future. Hope is a critical category in all eschatologies because hope has future as its horizon. Monica Hellwig succinctly defined Christian eschatology as "the systematic reflection on the content of our Christian hope" as well as "reflection on the risk of not attaining what our hope holds out to us."[3] Hellwig's definition reflects a speculative and systematic move on the part of the theologian, the move towards critically reflecting on the exhortation of 1 Peter 3:15: "Always be ready to give an explanation to anyone who asks you for a reason for your hope."[4] It seeks to investigate and explain the sacred writer's faith claim that Christian hope finds its content and ground in the definitive and final action of God in Jesus Christ. Her definition and accompanying exposition also reflect the effort to form a full and systematic understanding of Christian eschatology by relating reflection on the nature of the so-called *eschata* or final things/realities to the *Eschatos*, the Christ, and the *Eschaton*, Christ's Kingdom.

Hellwig's own systematic reflection is outlined by way of such eschatological subtopics as: the hermeneutics of eschatological statements, biblical and traditional symbols of hope, general and individual eschatology, and the need for a "spirituality" of Christian hope.[5] Her coverage of the topic is rather traditional. However, much like her theological contemporaries, Hellwig intimates that Christian eschatology stands in need of a spirituality of hope today, what she calls an "active or prophetic spirituality"[6] where hope animates concrete actions on behalf of the Kingdom in this world.[7] What is also important to note is that she views the discussion of Christian eschatology as a systematic one.

It is an exposition on the final topic of Christian systematic theology because it seeks to make reflective judgments on the nature of final and future realities in relation to the other major topoi of Christian theology. This is what a systematic theology attempts to accomplish; it seeks to draw theological topoi into an ordered and related whole.

Summarizing the state of contemporary eschatological reflection, Stephen Williams noted that the complexity of contemporary eschatological assertions is reflected in the nuanced thinking of theologians on four major consensual claims: that eschatology is central to Christian theological reflection today, that it is all about hope in God's promises for this world, that one's perspectives on christology figure largely in the discussion, and that Christian eschatology must serve as a stimulus to liberating action in this world.[8] To Williams, there are points of convergence on the contemporary scene, especially in terms of consensus on the matter of relating Christian eschatology to hopes for this world. There is greater emphasis on the "this-worldly" aspect of Christian eschatology where hope becomes task-oriented.

There are also, however, nuances within consensus, and those nuances all tend to revolve around the question of continuity versus discontinuity in eschatological reflection. Christian theologians readily identify Jesus Christ as the *Eschatos*. However, that very *Eschatos* is, for some, a symbol of continuity as fulfillment, for others, a symbol of discontinuity as rupture bringing about radical newness. Tracy's own christological understanding incorporates both incarnation and cross/resurrection in recognition of the tensive already-not-yet event of Jesus Christ as *Eschatos*. But this raises a systematic question: is eschatology more properly related to the doctrine of creation or of reconciliation? The way in which one answers this christological question can have related implications for eschatological understandings. This is perhaps best reflected in the contrast between the eschatological positions of Pannenberg (and eschatological theologians of history with their predominant focus on the future, hope, and consummation of creation) and Bultmann (and the so-called radical eschatologists with their predominant focus on the present, faith, reconciliation, and radical reversal). These issues tend to be the way eschatology is approached as the discussion of Williams's work and Gerhard Sauter's *What Dare We Hope?* demonstrates.

Again, what rises to the surface in all of these discussions are a series of assertions or propositions and inter-related systematic claims. One can see this pattern when the question of eschatology as continuity versus discontinuity points back to the Christian doctrines of creation and/or reconciliation. As another example, recall that Gerhard Sauter concludes his own reconsideration of Christian eschatology by making assertions about eschatology in terms of justification through hope. These assertions are directly related to the identification of Jesus as the Coming One, the One who comes in victory from God, justifying in faith and hope. Moreover, one need only look to the classical eschatological reflection of Karl Rahner, "The Hermeneutics of Eschatological Assertions,"[9] to see that much of contemporary Christian theology views eschatology from the perspective of making and explaining a series of assertions or reasoned propositions that are grounded in a sometimes ambiguous and mystifying biblical tradition. Rahner's classic operates from that very structural perspective. Scriptural revelations are assumed as he moves from one thesis and exposition logically to another in order to make eschatological claims about hope and future. Like so many others, he takes the systematic task quite seriously.

In examining the thought of Rahner, Sauter, or any of the other Christian theologians reviewed previously, I noted this concerted effort to wrestle with the ambiguity and complexity of the topic of Christian eschatology in a systematic way, a way that seeks to draw reflection about hope in a final future into the family of systematic topics. There is a certain amount of confidence and security in approaching Christian eschatology in this way; it becomes the final part of a total theological "package," summing up that package, as it were, by making speculations and assertions about the nature of final realities based on previous assertions.

Yet the question of an objectively unavailable future continues to bedevil the hopes of Christian eschatology, making statements about the nature of final realities somewhat ambitious. This is the case precisely because, as Paul notes and cautions in Romans 8: 24: "Now hope that sees for itself is not hope. For who hopes for what one sees?"[10] One cannot see the future with absolute clarity. Therefore, how can hope be just a matter of patiently enduring the present because of a certainty of the nature of the future? This is ultimately the direction of Rahner's thought as he claims that the future is present but hidden in the revelation of the Christ event. Where is an open future in a present certainty? Cannot such a stance lapse into the "eschatological fatalism" decried by the liberation theologians? Why exercise hope? Rather, should not hope be more a matter of yearning for and working towards positive possibilities stimulated by the sometimes ambiguous memory of a faith community as well as the ambiguities of our present? In this vein, recall that Moltmann points out that there is a certain logic problem inherent in the very term "eschatology;" it asserts a *logos* or final word on a final future that is yet open and unclear.[11]

Locating Tracy

It is perhaps at this point that the thinking of David Tracy as a revisionist Christian theologian can enter into the eschatological discussion. For Tracy does not offer contemporary Christian eschatology a series of systematic propositions or eschatological assertions; he has not joined in that form of eschatological discussion. In fact, as a revisionist theologian, he is not overly confident in systematic certainties because such certainties can evolve into hardened "isms," even in the matter of religion. Tracy's revisionist reading of the postmodern world cautions against absolute certainties about both the present and the future, and very few eschatological assertions or propositions can be found in his work.[12] What Tracy's work does offer or disclose are eschatological dimensions inherent in his investigation of the relationships between the two poles of a revisionist position: the Christian religious tradition and human experience. At the same time, having passed through modernity and into postmodernity, Tracy has shifted greater attention to recognizing differences within relationships. Hence his espousal of the notion of truth as at once disclosure and concealment and all of his language of "interruption" as well as his ongoing critique of the basic claims of modernity,[13] a critique that becomes stronger and stronger in his later writings. Tracy appreciates the liberations of the modern critical spirit but not modernity's tendency towards rationalism and optimism about the powers of the so called purely autonomous ego riding along the "asphalt highway of modern rationality."[14] Such a stance has been proven by history to be a failure and, quite importantly for eschatology, works against hope's positive future orientation. It really fixes itself in complacency with the present and with a certainty about the future. Thus, Tracy's postmodern anthropology is an anthropology of the "chastened subject,"[15] a "fragile" self open to an ambiguous future and chastened both by the realities of history and the hiddenness and incomprehensibility of God.

Tracy also decries the fact – and this is very important for the present study – that theology within a modern mindset tends to separate out reflective theology and lived spirituality, religious thought and religious devotion lived out in practice.[16] Concern about separating theology and religious practice was evidenced in Tracy's 1995 plenary address to the Catholic Theological Society of America on the matter of theodicy as well as in his appreciation for Louis Dupré's effort to re-connect spiritual traditions to theo/philosophical traditions in this postmodern world.[17] Tracy is vexed by modernity's "famous separations: thought from feeling, content from form, theory from practice."[18] Analysis of the movement of Tracy's project over time and across texts has surfaced his desire to overcome those separations by pointing out that certain eschatological namings inevitably evoke certain responses as all of a piece. Thus for instance and most recently, hope has become the appropriate and authentic response to the dialectical realities that Tracy recognizes in the ambivalences and atrocities of history and in retrieved but also reinterpreted classic and contemporary notions of God. Here Tracy's revisionist stance comes to the forefront. He takes seriously the critical rationality of modernity as well as the suspiciousness of postmodernity with its tentative openness to an ambiguous future. At the same time, he seeks to remember and restore the Christian tradition and identify the most appropriate response to both situation and tradition. That is what mutual critical correlation, the hermeneutic of the classic, and the hermeneutics of retrieval, critique, and suspicion are all about.

However, while recognizing dialectical realities, Tracy has not yet dismissed nor abandoned his analogical imagination, the theological method that he advocated for dealing with plurality in systematic theology. Tracy still supports an analogical imagination, the ability to "see similarities in difference" in "ordered relationships."[19] Indeed, this imagination forms the relational basis of all of his namings of God and the human situation across major texts.[20] And an analogical imagination is particularly suited to wrestling with plural interpretations in systematic theology because it seeks to see, disclose, and connect relationships conceptually and systematically into inter-locking thematic propositions in spite of plural interpretations.

Furthermore, Tracy's revisionist namings can be helpful for re-interpreting the traditional topoi of Christian eschatology. Recall Monica Hellwig's claims that a traditional treatment of Christian eschatology attempts to develop speculative propositions about the last things, such *eschata* as death, judgment, heaven and hell. Tracy does not really address the *eschata*; yet his theological keyword of limit serves as a possible heuristic with which to re-interpret the eschata of traditional Christian eschatology. So too, Hellwig claims that post-Vatican II eschatology focuses attention on the *eschaton* as the Kingdom of God in a renewed appreciation for the New Testament kerygma. But again, Tracy only briefly attends to the Kingdom or Reign of God as part of his christological discussions in *The Analogical Imagination*. Yet, Tracy's keyword, the whole, offers an eschatological heuristic with which to capture or describe the hoped for character of an eschaton. Furthermore, Sauter's claim that the radical eschatologists of the twentieth century rightly refocused eschatological reflection through the lens of Jesus Christ as the *Eschatos* certainly resonates with Tracy's christological as eschatological claims in *The Analogical Imagination*. Yet Tracy's critical journey into postmodernity with its sense of fissure and difference allows the keyword difference/otherness as radical and absolute mystery to serve as another heuristic with which to approach *Eschatos*. It is no wonder then that Tracy has become more and more interested in the mysterious and enigmatic Jesus of Mark's gospel.[21] In sum, Tracy's controlling theological namings may serve as new exploratory starting points for re-interpreting the traditional topoi of Christian eschatology by contributing a new language for dealing with those topoi. But Tracy himself does not develop these terms within the genre of a systematic eschatological exposition.

Therefore, Tracy himself does not offer the contemporary discussion a systematic treatment of Christian eschatology. His revisionist appreciation for the insights and suspicions of postmodernity serves to caution any facile attempts to make propositional claims about the nature of a final future – a truly ambiguous reality – and the One who stands at the core of that final future: the mysterious and ultimate reality we call God. Tracy's postmodern self has been chastened of those facile attempts. His revisionist contribution to the contemporary discussion of Christian eschatology is neither a full-blown systematic treatment like that of Moltmann, Hayes, or Lane nor a historical treatment like that of Sauter. At this time in his career, systematics is not Tracy's concern. Radical ambiguity and how to deal with it – how to live in its midst – preoccupy his thought. What Tracy does offer to the contemporary discussion are foundational elements, conceptual and perspectival tools with which to continue the task of creating a revisionist Christian eschatology for this postmodern age. His theological project offers a revisionist mindset and method surfacing theological keywords that have clear eschatological dimensions and that implicitly direct theological speculation towards action.

Shaping An Eschatological Imagination

At this point, I reiterate the constructive claim or thesis that a revisionist Christian eschatology for a world that has passed through critical modernity into suspicious and ambiguous postmodernity is best constructed as an eschatological imagination that takes on the shape of a rhetoric of virtue. An eschatological imagination is an exhortation to live an eschatological life as hope in action in the face of the uncertainty of the future but also in testimony to faith as trust in the finally transformative power of love. Hope predominates in an eschatological imagination because an eschatological imagination looks to the future as its horizon. But facing the ambiguity of the future, the Christian must also trust in hope's power to transform the future according to the criteria of love and justice. And hope and trust in the final power of love in the face of an ambiguous future is best served by exhortation, by the call to action – in a word – by rhetoric.

An eschatological imagination as a rhetoric of virtue thus contains several key and inter-related components or features, and these features give it a definitive revisionist shape. First and foremost, it is grounded in an honest if sober reading of the contemporary postmodern situation as well as in a related understanding of God appropriately retrieved from the Christian tradition. Here the retrieval of David Tracy's characterization of the present situation as well as of God, the Final Reality, as "interruptive" serves as a support base upon which to build an eschatological imagination. Metaphorically speaking, Tracy has done the spade work for this revised eschatology by offering as foundation a revised coherent, meaningful, and appropriate correlated characterization of the two poles under examination in revisionist theology.

A revisionist theological method from the perspective of David Tracy's sense of the morality of scientific knowledge and the public nature of theology seeks to discover correlations or coherent, meaningful, and true connections between two poles: the Christian tradition and common human experience. Such a method applies a hermeneutical and historical analysis to the Christian tradition (with the accompanying interpreted notion of truth as *aletheia* or disclosure/concealment within the classics of the Christian tradition) along with a phenomenological and philosophical analysis of common human experience (where truth takes on the shape of a transcendental argument) in order to arrive at those critical correlations. In Tracy's mind, such a methodology allows the faith claims of the Christian tradition to stand the test of intellectual honesty while being re-interpreted within the language and thought patterns of contemporary human experience and thinking.

In the previous chapters, we have followed this methodology in operation in Tracy's major texts and in doing so have unearthed not only Tracy's theological namings but also their eschatological dimensions. What is important to note is that those namings – as a foundational piece for an eschatological imagination as a rhetoric of virtue – share a commonality; those namings all disclose "interruption" as an essential feature of both God, the Final Reality, and the human condition within contemporary history. For Tracy, human beings live with interruption and act interruptively as God too acts to interrupt our pretensions to autonomy and self-sufficiency. Limit in its twofold dimension, the Whole in relationship to fragmentation, and the Different and the Other as Mystery in relation to plurality and ambiguity are all related namings that not only have eschatological dimensions but also carry with them a sense of interruption. When Tracy finally comes to describe God as the eschatological God precisely as one who is interruptive Mystery and these times as interruptive eschatological times from a Hegelian viewpoint of history as a "slaughter bench" of violence,[22] he does so in a coherent and intellectually honest way. In doing so, Tracy characterizes both tradition and the human condition by way of present retrievals of past understandings of God, particularly God as interruptive Mystery, in concert with present readings of history as interruptive, as the place where positive human achievements are laced with acts of barbarism and sin.

Interruption, Future and Hope

Such characterizations can certainly be helpful for a revised appreciation for the mystical tradition in Christian theology (where God is named as Mystery) as well as for a revised understanding of the nature of sin and human responsibility for its elimination. And such characterizations fit quite nicely with Tracy's notion that living authentic Christianity entails both a mystical and active prophetic dimension. However, an eschatological imagination, precisely as a rhetoric of hope, must step beyond the past and present and deal with the future. Eschatology has as its central focus hope in future and therefore can never be totally collapsed into a predominantly faith-oriented presentist perspective.[23] How then can the notion of interruption as distilled from Tracy's analysis of present conditions be adapted to an eschatological imagination that focuses on the future and, in doing so, serve as a foundational piece for structuring a revised Christian eschatology? I would suggest that the very notion of future as objectively unavailable and yet of fundamental human concern is of such a nature that it is itself interruptive. In this sense, interruption correlates coherently and meaningfully not only with Tracy's namings of God's actions and human actions and conditions in the present but also with the key concern of a revisionist eschatology: the future. Future is always ahead of us and coming towards us and as such interrupts and disturbs our past and present certainties in spite of the relatedness of past, present, and future. The future is an essential feature of human existence and of temporal reality, but is a feature that, as objectively unavailable, concerns us and always interrupts our sense of security in the present. If an eschatological imagination has to contend with future – and it does – it has to contend with future as yet another instance of interruption confronting and challenging human existence. God, history, and future *all* act on us interruptively. Therefore, interruption as a conceptual descriptor appropriated from Tracy's revisionist project quite adequately fits within the interrelated configuration of features making up a revised Christian eschatology as an eschatological imagination.

Furthermore, future as a fundamental but eschatological interruptive reality of existence really serves as the condition for the possibility of hope itself, for hope's focus is not on the present but looks to the future. There would be no need for hope in human existence if there were no future. Hope and future are intimately related. As Julia Kristeva has noted, the postmodern subject, the postmodern human being, is a "subject-in-process-on-trial."[24] Being in process can be interpreted as being in relationship[25] – not only with God and cosmos but also with and within time where past, present, and future are essential components of existence. We cannot escape the reality of being immersed in time, and this can be "trying," especially when one aspect of temporality is a future that is objectively unavailable, unclear, and uncertain. Again, the future is trying; it is interruptive. And yet to remain an active agent in existence, to remain alive, we must move within time and thus into the future. We can do so in hope, anticipating the achievement of positive possibilities or by drifting into the future in despair of ever achieving those possibilities. Regardless of the choice we make, the point is that the future serves as the condition for the possibility of hope (as well as of despair). Therefore, both future and hope are essential and related features of an eschatological imagination as a rhetoric of virtue. Future is entailed in the very nature of the eschatological and hope is the predominant virtue in an eschatological rhetoric because future conditions the possibility of hope. In other words, we hope because we live facing the future.

Furthermore and along these lines, hope in the light of a revisionist understanding of future as interruption itself serves as the condition for action, the particular action of moving beyond past and present and into that future. Hope activates one to move into the future. Even in common human experience – and separating ourselves for the moment from the final and ultimate hopes of Christian eschatology – human beings would stand frozen in time and fear making any movements into the future if they had not even the slightest mundane hope that their movements, their actions, would result in a positive future. Those who are essentially and fundamentally without a glimmer of hope are victims, the victims of despair, and do not act. They die. If the future conditions hope, then hope conditions action as living on into the future. Indeed, hope acts on and into the future. Thus, an eschatological imagination must concern itself with the virtue of hope in the face of the reality of future and it must concern itself with hope as action. This is not to dismiss the traditional understanding of virtue as infused grace from God but rather to give virtue a more postmodern activist sense.

Therefore, an eschatological imagination focused as it must be on interruption, future, and hope is a revision of Christian eschatology, a new way of thinking eschatologically as it were, in that it is action oriented rather than propositionally oriented. For the essential components of an eschatological imagination, i.e., interruption, future, and hope, are all action-oriented wherein an interruptive future acts on us and serves as the condition for the very possibility of the hope that moves us on into that very future. I noted above with reference to Williams's review of the literature that many contemporary approaches to Christian eschatology tend to gravitate towards the question of continuity versus discontinuity when making eschatological claims.[26] However and again as noted above, such a way of focusing eschatological reflection tends to direct that reflection towards making connections to systematic topics such as the doctrines of creation and/or reconciliation. This is all well and good to a point. But the question of continuity/fulfillment and discontinuity/radical rupture can tend to stay at the level of speculation and assertion about the nature of an unknown future, and radical interruptions in current history stand in need of more than speculation. These interruptions are better addressed by action than by speculative propositions. And, most importantly, the very notion of the future as interruption but also as the horizon for hope entails action.

Indeed, if we take seriously the claim that eschatology has as its focal interest hope and future, and if we do so supportive of and in concert with David Tracy's reasoned belief that interruptive ambiguity surrounds us and threatens our present as well as future and thus our hopes, I contend that we are best served by revising the focus of our eschatological thinking in the direction of action. Certainly, we should not wholly dismiss the "continuity versus discontinuity" conversation, but we should place it into the background in favor of a discussion that underscores the action orientation of an eschatological imagination. In this vein, eschatological thinking would be more fruitfully revised if framed by the categories of certainty versus possibility rather than by continuity versus discontinuity when talking about interruptive future and about eschatological hope as action. For a postmodern reading of God, world, and future is suspicious of absolute certainties, yet still hopes for and acts on positive possibilities.

Truth in Action and Rhetoric

Therefore, in the light of our contemporary sense of the future as objectively unavailable yet subjectively our concern, an important revisionist eschatological question might best be framed thus: how can we, in a critical revisionist sense, make truth claims about the future at all? If a revisionist perspective seeks to make public truth claims along with claims for the coherence and meaningfulness of its categories, must we despair of saying anything of truth value about the future in a kind of radical deconstructionist deferral because of future's objective unavailability and uncertainty? If that were the case, then eschatological reflection would be a futile exercise. Or is there a more fruitful avenue to explore in terms of the certainty/possibility issue? Can we re-think our understanding of truth within an eschatological imagination as action? To refer once again to Moltmann's contention about the oxymoronic nature of the very term, "eschatology," do we despair of any *logos* on eschaton or can we arrive at a different sort of *logos* and truth value?

I contend that with a revised eschatology in the form of an eschatological imagination we *can* make truth claims but neither by way of asserting absolute certainties nor by applying the criterion of scientific verification to eschatological hopes. Rather, we can make truth claims by way of an eschatological imagination wherein hope becomes more than a mere sentiment; wherein hope becomes action. In an eschatological imagination, the hope that is within one acts on positive possibilities rather than certainties and in doing so struggles to create the reality, the truth of those positive possibilities into the future. There are indeed different notions of truth: truth as scientific verification, truth as the end product of a logical argument, and even truth as *aletheia* as identified by Gadamer, Ricoeur, and David Tracy. But there is also the very pragmatic notion of truth as the reality that comes about as a result of chosen actions working to put possibilities into actuality. Truth can be the reality or the "outcome" created by action. We may not always be satisfied with the shape that truth as the outcome of certain actions may take – actions indeed sometimes have unintended and surprising outcomes – but we cannot deny that truth's reality, its truth value. Actions create truths. Moreover, even choosing not to act, to suspend action, is an act that will lead to future outcomes or realities. We are always acting even if some actions take the shape of "standing still" for the present, and all actions lead to certain outcomes, certain realities.

At this point, William James's notion of truth as transformative practice comes into play in an eschatological imagination and, in doing so, shifts the emphasis to the rhetorical feature of that eschatological imagination. In "The Will to Believe,"[27] James makes the argument that, in matters religious, faith is ultimately a matter of will, of opting and risking a choice and living one's life on that choice, accepting risk in faith but moving on in life nonetheless. The truth of certain kinds of claims such as faith claims cannot be submitted to the skeptical mindset of scientific and empirical verification for their authenticity, for scientific and empirical verification seeks truth by shunning error until certitude is established. Such a stance, when held up against the claims of religion, claims that are in James's mind live, forced, and momentous,[28] would freeze or suspend living religiously in favor of waiting for faith's verification according to the standards of science. James believes that human beings have a right to faith and to choose in matters religious even when scientific verifications fall short. His argument is summarized in the rhetorical language of Fitz James Stephens:

> We stand on a mountain pass in the midst of whirling snow and blinding mist, through which we get glimpses now and then of paths which may be deceptive. If we stand still we shall be frozen to death. If we take the wrong road we shall be dashed to pieces. We do not certainly know whether there is any right one. What must we do? "Be strong and of good courage." Act for the best, hope for the best, and take what comes....[29]

The Stephens quote rather poetically (and rhetorically) sums up James's thesis that we are always deciding, acting on those decisions, and thus creating outcomes. Even the decision to "stand still" in the midst of a snow storm on a mountain pass is an action that leads to the truth of a possible outcome: I may freeze to death. James's thesis further contends that human beings faced with religiously oriented options that cannot be submitted to the truth of scientific verification can act on those options, indeed, must act on those options if said options are ever to move from the realm of possibility to actuality. Thus, the truth of religious possibilities can only come to fruition by way of decisive action that can transform reality. As James notes, "In our dealings with objective nature [and truth as scientific verification] we obviously are recorders, not makers, of the truth."[30] However, in matters religious where truth cannot wait upon scientific verification, James claims: "There are, then, cases where a fact [truth] cannot come at all unless a preliminary faith exists in its coming."[31] In his own pragmatic way, James offers an illustration to make this point when he discusses relationships or "states of mind between one man and another. Do you like me or not?" He points out that one man being liked by another very much depends on the first man's faith in that possibility. Faith in the possibility opens up the way for that possibility to come to fruition.[32] Faith then *acts* on a perceived possibility and in doing so helps to create its reality, its truth. Conversely, unfaith in that possibility closes it off from any transformation into actuality. As James notes: "I [must] meet you half-way, [be] willing to assume that you like me, and show you trust and expectation."[33] The point is that in matters of the heart, and, correlatively, in matters as momentous and unscientifically verifiable as matters religious, the truth value of possibilities can only be discovered in action, in actively trusting and helping to create the reality of those possibilities. Faith as acting on a preferred possibility can help transform the present situation into a new reality, a new truth, a new outcome.

It is true that in "The Will to Believe" James focuses his attention on faith as choosing to act on live religious options, faith that, as active, helps to bring about the truth or reality of possible transformative outcomes in the present. But how can James's claim for religious faith's truth in transformative action be applied to an eschatological imagination as a rhetoric of hope for the future? The key to making the connection lies in the notion that both religious faith and eschatological hope entail an active trust. Religious faith actively trusts in possibility and not certainty, the possibility of transforming the present. So too, eschatological hope actively trusts in possibility and not certainty, the possibility of transforming the future. For a future interrupting the present also waits upon no scientific verifications. The future always comes upon us and presents us with the pressing challenge of a decision, a live option: to live either in hope or in despair. Eschatological disclosures force one not merely to reflect but to act on the momentous nature of that reflection, to live an eschatological life or to suspend that way of living for the short-term present security of a life refusing to realize and accept that real existence is existence ultimately on the edge of the future. Thus, the "how" of living eschatologically is choosing to live in active hope that seeks to transform the future.

Making that choice and acting on it is not easy however; it cannot rest on the comfortable certainty of scientific verification. We may take the wrong road and, in the words of Fitz James Stephens, "be dashed to pieces." Living eschatologically means living with the interruptive nature of the future but also living on possibilities, and that requires the courage that a rhetoric as persuasion offers. A rhetoric exhorts: "Be strong and of good courage" and, at the same time, act. Thus, hope as acting on possibility rather than certainty, on the possibility of working towards a preferred reality or truth, is always acting on a risk that positive possibilities may not come to fruition in the future. We are, after all, living in a sometimes threatening but certainly fundamentally ambiguous world. Hope as struggling to enact positive possibilities needs encouragement and therefore is best supported by a new genre for eschatology: eschatology not as speculation but as the persuasive word, as exhortation, a rhetoric encouraging action. As all students of classic rhetoric know, that genre is employed most often in times of crisis and threat and certainly when radical questions confront human beings to persuade towards a new way of thinking and acting. Rhetoric is useful and necessary when possibility rather than certainty holds sway. Rhetoric is useful – indeed necessary – when hoping for a future. Hence, an eschatological imagination for our interruptive world is best shaped as a rhetoric of hope, of virtue in action where struggling to exercise that virtue offers the opportunity to bring forth positive possibilities into the future. Hope and future, the concerns of eschatology, demand action, and action stands in need of the rhetorical power of the encouraging word.

Yet in a world of pluralism, how do we as Christians determine the shape of those positive possibilities and concomitantly act on them? Rhetoric points one towards thinking and acting in a certain way as opposed to other competing directions. How does Christian hope judge and act on what is a positive possibility amongst competing possibilities in a world of plurality and ambiguity? As noted above, hope hopes in a future that is objectively unavailable yet that is still a subjective human concern. This is the case because, once again, human beings are "subjects-in-process-on-trial," (both individually and corporately) and fundamentally enmeshed in relationship with God, world, *and* space and time and thus concerned about the future as a possibility to act upon. Being in process is trying not only because of the interruptive nature of future but also because it forces choices for hope's acting into that future. Therefore, as human beings, we have to make choices in the matter of directing our active hopes, and those choices can take on different shapes depending upon our judgments as to what are real, preferred, and positive possibilities – in the words of James – live options. In other words, we as human beings move into an unclear future and, in spite of future's lack of clarity, with some assumptions, some judgments, as to the plausibility of possibilities.

Therefore, to remain alive, to be truly human, we have to move into the future with hope. But something must fuel that hope. And for Christians, what fuels that hope and determines the shape of preferred and positive possibilities is the Christian story and its "program"[34] for living as it were. In other words, the Christian story, the decisive and final eschatological event of Jesus Christ, provides a schematic direction for hoping in the face of an uncertain future.[35] And this schematic direction offers a plausible possibility, for the actuality of transformation in the very story of Jesus' life, death, and resurrection provides fuel and direction for hope as acting on the preferred and chosen Christian possibility. That is why a Christian eschatological imagination entails critically reasonable witness – faith as testimony – to a schematic or direction for hope. A rhetoric needs a stimulus and direction for its encouragement. A Christian eschatological imagination as a rhetoric of hope trusts that the Christian story, precisely as eschatological and thus the final real possibility, fuels hope's transformative action in the direction of love and loving. For in the Christian schema for living, the focus is not on love as mere sentiment but on active loving as the final transformative power animating and liberating existence.

Herein lays the logic and value of the revisionist proposal of an eschatological imagination as a rhetoric of virtue in tune with the postmodern world and with faith in God as the Final Reality. For a revisionist Christian eschatology in a postmodern world then, *interruption, future, hope, and truth created in action directed by the Christian story* are inter-related eschatological categories, all re-thought in the light of unnerving plurality and ambiguity where there are more possibilities – both positive and negative – than certainties confronting humanity. In that re-thinking, an eschatological imagination emerges in a genre of rhetoric where hope in the future is directed towards action in the midst of interruptions and where hope's truth value lies in its struggle to transform the future according to the plausible but risky program for action that is embedded in the Christian story. Interruption within future thus points to hope as action, and interruption inherent in uncertainty in tension with possibility points to rhetoric. Hence, an eschatological imagination as a rhetoric of virtue, of hope acting on the plausible but risky possibilities of the Christian story, the Christian schema for eschatological living.

In this sense, a revisionist Christian eschatological imagination clearly mirrors the genre of classic rhetoric in both goal and structure. As Corbett and Connors note: "Classical rhetoric [is] associated primarily with persuasive discourse. Its end [is] to convince or persuade an audience to think in a certain way or to act in a certain way…during periods of…upheaval."[36] In an eschatological imagination, the goal is persuasion in the direction of risking a Christian eschatological life in response to the unnerving and interruptive ambiguity of the future. Moreover, classic rhetoric operates systematically, but not in the same way as does a systematic theology. It does not function as a systematic movement from thought to thought, from speculative propositions to further inter-connected propositions in the effort to arrive at a conceptual whole. That is what a systematic theology tries to accomplish as it seeks to order and inter-connect speculative propositions about the relationship of God-self-cosmos. Rather, the format or systematic structure of the genre of rhetoric is one where discovery and memory stimulate or move, attempt to persuade within a certain style of delivery, to living and acting in a particular way, and in doing so to create a new truth, a new reality, a new outcome. Rhetoric is communication that cannot stay inside of speculation but moves from a perceived preferred option (the Christian story and its program for action) to a call for action on behalf of that option. This is exactly the movement of a revisionist Christian eschatology as an eschatological imagination. For an eschatological imagination, the discovery of radical interruptions in the very nature of reality, in our history, and the very nature of future triggers the memory of an interruptive but ultimately gracious yet mysterious God and the program for living which that God offers as a real possibility. These discoveries and memories then move the Christian living on an eschatological imagination, living on active hope, towards a style or mode of speaking and acting. This is the eschatological *modus operandi* of acting as public, critically reasonable witness to a Christian schema that trusts in the final transforming power of the God of Love. This is the eschatological *modus operandi* of helping to create the truth of the real possibility of a future liberated by love and loving.

Active Hope's Arsenal of Practical Strategies

As I have noted again and again, a revisionist Christian eschatology in the form of an eschatological imagination as a rhetoric of hope is action oriented; it seeks to persuade towards a certain *modus operandi* so as to work with the eschatological God to create the real possibility of a world where the final animating power is the power of love. The Christian story directs a rhetoric of hope thus. The final question then for an eschatological imagination is how can the Christian live an eschatological existence practically and concretely? In a general sense, I have already answered that question. One acts out Christian eschatological existence by living on and actively practicing the virtues of faith, love, and hope, and especially hope when facing the ambiguous future. More concretely yet however, active hope, hope on behalf of a possible positive future in the face of future's interruptive nature, still stands in need of some practical supportive strategies.

At this stage, David Tracy's theological project offers an eschatological imagination a final foundational piece, a strategic piece fully resonant with an eschatological imagination's action orientation. In *Plurality and Ambiguity*, Tracy himself speaks of religion as an exercise of hope in the face of interruptive plurality and ambiguity. When he does so, religion becomes, in effect, a *strategy* or action plan for dealing with the present core realities of existence: limits, fragmentation, difference, otherness, plurality, and ambiguity – in a word – interruptions. And Tracy contends that the act of being religious in this present postmodern world must take on the practical and strategic shape of "resistance, attention, and solidarity with the other" in hope.[37] I would suggest that a Christian eschatological imagination, precisely as a rhetoric of virtue, of active hope directed towards the future and by trust in the final power of love, can appropriate these postmodern action strategies as part of hope's strategic arsenal. In other words, David Tracy's strategies for acting out religious existence in our postmodern present – resistance, attention, and solidarity – can also be appropriated by an eschatological imagination that attends to the ambiguous future. And that very appropriation can lend to the "practical" virtues of the tradition a revisionist understanding.

In this sense, resistance to assertions of certainties about a future objectively unavailable to us yet still our concern can bolster eschatological hope with a practical strategy: living the virtue of temperance. While Tracy speaks of religious resistance as the concerted effort to confront present day sinful interruptions and complacencies, temperance in support of eschatological hope can resist facile assertions of certainty claims about the future. Resistance as temperance can temper over-confidence in certainties while holding on to hope in possibilities. And precisely because eschatological hope acts on possibility and risk rather than certainty, tempering resistance also entails a certain measure of courage or fortitude. Again recall Fitz James Stephens' rhetorical exhortation in James's "The Will to Believe:" "Be strong and of good courage." Living on an eschatological imagination entails the courage to withstand over-confidence about the future *and* to risk enacting preferred possibilities into that future, even if those possibilities encounter their own resistances.

Moreover, Christian eschatological hope within a revisionist perspective must be supported by the strategic practice of attention, attention as critical and prudent witness to the true heart of the Christian story as the stimulus and directing schema for active hope. Here attention as prudence in support of eschatological hope must always strive in a critical, reasonable, and revisionist manner to strip away from the Christian story assertions that are fanciful and unreal, literally apocalyptic and mystifying. Prudence supporting eschatological hope must always attend to the central claim and animating feature of the

Christian story, the claim that love and loving can truly transform both present and future, and must direct hope's actions from that claim and into the future while yet critically reading the present. And prudence as a practical strategy of critically attending to the Christian schema or story knows that, in spite of whatever shape present historical circumstances may take, the preferred out-come for hope's actions into the future entails solidarity, solidarity with God, world, and others in acts of love and justice. Hope acting into the future must be animated and encouraged by the power of love and justice, must indeed work in solidarity with others for love and justice.

Resistance, attention, and solidarity, all strategic features of David Tracy's preferred way of living religiously in the present, thus can also be supporting strategies for an eschatological imagination's active hope. In a postmodern world facing an uncertain and ambiguous future, resistance can support and encourage hope's action into the future by way of acts of temperance and fortitude. And attention as a prudential and critical reading of the Christian program or schematic can direct hope's action into the future towards creating the preferred Christian reality or outcome: a future of solidarity in love always in concert with justice. The virtue of hope in action, the essential feature of an eschatological imagination as a rhetoric of virtue, itself can take on the concrete shape of the exercise of the practical virtues. In this way, the rhetoric of an eschatological imagination will not be an empty rhetoric. It will be a rhetoric encouraging the appropriation of concrete strategies for supporting and living out eschatological hope.

Concluding Remarks

In this final chapter, I have attempted to suggest the fundamental features of a revisionist Christian eschatology for our postmodern world. In this process, I have come to contend that an intellectually responsible and appropriate revi-sionist Christian eschatology can be best shaped in the form of a rhetoric of virtue wherein suspicions about certainty claims for the future can still find hope in possibilities. I name this rhetoric an *eschatological imagination* where interruptive future, hope acting on possibility, and truth as the outcome of that action are all essential features of that eschatological imagination. In making this constructive claim, I appropriate dimensions of the revisionist theologian David Tracy's theological project in order to address contemporary Christian eschatology in a critical, revisionist fashion.

Our journey into Christian eschatology began by noting Charles Hardwick's present day skepticism about Christian theology's lack of "candor" about the last things. Hardwick's criticism resonates with David Tracy's revisionist claim that all Christian theology – including eschatology – must appropriately remain faithful to the heart of the Christian message while in critical and reasonable conversation with existence as we now know it. In a word, Tracy maintains that we as theologians must remain faithful to the morality of scientific knowledge if we are to make public claims about the Christian vision in any time and place. And if that Christian vision entails an eschatological sense – and it does – then a revisionist understanding of Christian eschatology must operate from a candid investigation of the two essential poles of revisionist theology, both the tradition and the human situation in its totality, including the mysterious and ambiguous dimension of time.

In this vein, I have analyzed the thought of David Tracy as a revisionist Christian theologian in its progression over time and across texts in order to discover what might be appropriated fruitfully from that thought in the matter of Christian eschatology. I have discovered eschatological dimensions inherent in his namings of God and the human situation as well as what he considers to be adequate human responses to those namings. I have also discovered that Tracy's namings, arrived at by way of a revisionist perspective and methodology, can support a Christian eschatology as a rhetoric of virtue in important ways: the revisionist naming of God and reality as radically interruptive (as distilled from Tracy's own multiple namings) can be applied adequately and appropriately to eschatology's focal interest, the future, in an intellectually honest way. Moreover and secondly, Tracy's own consistent movement from namings to response as the active appropriation of virtued existence has served as an inchoate clue as to how the discussion of contemporary Christian eschatology might best be directed and shaped.

One might contend that Hardwick's skepticism about Christian eschatological reflection follows from the fact that Christian theologians tend to make propositional statements about eschatology's focal interest, i.e., the future, in relation to reflections on the revelations of the Christian tradition. This tendency can be problematic for eschatology, but not because of any lack of faith in revelation. The problem lies in making certainty claims about future because future should best be spoken of in the language of possibility. That is why we might be best served by moving reflection on Christian eschatology from the language of proposition to the language of encouragement and rhetoric where possibility and action move to the forefront. This is what an eschatological imagination as a rhetoric of virtue does; it builds on critical readings of God and the human situation as interruptive, applies interruption to eschatological hope's burning concern, the future, and in doing appropriates the core of the Christian message as a schematic stimulus to direct and encourage hope towards enacting a Christian future as the preferred and appropriate future for God, humanity, and cosmos. Action then – and the truth or reality that can come about as the result of action – becomes key to an eschatological imagination as a rhetoric of hope directed by faith in the Christian story. Indeed, hope as action in service to that Christian story and not mere speculation about that story and the future may be our only true, to appropriate James once again, live eschatological option when facing the interruptive mystery of God, the interruptive mystery of the present, and the interruptive mystery of the future. Hardwick will find no lack of candor in an eschatological imagination as a rhetoric of hope. He will find no mystifying speculations about the future. But he will find active hope facing interruptive future. Fitz James Stephens exhorts: "Act for the best, hope for the best." Making hope the act of resistance, attention, and solidarity with the other and with God, David Tracy puts it this way and in so doing serves as a foundation for this *eschatological imagination*:

> Whoever fights for hope, fights on behalf of all of us. Whoever acts on that hope, acts in a manner worthy of a human being. And whoever so acts, I believe acts in a manner faintly suggestive of the reality and power of that God in whose image human beings were formed to resist, to think, and to act. The rest is prayer, observance, discipline, conversation, and actions of solidarity-in-hope. Or the rest is silence.[38]

Notes

1. It should be noted that this final constructive chapter was published by the present author substantially much as it appears here as an electronic journal article entitled "An Eschatological Imagination: Constructing a Contemporary Christian Eschatology in the Light of David Tracy's Theological Project" in *Aggiornamento*, the E-Journal of the Institute for Religious and Pastoral Studies of the University of Dallas. Volume 2, Issue 2, 12/09/05. Used with permission of the publisher. All rights reserved.
2. David Tracy, *DWO*, p. 3.
3. Monica Hellwig, "Eschatology" in *Systematic Theology: Roman Catholic Perspectives*, Francis Schüssler Fiorenza and John P. Gavin, eds. (Minneapolis: Fortress Press, 1991), p. 349.
4. *NAB* Version.
5. See again Hellwig's "Eschatology," pp. 349–372.

6. Monica Hellwig, "Eschatology," p. 370.

7. One might recall from Chapter One that Hellwig's call for an active in-this-world eschatological spirituality is not altogether new; that call to action was present – if in an inchoate way – in the eschatological thinking of many of the twentieth century theologians under investigation (Rahner, Barth, Bultmann, Gutierrez, Lane, etc.). Moreover, more contemporary theologians have continued to echo this call. For instance, in "Time as Moral Space," William Schweiker contends that "new creation, as God's gracious renewal of conscience, is a way of life in the world.... To live the new creation is to dedicate one's life to combat all that unjustly demeans and destroys life...." See pp.136 and 138 in *The End of the World and the Ends of God,* John Polkinghorne and Michael Welker, eds. (Harrisburg, PA: Trinity Press International, 2000).

8. See again Stephen Williams's discussion in "Thirty Years of Hope: A Generation of Writing on Eschatology," *Eschatology in Bible and Theology: Evangelical Essays at the Dawn of the New Millennium,* Ken E. Brower and Mark W. Elliot, eds. (Downers Grove, IL: Inter-Varsity Press, 1997), pp. 243–262.

9. See again Karl Rahner, "The Hermeneutics of Eschatological Assertions" in *Theological Investigations,* Volume IV (Baltimore: Helicon Press, 1966), pp. 323–346.

10. *NAB* Version.

11. See again Moltmann's *Theology of Hope* (Minneapolis, MN: Fortress Press, 1993) beginning on p. 15.

12. See again his article in Volume 6 of *Continuum* (Summer, 1968) where he merely claims – and within the mainline of Christian eschatological thinking – that God acted finally and decisively in the person of Jesus Christ, that this act takes on the character of the "already-not-yet," and that Christian existence therefore is eschatological existence. See p. 176. See also *PA,* p. 113 where Tracy identifies God, the One who acted finally and decisively in the person of Jesus Christ, as the Final and thus the Ultimate Reality.

13. As overly optimistic, presentist oriented with its "more of the same" mentality. See again *PA,* p. 84.

14. David Tracy, "Fragments of Synthesis? The Hopeful Paradox of Dupré's Modernity" in *Christian Spirituality and the Culture of Modernity in the Thought of Louis Dupré,* Peter J. Casarella and George P. Schnee, eds. (Grand Rapids, MI: Eerdmans, 1998), p 13.

15. See again *PA,* pp. 82–83.

16. In this, albeit from the side of a postmodernity in critique of modernity, Tracy would appear to share an affiliation with the pre-modern view of theology as integrally tied to a spirituality of practice. He would be sympathetic to Bonaventure's claim that "we do theology so that we may become good people." Quoted from Bonaventure's *Sentences* in Zachary Hayes, *Bonaventure: Mystical Writings* (New York: Crossroad, 1999), p. 38.

17. See Tracy's "Evil, Suffering, Hope: The Search for New Forms of Contemporary Theodicy" in *Proceedings* of the Catholic Theological Society of America, Volume 50 (Santa Clara, CA: 1995), pp. 15ff. See also Tracy's "Fragments of Synthesis?" pp. 9–10.

18. David Tracy, "Evil, Suffering, Hope," p. 18. Such a vexation also reflects Tracy's appreciation for William James's understanding of religious experience as practically or action oriented. See Tracy's discussion to that effect in *DWO* beginning on p. 28.

19. See again Tracy's *AI,* pp. 421ff.

20. Recall from Chapter Three that the analogical imagination is not merely a method appropriate for dealing with pluralities of interpretation; it is also – quite importantly – the gift, the grace, of seeing and appreciating relationships even if those relationships are relationships in and as difference. Recall from analysis in Chapter Four that the radical difference and otherness which characterizes humanity and all of reality reflects the radically Different and Other Mystery of God in whose image "human beings were formed." See PA, p. 114.

21. See his reference to the "fragmentary" and mysterious nature of Mark's gospel in "The Hidden God: The Divine Other of Liberation" in Cross Currents 46/1 (Spring, 1996), beginning on p. 12.

22. See David Tracy's "The Post-Modern Re-naming of God as Incomprehensible and Hidden" in Cross Currents 50/1–2 (Spring, Summer, 2000), pp.240ff.

23. This is not to say that David Tracy does this, even though he is appreciative of Bultmann's contributions to Christian theology. As noted in Chapter One, Bultmann's existentialist approach to Christian eschatology tends to focus on one's private, personal, authentic faith decision for Jesus Christ in the present, my present. While Tracy himself appropriates existentialist language as well as the thought of Bultmann and Karl Jaspers in BRO and AI, his focus clearly turns to future, hope, and the turn from the self to the other in PA and later writings.

24. As noted in Tracy's ONP, p. 17.

25. This postmodern sense of the subject-in-process-on-trial again indicates a shift, a shift away from the existentialist tendency to focus on individual authenticity in personal decision-making and towards the relational responsibility of the ethical turn to the other. Kristeva makes this shift as does David Tracy himself with his postmodern notion of radical difference and otherness lying at the core of all reality evoking ethical responsibility to others.

26. This was not only the case in past twentieth century discussions (e.g., Pannenberg's historical orientation with its sense of continuity as over against Bultmann's radical orientation with its sense of discontinuity). The question of continuity/discontinuity continues especially in the dialogue between twenty-first century scientists and theologians. See John Polkinghorne's The God of Hope and the End of the World (New Haven: Yale University Press, 2002). See p. 149 especially where Polkinghorne asserts that the claims of science about the universe and the faith of theologians about the end time should be dealt with in terms of a "tension between continuity and discontinuity."

27. See "The Will to Believe" by William James in The Internet Encyclopedia of Philosophy, http://users.compaqnet.be/cn111132/wjames/The_Will_To_Believe.htm.

28. See "The Will to Believe," #1.

29. Quoted in James's "The Will to Believe," #9.

30. See "The Will to Believe," #8.

31. See "The Will to Believe," #9.

32. Recall that John Henry Newman made a similar claim. See again note 48 in Chapter Two of this present study.

33. See "The Will to Believe," #9.

34. Here Tracy's notion that the "event" of Jesus Christ is both a "gift and command" is of value. The revelation of Jesus Christ is not only a gift offered but a command to follow a certain program for living.

35. Along these lines, N. T. Wright makes a similar claim when he notes: "All our language about the future . . . is like a set of signposts pointing into a bright mist. The signpost doesn't provide a photograph of what we will find when we arrive but offers instead a true indication of the direction we should be traveling in." See Wright's *Surprised by Hope: Rethinking Heaven, the Resurrection, and the Mission of the Church* (New York: Harper Collins, 2008), p. 107.
36. Edward P. J. Corbett and Robert J. Connors, *Classical Rhetoric for the Modern Student* (Oxford: Oxford University Press, 1999), p. 16.
37. David Tracy, *PA*, pp. 72ff.
38. David Tracy, *PA*, p. 114.

BIBLIOGRAPHY

Selected Writings by David Tracy

Blessed Rage for Order: The New Pluralism in Theology. Chicago: University of Chicago Press, 1996.

Dialogue with the Other: The Inter-Religious Dialogue. Grand Rapids, Michigan: Eerdmans, 1990.

"Eschatological Perspectives on Aging." *Toward a Theology of Aging.* Seward Hiltner, ed. New York: Human Sciences Press, 1975.

"Evil, Suffering, Hope: The Search for New Forms of Contemporary Theodicy." *Proceedings of The Catholic Theological Society of America.* Volume L, Santa Clara, CA: Santa Clara University Press, 1995.

"Fragments of Synthesis? The Hopeful Paradox of Dupré's Modernity." *Christian Spirituality and the Culture of Modernity: The Thought of Louis Dupré.* Peter Casarella and George Schnee, eds. Grand Rapids, Michigan: Eerdmans, 1998.

"God, Dialogue, and Solidarity: A Theologian's Refrain." *The Christian Century* 107 (October, 1990).

"Horizon Analysis and Eschatology." *Continuum* 6 (Summer, 1968).

On Naming the Present: God, Hermeneutics, and Church. New York: Orbis, 1994.

Plurality and Ambiguity: Hermeneutics, Religion, Hope. Chicago: University of Chicago Press, 1987.

The Achievement of Bernard Lonergan. New York: Herder and Herder, 1970.

The Analogical Imagination: Christian Theology and the Culture of Pluralism. New York: Crossroad, 1981.

"The Christian Understanding of Salvation-Liberation." *Buddhist Christian Studies* 7 (1987).

"The Hermeneutics of Naming God." *Irish Theological Quarterly.* 57/4 (1991).

"The Hidden God: The Divine Other of Liberation." *Cross Currents* 46 (Spring, 1996).

"The Post-Modern Re-Naming of God as Incomprehensible and Hidden." *Cross Currents*. 50/1–2, Spring/Summer 2000.

"The Uneasy Alliance Reconceived: Catholic Theological Method, Modernity, and Postmodernity." *Theological Studies*. 50, 1989.

"Theology and the Many Faces of Postmodernity." *Theology Today*. 51/1 (April, 1994).

General Selected Bibliography

Balthasar, Hans Urs von. "Some Points of Eschatology." *Explorations in Theology*. Volume I, San Francisco: Ignatius Press, 1989.

—— *Theo-Drama: Theological Dramatic Theory. Volume V: The Last Act*. San Francisco: Ignatius Press, 1998.

Barth, Karl. *Death to Life*. Adolph Portmann, ed. Chicago: Argus Communications, 1968.

—— *The Epistle to the Romans*. Oxford: Oxford University Press, 1968.

—— *Church Dogmatics, IV.1: The Doctrine of Reconciliation*. G. W. Bromiley, trans., Edinburgh: T. & T. Clark, 1956.

Bauckham, Richard and Hart, Trevor. *Hoping Against Hope: Christian Eschatology in Contemporary Context*. London: Darton, Longman, and Todd, Ltd., 1999.

Baum, Gregory. "Radical Pluralism and Liberation Theology." *Radical Pluralism and Truth: David Tracy and the Hermeneutics of Religion*. Jennifer L. Rike and Werner Jeanrond, eds. New York: Crossroad, 1991.

Bernstein, Richard J. "Radical Plurality, Fearful Ambiguity, and Engaged Hope." *Journal of Religion*. 69 (1989).

Bloch, Ernst. "Man as Possibility." *The Future of Hope*. Walter H. Capps, ed., Philadelphia: Fortress Press, 1970.

Braaten, Carl E. "The Significance of the Future: An Eschatological Perspective." *Hope and the Future of Mankind*. Ewert H. Cousins, ed. Philadelphia: Fortress Press, 1972.

—— "The Recovery of Apocalyptic Imagination." *The Last Things: Biblical and Theological Perspectives on Eschatology*. Carl E. Braaten and Robert W. Jensen, eds. Grand Rapid, Michigan: Eerdmans, 2002.

Bonaventure, St. *The Breviloquium*. José de Vinck, trans. Paterson, New Jersey: St. Anthony Guild Press, 1963.

—— *The Soul's Journey Into God*. Ewert Cousins, trans. Mahwah, New Jersey: Paulist Press, 1978.

Bultmann, Rudolph. *History and Eschatology: The Presence of Eternity*. New York: Harper and Row, 1957.

—— *Jesus Christ and Mythology*. New York: Charles Scribner's Sons, 1958.

Collins, John J. *The Apocalyptic Imagination: An Introduction to Jewish Apocalyptic Literature*. Grand Rapids, Michigan: Eerdmans, 1998.

Corbett, Edward P. J. and Connors, Robert J. *Classical Rhetoric for the Modern Student*. Oxford: Oxford University Press, 1999.

Cousins, Ewert. ed. *Hope and the Future of Man*. Philadelphia: Fortress Press, 1972.

Daugherty, Kevin. "The Eschatology of David Tracy." *Southwestern Journal of Theology.* 36 (Spring, 1994).

Dulles, Avery. "Method in Fundamental Theology: Reflections on David Tracy's *Blessed Rage for Order.*" *Theological Studies.* 37/2 (June, 1976).

Eliade, Mircea. *The Sacred and the Profane: The Nature of Religion.* New York: Harcourt, Brace & World, 1959.

Eliot, T. S. *Collected Poems 1909–1962.* New York: Harcourt, Brace & Jovanovich, 1963.

Gadamer, Hans Georg. *Truth and Method.* New York: Crossroad, 1982.

Grillmeier, Aloys. *Christ in the Christian Tradition: From the Apostolic Age to Chalcedon.* New York: Sheed and Ward, 1964.

Guarino, Thomas. "Revelation and Foundationalism: Toward Hermeneutical and Ontological Appropriateness." *Modern Theology.* 6/3 (1990).

Gutierrez, Gustavo. *A Theology of Liberation.* Maryknoll, New York: Orbis, 1988.

Hanson, Paul. "Apocalypticism." *Interpreter's Dictionary of the Bible.* Supplementary Volume, Nashville: Abingdon Press, 1982.

Hardwick, Charles. *Events of Grace: Naturalism, Existentialism and Theology.* Cambridge: Cambridge University Press, 1996.

Hayes, Zachary. *Bonaventure: Mystical Writings.* New York: Crossroad, 1999.

—— *Visions of a Future: A Study of Christian Eschatology.* Collegeville, MN: Liturgical Press, 1989.

—— "Visions of a Future: Symbols of Heaven and Hell." *Chicago Studies.* (1985).

Heidegger, Martin. "The Way Back into the Ground of Metaphysics." in *Primary Readings in Philosophy for Understanding Theology.* Diogenes Allen and Eric O. Springsted, eds. Louisville: Westminster/John Knox Press, 1992.

—— *Poetry, Language, Thought.* Albert Hofstadter, trans. New York: Harper and Row, 1971.

Hellwig, Monica. "Eschatology." *Systematic Theology: Roman Catholic Perspectives.* Volume II, Minneapolis: Fortress Press, 1991.

James, William. "The Will to Believe." *Internet Encyclopedia of Philosophy.* http://users.compaqnet.be/cn111132/wjames/The_Will_To_Believe.

Johnson, Elizabeth, C.S.J. "The Theological Relevance of the Historical Jesus: A Debate and a Thesis." *The Thomist.* 48/1 (January, 1984).

Käsemann, Ernst. *New Testament Questions of Today.* Philadelphia: Fortress, 1969.

Lane, Dermot. *Keeping Hope Alive: Stirrings in Christian Theology.* Mahwah, New Jersey: Paulist Press, 1996.

Lash, Nicholas. *A Matter of Hope: A Theological Reflection on the Thought of Karl Marx.* London: Darton, Longman & Todd, 1981.

Letter on Certain Questions Concerning Eschatology. Sacred Congregation for the Doctrine of the Faith. Boston: Daughters of St. Paul, 1979.

Lonergan, Bernard. *Method in Theology.* Toronto: University of Toronto Press, 1971.

Malcolm, Lois. "The Impossible God." *Christian Century.* 119/4 (February, 2002).

Martinez, Gasper. *Confronting the Mystery of God.* New York: Continuum, 2001.

McCarthy, John P. "David Tracy." *A New Handbook of Christian Theologians.*, D. Musser and J. Price, eds. Nashville: Abingdon Press, 1996.

Metz, Johannes B. *Faith in History and Society.* New York: Seabury Press, 1980.

Moltmann, Jürgen. *The Coming of God: Christian Eschatology.* Minneapolis, MN: Fortress Press, 1996.

—— "Is There Life After Death?" *The End of the World and the Ends of God.* John Polkinghorne and Michael Welker, eds. Harrisburg, PA: Trinity Press International, 2000.

—— *The Experiment Hope.* London: SCM Press, 1975.

—— *The Theology of Hope.* London: Minneapolis: Fortress Press, 1993.

Newman, John Henry. *An Essay in Aid of a Grammar of Assent.* Notre Dame: University of Notre Dame Press, 1979.

Ogden, Schubert. *Doing Theology Today.* Valley Forge, PA: Trinity Press International, 1996.

—— *The Reality of God and Other Essays.* New York: Harper and Row, 1966.

Origen. *On First Principles.* G. W. Butterworth, trans. Gloucester, Massachusetts: Peter Smith, 1973.

Pannenberg, Wolfhart. *Systematic Theology,* Volume III, Grand Rapids, Michigan: Eerdmans, 1998.

—— "The Task of Christian Eschatology." *The Last Things: Biblical and Theological Perspectives on Eschatology,* Carl E. Braaten and Robert W. Jensen, eds. Grand Rapids, Michigan: Eerdmans, 2002.

Peters, Ted. "David Tracy: Theologian to an Age of Pluralism." *Dialog.* 26 (1987).

Polkinghorne, John. *The God of Hope and the End of the World.* New Haven, Connecticut: Yale University Press, 2002.

Rad, Gerhard von. *Old Testament Theology, Volume II.* New York: Harper and Row, 1965.

Rahner, Karl. "A Fragmentary Aspect of a Theological Evaluation of the Concept of the Future." *TI.* Volume X, New York: Herder and Herder, 1973.

—— "Eternity from Time." *TI.* Volume XIX, New York: Crossroad, 1983.

—— *Foundations of Christian Faith: An Introduction to the Idea of Christianity.* New York: Crossroad, 1993.

—— "On the Theology of Hope." *TI,* Volume X, New York: Herder and Herder, 1973.

—— "The Hermeneutics of Eschatological Assertions." *TI.* Volume IV, Baltimore: Helicon, 1966.

—— "The Inexhaustible Transcendence of God and our Concern for the Future." *TI.* Volume XX, New York: Crossroad, 1981.

—— "The Question of the Future." *TI* Volume XII, New York: Seabury Press, 1974.

—— "Utopia and Reality: The Shape of Christian Existence Caught between the Ideal and the Real." *TI.* Volume XXII, New York: Crossroad, 1991.

Ratzinger, Joseph. *Eschatology: Death and Eternal Life.* Washington: Catholic University of America Press, 1988.

Ricoeur, Paul. "Toward a Hermeneutic of the Idea of Revelation." *Harvard Theological Review.* 70/1–2 (1977).

Rike, Jennifer L. "Introduction: Radical Pluralism and Truth in the Thought of David Tracy." *Radical Pluralism and Truth: David Tracy and the Hermeneutics of Religion.* New York: Crossroad, 1991.

Sauter, Gerhard. *What Dare We Hope? Reconsidering Eschatology.* Harrisburg, PA: Trinity Press International, 1999.

Scanlon, Michael J., O.S.A. "The Postmodern Debate." *The Twentieth Century: A Theological Overview.* Gregory Baum, ed., New York: Orbis, 1999.

Schillebeeckx, Edward. *Jesus: An Experiment in Christology.* New York: Crossroad, 1991.

Schweiker, William. "Time as Moral Space: Moral Cosmologies, Creation, and Last Judgment." *The End of the World and the Ends of God.* John Polkinghorne and Michael Welker, eds. Harrisburg, PA: Trinity Press International, 2000.

Schweitzer, Albert. *The Quest of the Historical Jesus: A Critical Study of Its Progress from Reimarus to Wrede.* New York: Macmillan, 1964.

Scott, Nathan A., Jr. "Hermeneutics and the Question of the Self." *Radical Pluralism and Truth: David Tracy and the Hermeneutics of Religion.* New York: Crossroad, 1991.

Shea, William M. "Review Symposium on David Tracy's *The Analogical Imagination.*" *Horizons.* 8/2 (Fall, 1981).

Stiver, Dan R. *Theology After Ricoeur: New Directions in Hermeneutical Theology.* Louisville: Westminster John Knox Press, 2001.

Tanner, Kathryn. "Eschatology without a Future!" *The End of the World and the Ends of God.* John Polkinghorne and Michael Welker, eds. Harrisburg, PA: Trinity Press International, 2000.

Troeltsch, Ernst. *The Christian Faith.* Minneapolis: Fortress Press, 1991.

Weinsheimer, Joel. *Gadamer's Hermeneutics: A Reading of Truth and Method.* New Haven: Yale University Press, 1985.

Weiss, Johannes. *Jesus' Proclamation of the Kingdom of God.* Chico, California: Scholars Press, 1985.

Williams, Stephen. "Thirty Years of Hope: A Generation of Writing on Eschatology." *Eschatology in Bible and Theology: Evangelical Essays at the Dawn of the New Millennium.* Ken E. Brower and Mark W. Elliot, eds. Downers Grove, Illinois: Inter-Varsity Press, 1997.

Wright, N. T. *Surprised by Hope: Rethinking Heaven, the Resurrection, and the Mission of the Church.* New York: Harper Collins, 2008.

INDEX